Goodbye, Judge Lynch

Goodbye, Judge Lynch

The End of a Lawless Era in Wyoming's Big Horn Basin

JOHN W. DAVIS

UNIVERSITY OF OKLAHOMA PRESS : NORMAN

ALSO BY JOHN W. DAVIS

A Vast Amount of Trouble: A History of the Spring Creek War
(Boulder, 1993; Norman, 2005)

Wyoming Range War: The Infamous Invasion of Johnson County (Norman, 2012)

Library of Congress Cataloging-in-Publication Data

Davis, John W., 1943–
Goodbye, Judge Lynch : the end of a lawless era in
Wyoming's Big Horn Basin / John W. Davis.
p.   cm.
Includes bibliographical references and index.
ISBN 978-0-8061-3774-2 (paper)
1. Gorman, James, 1880?–1903—Trials, litigation, etc.
2. Trials (Murder)—Wyoming—Basin.
3. Lynching—Wyoming—Basin—History—20th century.
4. Criminal justice, Administration of—Wyoming—Big Horn County—
History—20th century.
5. Public policy (Law)—Wyoming—Big Horn County—History—20th century.
I. Title.

KF224.G67D38 2005
364.9787'33'09041—dc22
2004059889

The paper in this book meets the guidelines
for permanence and durability of the
Committee on Production Guidelines for Book Longevity
of the Council on Library Resources, Inc. ∞

◆

Contents

List of Illustrations   vii

List of Maps   ix

Preface and Acknowledgments   xi

1. The Gormans   3

2. The 1880s   14

3. The 1890s   24

4. The Trial   41

5. The Second Trial   58

6. Joseph Walters   72

7. Judge Lynch Appears   81

8. Lynching in America   99

9. A Big Horn County Grand Jury   107

10. Sheep and Cattle   117

11. The Spring Creek Raid   126

12. The Reaction   133

13. Another Grand Jury   141

14. The Cattlemen Fight Back   151

15. The Brink Trial Begins   162

16. The Brink Trial Concludes   182

Epilogue   197

Notes   213

Bibliography   247

Index   253

♦

Illustrations

Dry Fork of Brokenback Creek   6

Edward Elmer Enterline   47

Big Horn County Courthouse, 1909   88

Percy W. Metz   125

The Allemand family   127

W. L. "Billy" Simpson   163

Herbert Brink   165

The Spring Creek Five   167

The jury in *State v. Brink*   169

Fraternal Hall in Basin   171

Charles David "Bounce" Helmer   176

Denver Post story of the Spring Creek Raid   180

Joe LeFors   199

Wyoming State Penitentiary baseball team, ca. 1911   201

Wanted flier for George Saban (front)   204

Wanted flier for George Saban (back)   205

Spring Creek Raid historical marker on Highway 434   206

Maps

Wyoming, 1880   9

Northern Wyoming, 1890   25

Big Horn Basin, 1909   122

◆

Preface and Acknowledgments

About ten years ago, I completed the manuscript for *A Vast Amount of Trouble: A History of the Spring Creek Raid,* and I promised my wife (and myself) that I would not begin a new project for a while. Writing this book about the worst of the Wyoming sheep raids took a huge amount of time from a lot of important things, such as the practice of law and fly-fishing and pheasant hunting, not to mention my family. So, for several years after the book was published, I resisted the urge to charge off in some new direction.

The trouble is that once you have written a book about a topic, you remain interested in all the aspects of that subject. People kept feeding me intriguing information related to *A Vast Amount of Trouble,* and one item, the 1902 murder of Tom Gorman, kept coming up. When I wrote about the Spring Creek Raid, I knew the case of *State v. James Gorman* had conditioned the Big Horn County authorities in powerful ways, but I did not know the full story, certainly not as thoroughly as I did *State v. Brink,* the primary case that arose from the raid.

I started looking into *State v. Gorman,* doing things such as visiting Fred and Gloria Cutt (who now own what was the Gorman place), looking up contemporaneous newspaper articles and the original court files. These last two inquiries, though, led to frustration. I learned that the

PREFACE AND ACKNOWLEDGMENTS

1902 and 1903 issues of the *Big Horn County Rustler*, the only newspaper published in Basin during those times, were not available. Nor were the original court files. During all this, I kept bumping into hints about Maggie Gorman, the wife of the murder victim—that she was a very good-looking woman and that this was a factor in the murder case.

I went to the State Archives in Cheyenne in order to cast a broader net for newspaper stories. I had the dates of the key events, initial arrests, and first and second trials, and the time of the raid on the Big Horn County jail, and so I started looking through newspapers published in Wyoming around these dates. This inquiry proved very productive, as I found one informative article after another about the Gormans, especially one dated October 1902 about the first trial, printed in the *Cheyenne Daily Leader*. Then, too, I found the district court journal in a back room of the Big Horn County Courthouse. Court records usually lack the really interesting information found in newspapers, but they provide a set of basic, incontrovertible facts, an invaluable check of the accuracy of the newspaper stories.

As I spoke to many people about Maggie Gorman, the impression that she was exceptionally attractive kept being reinforced. I started searching for a photograph. The area museums generally have very good collections of photographs, but none of a person I could identify as Maggie Gorman. So I started looking for Maggie, hoping to find a living member of the family, someone who might supply what had become my holy grail, a photograph of Tom Gorman's widow. I knew Maggie Gorman and her daughter had left the Big Horn Basin in 1903, but had no notion where she had gone. After much flailing around, I learned where Maggie's family had gone after about 1908 and where Maggie was in the 1920s. But then Maggie's trail faded out entirely.

Still, at this point the story had captivated me, and I could not let it go. As I delved more and more deeply into the Gorman case, I realized what a remarkable and complicated event it was. And I realized how important the Gorman case was to the final victory of law and order in the Big Horn Basin, to the area's thirty-year progression from raw frontier to what could fairly be called a mature society. Many things were no longer a mystery; for instance, why the authorities in 1909 felt so strongly about stationing militia about the Big Horn County Courthouse. Even more, I was fascinated by Maggie Gorman, this ill-starred young woman whose God-given good looks started such a tragic chain of events. All of which meant I had little choice but to write another book. Once a person has written one book, it seems the normal immunity from such an urge has been weakened so badly that other books are inevitable.

Anyone who does historical research in Wyoming appreciates the people of our state. Whether found in the state archives in Cheyenne, in various libraries, or in the offices of clerks of court, they are invariably gracious and helpful. This is one of the very nice aspects of living in the least populated state in the union.

It seems it is no longer possible to write a book without the extensive use of a computer. These beasts, though, are cantankerous and contrary, constantly at risk for disaster. My secretary, Pam Gaulke, comes as close to taming the savage creatures as anyone does, and without her, I do not believe I could have completed a single chapter.

I want to give special thanks to Fred and Gloria Cutt; to the very patient people at the University of Oklahoma Press, especially Chuck Rankin; and, of course, to my tolerant wife, Celia.

Goodbye, Judge Lynch

1

◆

The Gormans

In the spring of 1902, Thomas C. Gorman and his wife, Margaret, lived a few miles north of Ten Sleep, Wyoming, on the Dry Fork of Brokenback Creek, a small stream issuing out of the Big Horn Mountains. The Gormans's tiny outpost lay at the base of this large mountain range, along the eastern rim of the Big Horn Basin of northern Wyoming. Tom Gorman and Maggie McClellan had been married in Buffalo, Wyoming, on September 19, 1898, when Maggie was barely eighteen; Tom had been considerably older—twenty-eight.[1]

The Gormans leased their house from Henry E. Miller, who had moved upon the land in April 1899 and built a small log house as part of proving up his homestead claim. This house, only about 430 square feet, still stands where it did originally, about thirty or forty feet from the Dry Fork stream (which, true to its name, usually does not flow water). The house is on the floor of a small canyon so tightly tucked into the mountains that from the house, only the canyon interior is visible. The high peaks of the Big Horn Mountains, when viewed from a distance, look like huge rock formations sitting atop a forested plateau, what John McPhee referred to as "crowns on tables." From within Dry Fork Canyon, however, that view is lost in a reduced horizon. The floor of the canyon is very narrow, about two hundred feet wide, and is filled with box elder, cottonwood, and sagebrush. When the sun lowers, the canyon quickly becomes dark. The house has always been off the beaten path, so that a visitor must divert from a county road, and only after one travels a mile or more into the mountain does the house come into view.[2]

In 1900, Tom Gorman asked his younger brother, Jim, to come out to Wyoming from Pennsylvania. This was probably a happy event; Tom had last seen his brother when Jim was only seventeen or eighteen, but this is an age when young men change quickly, and perhaps Tom was surprised by the twenty-year-old man who arrived in Wyoming. The great complication here was that Maggie Gorman, by almost all accounts, was remarkably attractive. Whatever there is about a woman that men find appealing, Maggie had it. She had that quality that eludes so many who seek it—desirability. Many years after her brief and tragic time of infamy, people in the Ten Sleep country still talked about the aura of Maggie Gorman.[3]

Jim Gorman resided with Tom and Maggie when they lived south of Ten Sleep on the George B. McClellan ranch and when they moved to the Ed Miller place north of Ten Sleep, but there were frequent disagreements between the brothers. In the fall of 1901, Tom objected to the attention his younger brother showed Maggie and drove Jim away at rifle point. It was not long, though, before Jim Gorman came back into the picture.

The following spring, something drew him back to his brother's home, and it was probably Maggie, whether because she encouraged him, or simply because she was a "fine looking woman." Although Jim returned to his brother's home, Tom and Jim Gorman continued squabbling. Later accounts conflict sharply as to why and how it happened, but there is no question that on April 20, 1902, Jim Gorman killed his brother, burying a hatchet in Tom Gorman's head.[4]

That spring, Tom had been freighting to and from Casper with his partner, Fred Bader. In April, after they finished a trip, Tom wanted to work on his wagons, and the horses needed a rest, so he and Bader decided not to start out again for a couple of weeks. For a time, people in the area were not particularly concerned at not seeing Tom Gorman, but then neighbors started inquiring about him and were given unsatisfactory and inconsistent answers as to where he had gone—there were ambiguous references to Canada.[5]

Things came to a head when Fred Bader went to the Gorman home in June to ask about Tom. The Gormans had a little girl, probably born in late 1900, whom Fred Bader described as "a pretty little golden haired girl—they named her Rose." Almost one hundred years later, one of Fred Bader's children recounted conversations with his father about this visit, and the one thing he remembered most distinctly was his father's description of how strangely the little girl was acting. Fred asked her where her father was, and little Rose said something about "under the wagon."[6]

Of course, all of this led to great suspicion. Bader and other neighbors contacted the authorities, asking the sheriff of Big Horn County, Dudley Hale, to come out and investigate. In the meantime, Jim and Maggie took a wagon and a buggy, filled them with provisions and bedding, and headed north toward Montana.[7]

Hale did come to the Dry Fork , found "suspicious conditions," and traced the body of Tom Gorman to a small washout, where it was buried about one hundred yards from the house, underneath "a thin covering of dirt, sagebrush and stones." There had been an attempt to burn the body. Dr. C. Dana Carter and the assistant county attorney, Clarence A. Zaring, were called to the scene; an inquest was quickly held, with the conclusion that Tom Gorman met his death by murder. These events apparently happened in a hurry, because during this time it was learned that Jim Gorman and Maggie Gorman had been seen "traveling north." Deputy Frank James pursued the two Gormans, finding them in a camp on Dry Creek near Germania (now Emblem).[8]

Maggie and Jim were brought back to the county seat, Basin City; Jim was placed in the county jail, and Maggie was kept in a private house, under guard. On June 14, 1902, they appeared before F. T. Brigham, justice of the peace, on a charge of first-degree murder, and both pleaded not guilty.[9]

Shocking though this crime might have been, in many ways it was a garden-variety murder case, the kind of incident that the American

Dry Fork, Brokenback Creek, looking east. Photograph by author.

criminal justice system had been processing routinely since Americans were colonists of the British Empire. In the Big Horn Basin, however, the prosecution of crime had been anything but routine. Indeed, the Gorman murder case became a test, a trial not only of Jim Gorman but of the political maturity of the citizens of Big Horn County (the Wyoming county enclosing most of the Big Horn Basin). Based on the dismal history before 1902, which demonstrated time and again a shocking absence of law and order, there was a profound question as to whether these citizens would pass that test.

In 1902, the Big Horn Basin had been settled for only twenty-three years. Before 1879, it had been the residence of just one white man, J. D. Woodruff. The basin covers a huge area, almost three times the size of the state of Connecticut. Woodruff could do something, though, that not one of the teeming millions in the verdant state of Connecticut could ever do. That lone man could walk to a nearby hill and view the entire, magnificent expanse of his home. He could stand and turn, and turn, and in every direction see hills and ridges and mountains stretching and looping before him. He could see a very big sky framed on every horizon by a mountain. To the east, almost a 180-degree sweep, he could see the broad-shouldered Big Horn Mountains, deep blue, capped by white, and rising over 13,000 feet. To the south, he could see the Bridger, Lysite, and Owl Creek Mountains; to the west stretched another huge chain of blue and white mountains, the Absarokas, and to the north, the Pryors. Within this massive arena, Woodruff could watch the slow unfolding of weather; view the entire panoply of a winter front, and in the summer see the coming of forty-mile storm lines, black, angry, trampling armies in the sky, ponderously flashing and fuming. Standing on that nearby hill, Woodruff would have felt that he was lord of all he surveyed.[10]

Events in the latter part of the 1870s, however, would forever alter Woodruff's spectacular home. As a consequence of the 1876 Custer battle (an engagement that took place fifty miles off the northeast corner of the basin), the Sioux hunting grounds to the east of the Big Horn Mountains were abolished, and the basin lay open. In 1879, the Big Horn Basin was finally invaded by other "lords," and livestock poured in. The last two decades of the nineteenth century became an era of cattle kings in the Big Horn Basin, and, indeed, throughout the territory and state of Wyoming. The United States owned almost all of Wyoming, a public domain open to all. Thus, the sparse but nutritious grasses in the high valleys of Wyoming drew men determined to be the first to claim the bounty of the public land.

It was 1879 when Judge William A. Carter, the sutler at Fort Bridger, sent Pete McCulloch into the western half of the Big Horn Basin with a herd of almost 4,000 cattle. In 1879, Henry Clay Lovell brought in two herds, and Otto Franc drove 1,200 Oregon cows to the Greybull River in the far western part of the basin, beginning the famous Pitchfork Ranch. Franc spent the first winter on the Greybull River, forty miles downstream from where it issues from the Absaroka Mountains. In 1880, he moved the headquarters far upstream, to the striking mountain setting the Pitchfork still occupies. The same year, Angus J. McDonald started his ranch on Gooseberry Creek. In 1881, George Baxter established the LU Ranch on Grass Creek, south of Gooseberry; Worden Noble placed a herd at the junction of Ten Sleep Creek and Nowood River, on the east side of the basin; and John Luman brought a herd to Paintrock Creek, north of Noble's ranch. In 1882, another cattle company was established on Ten Sleep Creek, the Big Horn Cattle Company (Bar X Bar). This company was supported by English capital but was managed by an American, Milo Burke.[11]

The early cattlemen were energetic entrepreneurs, and they built huge ranches, employing rowdy young men as cowboys to round up, brand, and drive thousands of head of cattle. In their drive to tame one of the last empty corners of America, however, the cattlemen cared little that they were also creating an immense and complicated social predicament— how to create law and order out of nothing. It was the same problem confronted by settlers from Boston to Boonesboro to the gold fields of Montana, what Bernard DeVoto referred to as "the pitched battle between the lawless of the frontier and the frontier as a developing social stability." Constructing civil institutions—a system of sheriffs, deputies, lawyers, courts, and jails—to wrest order from chaos takes a long time and a massive amount of effort.[12]

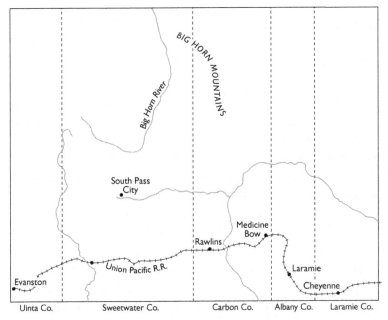

Wyoming, 1880

The early cattle ranches could sustain only a tiny population, but for many years, this handful of people in northern Wyoming suffered a barrage of violence—murders, attempted murders, and aggravated assaults. Before the turn of the century, in a population that ranged from several hundred people to four thousand, there were more than twenty killings in the Big Horn Basin. Most went unpunished. What little "law enforcement" there was usually came in the form of private vengeance.[13]

Wyoming was a territory in 1879, having been organized for only about ten years. The infant government had made great efforts to address persistent lawlessness, enacting a complete set of criminal statutes; there were even five county governments to enforce the laws. The territorial legislature had borrowed wholesale from the statutes of Nebraska, Nevada, Colorado, and, especially, Ohio, and had thereby provided the fledgling jurisdiction with a full set of basic rules of proscribed conduct (as in murder, robbery, and arson statutes), as well as procedural rules to follow when those rules were violated. The statutory arrangement looked very much like the structure followed throughout the next century, a system using justices of the peace and district courts.[14]

Providing a full set of necessary statutes, however, was the easy part. The cowboys hired by the early cattlemen (and for about fifteen years after 1879, the great majority of the people who arrived in the basin were men who worked as cowboys) were young, most in their teens or twenties, men drawn to the life by a need for adventure and physical challenge. Victor Arland, who founded the first town in the Big Horn Basin, wrote: "The cowboys are singular characters, very violent and without their equals in their spirit of independence; . . . In the towns of the Far West they are getting a most deplorable reputation through their audacity and lack of restraint." Applying statutes so that they suppressed the conduct of these zestful young men posed a huge problem.[15]

In 1879, every one of the five county seats was in far southern Wyoming, along the Union Pacific Railroad, and thus criminal prosecution could take place only in southern Wyoming. Most of the Big Horn Basin was in Sweetwater County, county seat Green River, and a slice on the east was in Carbon County, county seat Rawlins. A modern highway map shows a distance of 211 miles from Worland, in the southern half of the basin, to Rawlins, and 293 miles from Cody to Green River; but modern transportation systems are not remotely like those of 1879. In practical terms, Green River and Rawlins were farther from the Big Horn Basin in 1879 than they are now from Outer Mongolia, and criminal prosecution was nearly impossible.[16]

There were no roads leading south from the basin, only trails. At least one yearly trip to the Union Pacific had to be made, though, because in the early 1880s this was the nearest railhead, the only real opening to a market to sell cattle and to get supplies. E. W. Copps declared that the cattle drive from Buffalo to Rawlins, a trip that did not require a traverse of mountains, took eighteen days. Coming from the basin, however, a cattle owner first had to get out, and any exit required going over an 8,000-foot pass, such as Birdseye Pass or Cottonwood Pass; thus, David John Wasden's estimate of six weeks for a round trip seems about right.

Of course, the return trip, when cattle were not being driven, usually did not take as long but still was arduous. Owen Wister describes a 263-mile excursion from Medicine Bow "deep into cattle land," a trip taking several days by wagon, while "swallowed in a vast solitude." His description sounds like a journey north into the Big Horn Basin.[17]

Government crept a little closer to the basin in March of 1881, when Johnson County started operating. Johnson County was actually declared as Pease County by the territorial legislature back in 1875, when most of the county was Sioux hunting grounds, and only the most courageous or foolhardy white man ventured there; it would be six years before county operation could begin. Johnson County extended over a very large area, including most of the Powder River Basin, most of the Big Horn Mountains, and the Big Horn Basin east of the Big Horn River. Still, as of March 29, 1881, for the eastern half of the basin, there was now a county seat on Clear Creek, at present-day Buffalo. It provided, or soon would provide, a courthouse and a jail within a hundred miles—at least as the crow flies—for half of the basin. Of course, it would take a mighty crow indeed to make a direct flight over 13,175-foot Cloud Peak, the highest point in the Big Horn Mountains.[18]

The vast distance of the basin from places of authority had a strong practical effect. Shortly after the arrival of the cattlemen, in April 1881, a buffalo hunter, Jim White, was murdered at a place near where Shell Creek emerges from the Big Horn Mountains. This was only a month after Johnson County began; a sheriff had just been appointed, and the courthouse and jail were still under construction. The complaint in the first Johnson County criminal case is dated July 1881, but the first district court proceeding did not occur until the following year. In any event, there is no record of Johnson County authorities even investigating the murder of Jim White.[19]

The fundamental building block for Wyoming territorial government was the election precinct; each precinct had a justice of the peace and a constable. Johnson County had established precincts at Upper Powder River, Crazy Woman, Clear Creek, Piney, Big Horn, Sheridan, Bingham, Tongue River, but none in the Big Horn Basin. In fact, the first election precinct established in the Big Horn Basin was not by Johnson County, but by Sweetwater County. In September 1882, Sweetwater County created the first governmental organization in the basin when it declared an election precinct at Gooseberry; Angus McDonald's ranch house was set as the site of an election to vote upon a justice of the peace and a constable. (A justice court is commonly referred to as an "inferior court," meaning that its civil and criminal jurisdiction is limited to less serious matters than those addressed in district court, and a constable's duties are normally confined to the cases addressed by a justice of the peace in justice court.)[20]

Between 1881 and 1883, Sweetwater County officers dealt with a few matters concerning the Big Horn Basin, such as making numerous payments for wolf bounties (for example, $109, at $1 per wolf, to H. C. Lovell alone) and addressing property tax disputes. The first time any matter connected with the Big Horn Basin came before the Johnson County commissioners was on July 16, 1883, when the attention of the board was called to the need for a bridge across Ten Sleep Creek. The site of this bridge was about fifty miles southwest of Buffalo, Wyoming, by a direct line, but a direct route requires passage over the Big Horn Mountains, including a traverse of Powder River Pass, elevation 9,666 feet, impassable by horse or wagon for about half the year.[21]

The county seat for the western half of the basin remained at Green River, in Sweetwater County, until 1884. As noted, Sweetwater County officials' dealings with the basin were only cursory, but there was an active population of men west of the Big Horn River, and violence was there, as shown by an 1882 event that John William "Josh" Deane described. Deane wrote of three men who identified themselves as "sheriffs," on the trail of two strangers with whom Deane had just spent some time. Deane pointed out the direction in which the two strangers had gone and a few hours later rode in that direction. He found three bodies in an aspen grove, the two strangers and another man Deane knew, men who had just been gunned down, evidently without a battle. Deane said, "The sight sickened me, though I was not unaccustomed to brutalities." Perhaps these three "sheriffs," were actually law enforcement officers, but if so, they carried out summary executions, followed, apparently, by no official action of any kind.[22]

In 1884, Fremont County was created, carved out of the northern part of Sweetwater County, with its county seat at Lander. The new county was even larger than Johnson County, comprising about 15,000 square miles. As with Buffalo, Lander is outside the Big Horn Basin; a traverse over the Owl Creek Mountains is necessary to go from the southwestern part of the basin to Lander. A trip from most of the early ranches in the western Big Horn Basin, those around present-day Cody and Meeteetse, to Lander, is a trip of more than a hundred miles; by road today, the distance from Cody to Lander is 163 miles. Still, Lander was much closer than Green River was, cutting off another hundred miles and avoiding a southward trip over South Pass.[23]

Until 1897, this was the arrangement for criminal justice in the Big Horn Basin; west of the Big Horn River, all arrests, trials, and convictions were conducted out of Lander. East of the river, any such activity had to go through Buffalo. From 1884 to 1897, there was ample business for the men of law enforcement, but, as will be seen, time and again their efforts were frustrated by distance and terrain.

2

♦

The 1880s

The cattle industry remained dominant in the Big Horn Basin throughout the 1880s, and the extensive problems of law and order resulting from the isolation of the basin remained at least through the end of the decade. Life in the basin changed in other ways, though. In the early 1880s, a closer railhead arrived, and shortly thereafter, a town was founded. The Northern Pacific Railroad had moved through southern Montana, creating Billings, and after 1883, the time required for a cattle drive to a railhead was halved for most of the ranches in the basin.[1]

In March 1884, Victor Arland and his partner, John Corbett, decided to move their trading post from Cottonwood Creek on the Stinking Water (Shoshone River) to Meeteetse Creek, some thirty-five miles south. Arland was a Frenchman who already had an interesting career in the United States. He arrived in 1870, prospected in the Black Hills in 1875, and moved into the Big Horn Basin in 1880. At first, the trading post was at Trail Creek and supplied "the needs of the hunters and trappers of this region and of the Indians, Crows and Shoshones, who are hunting in this vicinity."[2] Trail Creek led to Cottonwood Creek, and then to Meeteetse Creek. Arland wrote a friend about the excellence of his latest location, being directly in the center of cattle raisers of this area . . . The country is really good only for cattle raising. There are at the present time about 30,000 head of cattle between Stinking Water and Greybull. In a radius of 20 miles of here, there are about 15 cattle ranches.

We have a coach from Fort Washakie twice a week. We hope that the coach will come directly from Fort Washakie the first of July, passing right by our place. . . .

We are in the process of building several buildings such as a store, a restaurant, . . . We have at the present moment 5 employees. . . . There are days when we have 10–20 men to feed, and then for several days, there will be scarcely one or two passers-by.[3]

Arland's little town met all the needs of the local cowboys: food, gambling, drink, and sex. The local ranchers did not like their cowboys to frequent Arland, but a great many of them did.

Arland made further note of a store about four miles from his establishment, in "Old Meeteetse," farther downstream on Meeteetse Creek. In 1884, a man named George Smith visited a saloon there, but when he came out, he confronted one McWallace, against whom he apparently had an old personal grudge. Smith called McWallace a name, and McWallace fired a shot at Smith, killing him instantly. McWallace was asked why he did that, but he made no reply and rode back to his camp; not long after, he left the Big Horn Basin and went to Green River, Wyoming. George Smith's widow and her sister, Maude Baker, wanted Smith's death avenged. Baker had a persistent suitor named Ira Hamilton, and she told him that if he would go with her, follow McWallace, and kill him, then she would marry Hamilton. So Hamilton, Baker, and Smith's brother went after McWallace, riding down to Green River.

Tom Osborne described what happened next: "The three stationed themselves at the corner of McWallace's barn and as he came out to feed his stock they shot, killing McWallace. This murder was a mystery to the people of that section. Maude, Smith and Ira left immediately. Maude and Ira were married and as far as I know they are happily living together."[4]

Obviously, no arrest followed the murder of McWallace, but in the fall of 1884, authorities actually made an arrest in the Big Horn Basin. After his employer, S. W. Hyatt, fired him, Harry Anable and a cohort, Jack Knight, stole horses, mules, and "personal property" of Hyatt, D. A. Patch, and J. F. Buckingham. Anable and Knight fled the area, going over the mountains to the Big Horn Basin, following what had already become a common practice for those on the wrong side of the law. They were unlucky, though, because the Johnson County sheriff, Frank Canton, and his deputy, Tom Adams, pursued them and made arrests in the Nowood country. The two miscreants were brought back to Buffalo for trial; both received three-year prison sentences and were sent to the Joliet, Illinois, prison facility, then used by the territory of Wyoming.[5]

When Fremont County began operation in 1884, it significantly increased governmental involvement in the Big Horn Basin, although this involvement was still feeble by modern standards. Of course, Fremont County inherited the Gooseberry Precinct at the McDonald Ranch, but it also added an Owl Creek Precinct (at Torrey's Headquarters) and a Meeteetse Precinct (located at the old Meeteetse Post Office). More than that, one of the new county commissioners was Angus J. McDonald himself, the proprietor of the ranch on Gooseberry Creek. Later in 1884, steps were finally taken in Johnson County to bring a governmental presence to the eastern half of the Big Horn Basin. On September 6, 1884, a precinct for Ten Sleep was established, and an election was set to elect a justice of the peace and a constable for the precinct. The polling place was set at the headquarters of the Big Horn Cattle Company ranch, which was then located on Little Canyon Creek, twenty miles south of the junction of Ten Sleep Creek and the Nowood River.[6]

The population of the Big Horn Basin grew in the first part of the 1880s, and Johnson and Fremont Counties kept creating new election precincts. On October 4, 1884, the Fremont County Board of Commissioners added the Stinking Water Precinct, an area near present-day Cody; Pete McCulloch was named as one of the election judges. On September 17, 1886, another precinct on the Stinking Water was created, called Corbett. At almost the same time, the Johnson County commissioners issued a declaration of the 1886 election, and it showed Big Horn Basin precincts at Ten Sleep (announced voting place: Waln Brothers Ranch), Paint Rock (Hasbrouck's store), Shell Creek (W. H. Hunt's Ranch), and Mahogany Buttes (Ritchie Brothers Ranch).[7]

There were civic improvements too. At the second meeting of the Fremont County commissioners, on May 6, 1884, a county road was declared along the stagecoach route from Fort Washakie to the Stinking Water, and on April 9, 1886, Otto Franc and seventy others presented a petition asking for a bridge across the "Grey Bull" at the stage crossing. On October 10, 1885, the Johnson County commissioners let a bid for a bridge on "Paint Rock Road." The Fort Washakie stage provided rough transportation of passengers but did not include mail service. Until 1888, the delivery of mail from Fort Washakie to the western half of the basin was the personal enterprise of Josh Deane.[8]

During this time, the big ranches continued with their business, carrying out twice-yearly roundups and getting their cattle to market; cattle prices were quite favorable. However, livestock theft had quickly become a problem. Indeed, from the very beginning, the criminal case files in Johnson and Fremont Counties show the most common charge to be some variant of livestock theft. The authorities took the problem seriously and tried to curb such crimes, even in the vast spaces of the Big Horn Basin. At times they were overzealous, such as when Christopher Gross, acting as both a cattle inspector and a deputy sheriff, sought to make an arrest of George Stevens for stealing horses. On the morning of November 30, 1885, Gross and two others surprised Stevens at a small cabin on Spring Creek, a little stream that empties into the Nowood River seven miles south of the present location of the town of Ten Sleep. Stevens apparently objected to the arrest, and Gross shot and killed him, then took Stevens's body to Buffalo. Not everyone in Johnson County, however, believed that summary execution was appropriate for a crime against property. In 1888, Gross was indicted by a Johnson County grand jury for assaulting and killing Stevens; he was tried before a jury but acquitted. This debate over life versus property would be heard again in Johnson County.[9]

In 1886, cattle prices began to slip. Cattlemen, hoping for an upturn in prices, placed even more cattle on a range that was already overburdened. During that year, the town of Arland continued to be a violent place. A. A. Anderson came through the town that year and reported a dispute between Victor Arland and a broncobuster named Joe Crow:

> Joe Crow had got into a dispute with Arland. He pulled his six-shooter and opened fire. He shot off one of Arland's locks of hair, put a hole through the sugar scoop, and kept shooting, while Arland, in the meantime was hunting for his gun behind the bar. He did not find it, but when Joe emptied his, Arland picked up a beer bottle and came from behind the bar. Joe Crow ran out of the saloon with Arland after him, and got caught in a barbed wire fence, where Arlan proceeded to knock him senseless with the beer bottle.[10]

In 1886, a girl from the house of ill fame in Arland was found in a lane, showing signs of strangulation. She soon died. In yet another incident, a Mexican named Tauhoundus was shot and subsequently died. He had earlier traded a horse for a man's daughter; the daughter lived with Tauhoundus for a while, but then she came to Arland to get away from him. Tauhoundus rode to Arland to get the girl, and in the process got into a gunfight with the Red River Kid, who was "too quick for him" and shot Tauhondus through the arm and upper shoulder. A man named Jack McGreggor proceeded to take Tauhoundus to Lander by wagon, but by the time he crossed Owl Creek Mountains, the Mexican had died.[11]

There is no report of a response by anyone in authority to any of the above incidents. The authorities could be quite stern, though, when they had a malefactor in hand. William Booth committed a murder near Buffalo, which was bad luck for him. He was quickly arrested, tried, and convicted. District Judge Jacob B. Blair sentenced Booth and declared that he would be, "hung by the neck until you are dead, dead, dead." And Booth was. After a brief and abortive attempt at an appeal, a scaffold was promptly erected next to the jail and the sentence carried out.[12]

Bad as the complete absence of law and order was, 1886 had a deeper calamity in store for the Big Horn Basin, and for the northern plains. The infamous winter of 1886–1887 caused horrendous losses of cattle (estimated at 50–90 percent) and the bankruptcy of many large ranches. Several people froze to death, including two within fifteen miles of Arland. While it thinned the ranks of the big cattlemen, however, it increased those of the small cattlemen, as they moved into valleys made newly vacant. For example, many of the first deeds (United States patents) for good cattle lands in places such as Little Canyon Creek (near Big Trails), Canyon Creek, the Nowood River, and Spring Creek date from claims made during or just after 1887.[13]

The year 1887 appears to have been relatively peaceful, perhaps because the people of the Big Horn Basin were stunned by the winter. Wasden reports one incident, in which two men were killed while sleeping at a temporary camp, where Gooseberry Creek flows into the Big Horn River. The murderer apparently robbed his victims and then went on to Hyattville, where he got "uproariously" drunk and bragged about his crime. He was arrested by constable B. F. Wickwire and taken to Lander, but then he escaped.[14]

The next year made up for the comparative lull of 1887. All through the 1880s, Victor Arland had been writing a series of fascinating letters to his friend Camille Dadant, of Hamilton, Illinois. On March 12, 1888, he wrote a hair-raising letter that spoke volumes about the climate of violence in the Big Horn Basin at that time. Victor casually tells his friend, "I was obliged to kill a man ["Broken Nose" Andy Jackson] in order to avoid being killed myself. Immediately I sent for the Justice of the Peace, who came to the scene, investigated the whole affair, and convoked a jury which rendered a verdict of justifiable homicide." Arland did not mention to Monsieur Dadant that the friction between him and the slain man had arisen over a woman, Rose Williams, the madam of the house of ill repute in Arland.[15]

Arland went on to explain to his friend, "I must tell you that twice I've been attacked by these 'bad men' and that it is only through my agility and cool-headedness that I escaped being assassinated." Arland gave his version of the dispute with Joe Crow, whom he identified as a horse trader, a "violent and hot-headed character," who shot at Arland. But then,

Arland wrote, Crow fled and hid in terror, fearing arrest or worse. Arland heard of this and sent him word that if he would come to his place, he (Arland) would forgive him, "on condition that he would behave himself toward me." Arland wrote that, "Afterwards, that man would have died for me."[16]

Arland told Dadant of a second murderous event, when a man named Thomas Brady, "a rascal of the worst sort, fired a revolver shot at me point blank because I hadn't wanted to lend him some money to gamble. Fortunately, I was quick enough to thrust his gun aside with my hand." Arland reported that the sleeve of his shirt was burned and his wrist was singed, and he had Brady arrested, although Brady then escaped from jail and was never tried.[17]

Charles Lindsay, in his 1932 Ph.D. thesis, wrote with great authority about the Big Horn Basin of the late 1880s. The basin had a reputation as a center for criminal activity, a place where "rustlers were becoming common and daring." Lindsay was skeptical, though, that the problem was exactly as presented by the large cattle interests. He noted two deaths in 1888 (Henry Gormand and J. C. Inglas) but observed that the killing of Inglas involved an argument over horses, not cattle, and stated that, "Killings in the remoter corners of the range that had no relationship to cattle rustling could easily be given one." Lindsay quoted Frank Canton's report to the Wyoming Stock Growers Association, "I have never known them [rustlers] to be so bold as at the present time," but Lindsay pointed out that many of the charges made at that time were greatly overblown, such as the assertion that the rustling gangs were "hand in glove with local county officials."[18]

As can be seen, the perspective of the Stock Growers Association toward cattle theft was formed well before 1892, the year of the Johnson County Invasion; in 1888, crimes involving cattle already carried a political overtone. Lindsay refers to Deputy Jack Hill, who was apparently the first deputy from Johnson County in the Big Horn Basin. The first deputy from Fremont County was probably A. J. Robinson, who was appointed on November 1, 1890, following a petition by fifty-one citizens of the basin asking for a deputy. There had been constables, but these were part-time positions tied to a local justice of the peace, not the full-time job carried out by a deputy sheriff covering a large part of the county.[19]

July 1888 witnessed the disappearance and possible robbery and murder of a woman, Edna Wilson. Edna was quite popular, being one of the rare single women in the area. She visited her sister on the Greybull River, attended a dance, and left at about 2 A.M. in the company of Al McComb. She was seen with McComb over the next few days, but then she disappeared. McComb had acted strangely during that time and soon left the area for Montana, but before doing so, he supposedly told a man named Harry Cheeseman that he and Edna had started for Casper, but that she was drowned while crossing the Big Horn River at the mouth of Owl Creek. About eight months after her disappearance, Edna's horse and saddle (but not Edna) were found washed up on an island in the Big Horn River, near the future site of Worland; the horse's head had been severed. Historians disagree about what all this meant, but whether foul play or accident, it was yet another instance of a suspicious death followed by no official action.[20]

Oddly, the authorities sometimes prosecuted cases arising in the Big Horn Basin that did not seem to represent a great threat to that society. J. P. Fister from Corbett was indicted on July 2, 1888, by a Fremont County grand jury for the crime of criminal libel, an offense no longer a crime.[21] The indictment alleged that Fister did

> feloniously, unlawfully and maliciously write and publish of and concerning one Austin M. Bunce and one Mary Stewart a certain false, scandalous and malicious libel of the tenor following:
>
>   . . . It will no doubt give you pain to read the few lines below written, but it also pains me to write this. . . . Mr. Bunce and Mrs. Stewart are getting too loving for the good of all parties concerned and the only way to brake it up is your immediate return home. This you may not think possible but my information is correct or I would not have written this for she is my sister.
>
>   Yours,
>   J. P. Fister.

With the intent to impeach the virtue and reputation of the said Austin
M. Bunce and the said Mary Stewart and thereby expose them to
public hatred, contempt and ridicule.[22]

The case record does not reveal how this charge was finally resolved.

Sheridan County was created in 1888 and included land in the Big
Horn Basin east of the Big Horn River and north of what is now Greybull.
Johnson County vigorously opposed this new county, to the point of filing
a lawsuit to enjoin its operation, and carrying the case to the Wyoming
Supreme Court. The case was finally resolved by a decision of the Wyo-
ming Supreme Court dated June 12, 1888, vacating the injunction against
Sheridan County.[23]

In 1889, an unusual year, there were no reported killings within the
Big Horn Basin. It was by mere chance, though, that Dab Burch and
Pistol Billy Rogers were not killed in September, when they got into a
gun duel at the LU Ranch over a woman. Each took ten steps backward
and started blazing away at the other, scoring one brutal wound after
another. Billy shot Dab through the lungs and out the left shoulder, and
Dab fell to the ground but retaliated by shooting Billy through the chest.
Billy shot Dab through the eyebrow, but the bullet did not go through
Dab's brain, instead ranging over his skull. A third bullet ran up Dab's leg
and penetrated his wrist. Then Dab shot Billy through the groin, a serious
injury evidently attended by a great deal of bleeding, a deep wound from
which the bullet was never removed.

A doctor was brought from Lander, although it seems this should have
been a wasted effort. Both men were still alive, however, when the doctor
arrived, and he removed all but one of the bullets. The two men then
occupied the same room for several weeks and slowly recovered. They
talked together, of course, and perhaps they settled their differences, as
some people asserted. When they finally recovered, they avoided each
other's company, though, going to different ranges, and it seems more
likely that rather than parting amicably, each just decided that he had had
quite enough of the other.[24]

The last month of the 1880s witnessed a sad but not surprising event, when Victor Arland's letter writing ceased forever. In December 1889, Arland traveled to Red Lodge, Montana (about fifty miles north of Cody), with Rose Williams and John Dyer. He was at a local saloon playing poker when he was shot and killed. The shot came from outside the saloon, through a window, and when people rushed to the door, they heard only hoofbeats in the darkness. No arrests were made, but it was suspected that a friend of Broken Nose had done the deed.[25]

3

♦

The 1890s

Wyoming became a state in 1890, and it entered the union with 62,555 residents. The vast majority of those 62,555 souls lived in the southern half of the state; by 1890 the population of the Big Horn Basin was probably still fewer than 1,500 people. An 1890 map of Wyoming shows four tiny towns in the Big Horn Basin, and the only one extant is Meeteetse.[1]

The residents of the basin were acutely aware of the deficiencies of their government and badly wanted a county government seated within the mountains that ringed their home, a place with a resident sheriff and courthouse. This possibility was strongly enhanced when, in 1888, Colonel William Douglas Pickett, who resided in the Big Horn Basin, was elected to represent Fremont County in the territorial house of representatives. Pickett had been a distinguished officer in the confederate army and first came to the basin in September 1879. In spring 1883, he established a ranch near the Pitchfork Ranch, on a tributary of the Greybull River (the smaller stream is now known as Pickett's Creek).

Pickett was an energetic and competent man, and he directed his efforts toward creating a new county to encompass the Big Horn Basin alone. Unfortunately, it was a complicated time, with statehood looming. As part of drafting a constitution, many propositions were afoot setting

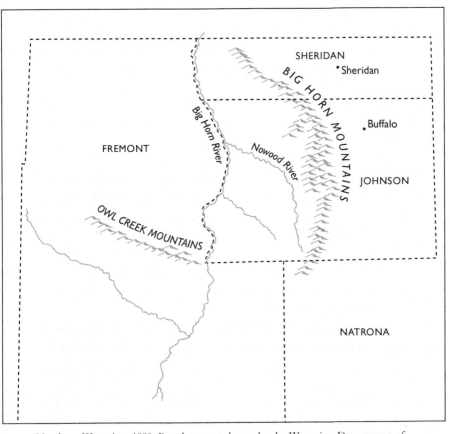

Northern Wyoming, 1890. Based on map drawn by the Wyoming Department of
State Parks and Cultural Resources.

standards for the creation of new counties. Legislators forwarded and supported bills based on the leanings of their constituencies. Sheridan County wanted to free itself of lands in the Big Horn Basin and thus proposed that county organization be allowed with as few as 500 citizens and a relatively low property valuation. Johnson County, however, saw the loss of Big Horn Basin lands as diminishing its already poor financial base and thus insisted that county creation be allowed only with at least 1,500 citizens and a relatively high valuation.[2]

Pickett perceived that the standards to be set in the new Wyoming Constitution would not help the Big Horn Basin become a county, and thus he turned to legislation that he thought would survive the enactment of the constitution. Before the constitution was approved and Wyoming became a state, Pickett succeeded in getting legislation passed to establish Big Horn County, though organization was delayed until after February 2, 1892. The new county was to include the entire Big Horn Basin, except for a thin southern strip just north of Wind River Canyon, which would remain in Fremont County.[3]

In the meantime, Fremont and Johnson Counties continued to do their best to enforce the criminal law of the new state. In April 1891, a sordid tale unfolded, which actually worked its way through the courts, but with disappointing results. James and Mary McDermott lived on the Nowood River, a few miles west of Bonanza, and their nearest neighbors were two brothers, Tom and Peter Madden, with whom they had been friendly. The trouble apparently began because of an affair between James McDermott and one Helen Martin, which caused great conflict in McDermott's marriage. On April 1, Mary McDermott fled, taking her youngest child, a baby girl, to the Madden Ranch. James McDermott, who possessed a volcanic temper and, apparently, the "mental disorder" of paranoia, learned his wife had gone to the Maddens and threatened to "clean up the whole outfit of you" if his wife did not return by sundown.[4]

Mary McDermott did not return, and James McDermott marched over to the Maddens, carrying with him, strangely, little Phil McDermott (one year, eight months, and fourteen days old). The parties later gave conflicting versions of what then happened. Tom Madden said James

McDermott confronted him, fired a shot at him with a pistol, and that he (Madden) then charged McDermott, shooting at him with his pistol, but just as he shot, McDermott pulled little Phil up as a shield. McDermott said he was shot down as he pleaded for his life. Under either version, little Phil was shot in the head and killed, and McDermott suffered a serious wound from which he was expected to die. He did not and was arrested and taken to Buffalo.[5]

The incident was investigated by Johnson County sheriff W. C. Angus and "his Basin deputy," and McDermott was charged with the death of his son. While waiting for judicial proceedings to begin, however, James McDermott made some pronouncements from the Johnson County jail. He "frequently assured those who were in attendance upon him that he would put Madden in the penitentiary or else drive him from the country." In furtherance of this declared objective, McDermott wrote "an old stockman on Grey Bull named Tatman," and told him that in 1888, he and Tom Madden had stolen a large number of horses from Tatman, driven them to Nebraska, and sold them for "a good figure per head"; McDermott added that this scheme was Madden's and that he "had been merely an unwitting accomplice."[6]

Tatman immediately went to Bonanza and confronted Mary McDermott, who admitted the event but said that her husband had been the instigator and had kept all the money from the sale of the horses. She then added that her husband had made several thefts from the mails. The May 21, 1891, edition of the *Buffalo Bulletin* carried a story declaring the vindication of a man who had been falsely accused of stealing money that James McDermott had apparently taken from the mails.[7]

James McDermott and his attorneys chose to challenge the murder charge against him at the preliminary hearing. This hearing is normally a quiet proceeding before a justice of the peace, almost a walk-through, in which law officers provide the results of their investigation, which are usually sufficient to meet the light standards of proving the probability that an offense was committed and that the accused had committed it. The June 15, 1891, preliminary hearing in *State v. McDermott,* however, was turned into a full-blown trial in which all the principal witnesses,

including the defendant, testified at length. McDermott turned the tables
on his wife, declaring that the problems started because of her infidelity;
he testified that at dinner on April 1, he "discovered 'unspeakable' evidence
of his wife's infidelity"; then he spoke of little Phil (and broke down and
wept), his trip to the Madden house, and how Tom and Peter Madden
declared their intention to kill him. James McDermott was apparently a
good witness, and Tom Madden was not, because at the end of the evidence, Justice Joseph Reimann declared that he did not believe Tom
Madden and that the evidence was insufficient; he discharged the prisoner.
The *Buffalo Bulletin* reported that, "Great applause followed this decision,
and many men pushed forward and shook McDermott's hand." Immediately afterwards, McDermott was arrested for mail theft; Tom Madden
had already been arrested for horse stealing.[8]

On August 20, 1891, the *Buffalo Bulletin* reported an interview of
James McDermott that was conducted in the Johnson County jail (he was
convicted of the charge of mail theft). McDermott claimed that he had
been misrepresented by false stories that he had stolen cattle (he did not
deny the theft of horses) and that he had been postmaster at the time of
alleged theft in the mails (he said that he had never been a postmaster).
The reporter who conducted the interview was obviously skeptical about
the damage to McDermott's name, and one of the headlines to his story
read, "James McDermott Fears His Reputation Is Being Injured by the
State Press."[9]

In December 1892, James McDermott swore out a complaint against
Peter Madden and Mary McDermott for "cohabitating in a state of
adultery" but failed to appear to testify on this charge. In January 1893,
James McDermott sued his wife and Madden for selling his cattle while
he was in jail.[10]

In spring 1893, James McDermott returned to the Big Horn Basin and
went to the Madden place, ostensibly to pick up some of his property.
Mary McDermott was there, as was Peter Madden (Tom Madden had
been sent to prison for horse stealing). A gun battle predictably ensued
and James McDermott shot and killed Peter Madden. McDermott was
tried for murder, pleaded self-defense, and was acquitted. The district

judge admonished the jury, declaring that the verdict was indefensible. Indeed, it is hard to see how self-defense could conceivably be justified when McDermott went to his avowed bitter enemy's home with gun in hand and got into a gun battle. Nevertheless, thus ended a particularly nasty frontier feud. By the rough standards of the day, perhaps justice was done for the McDermotts and the Maddens, but the various judicial proceedings could not have inspired confidence in the wisdom of the courts.[11]

In 1891, Fremont County brought criminal charges against Bill A. Gallagher, a cowboy who resided in the Big Horn Basin. On October 21, 1891, a complaint was made against Gallagher in the justice court of Will L. Simpson, declaring that Gallagher improperly branded a bay horse that was the property of Charles and Ghodderton, and that he did so at the Baxter ranch (LU Ranch on Grass Creek). One of the sureties on his $200 bond was Belle Drewry, an Arland prostitute. On December 24, 1891, charges were filed against Gallagher for allegedly altering a ten-dollar check from Robert A. Torrey to D. J. Rice to forty dollars and presenting it to First Lander Bank of Amoretti and Parks. Gallagher pleaded not guilty to these charges and was allowed bond. He apparently served time in the local jail for the charged offenses.[12]

In 1892, Big Horn County was formed. When the governor of Wyoming was petitioned to organize Big Horn County, however, Fremont County brought a lawsuit to stop the organization of the county. The contentions went back to the issues with which Pickett had earlier struggled. Fremont County asserted that Pickett's legislation had not trumped the Wyoming Constitution but had done exactly the opposite, and that the constitution's minimum population and property value requirements for creation of a county should prevail. It would be three years before a Wyoming Supreme Court decision finally resolved the question, and in the meantime, Big Horn County was put on hold; the Big Horn Basin remained within Fremont and Johnson Counties.[13]

In the early 1890s, there was big trouble in that part of Johnson County east of the Big Horn Mountains, culminating in an astonishing event, during which normally law-abiding men deserted "the established order of things and by adopting Judge Lynch's tactics, set at defiance the laws of a state as well as a nation." (The phrase "Judge Lynch" was a common euphemism of the day, an expression concocted from the sarcastic observation that a case was being referred to a higher court, to be heard by Judge Lynch. The "higher court" was a lynch mob.)[14]

In 1891, near Buffalo, the Johnson County seat, two small ranchers had been ambushed and killed as part of the growing conflict between large and small cattlemen over mavericks and rustling. This was just a prelude, however, to the notorious Johnson County Invasion. In April 1892, twenty-five men, including many of the largest landowners and ranchers in the state of Wyoming, accompanied by twenty-five Texas gunmen, made an imperious drive north into Johnson County. They were heavily armed, and their intent was to kill those they termed "rustlers," as well as county officials and community leaders. They were able to gun down two men, Nate Champion and Nick Ray, before the small ranchmen of Johnson County rallied to save their homes and forced the invaders to take refuge at the TA Ranch, south of Buffalo. The cavalry from Fort McKinney (at Buffalo) rescued the invaders just in time and took them into their custody, but then the enormous political power of the invaders kicked in. These willful men proved impossible to convict, even though evidence of their guilt was overwhelming. All the invaders had to be turned loose on bail because of the ruinous costs of keeping them. Most of the defendants then left Wyoming, never to return, and witnesses were made unavailable. Johnson County's effort to enforce the law finally ended in abject failure in a Cheyenne courtroom in January 1893. The State of Wyoming provided no assistance, although Johnson County expected it from the beginning.[15]

The harsh and angry conflicts between big cattlemen and small cattlemen in Johnson County were not confined to the part of the county east of the Big Horn Mountains. West of the Big Horn Mountains, in the Big Horn Basin, the same fear and anger polluted relations among neighbors. On October 1, 1892, two men suspected of rustling, Dab Burch (evidently recovered from his gunshot wounds at the hands of Billy Rogers) and

Jack Bedford, were killed near Bonanza by range detectives in the employ of the big ranchers in the basin. These detectives, Joseph Rodgers, James Wickham, and John Peverly, had been directed by the Bonanza justice of the peace, Walter W. Peay, to act in a law enforcement role—to bring Bedford and Burch from Bonanza to Buffalo to face misdemeanor charges. Bedford and Burch were tied to horses in preparation for the long trip over the Big Horn Mountains, but only a short distance east of Bonanza, they were gunned down while still tied to their horses. All the circumstances pointed to the killings being cold-blooded retribution. No arrests were made, and it was not until November 28, 1892, that Rogers, Wickham, and Peverly were charged in Johnson County with first-degree murder. By the time a posse was formed to make arrests, Otto Franc had plenty of time to spirit the men away to Montana. Once again, the remoteness of law enforcement authorities frustrated the application of the law.[16]

Through the next few years, from 1893 to 1896, grave problems with crime continued in the Big Horn Basin, although there did seem to be a change in the types of crimes being prosecuted in the basin. During this time, the criminal records of Johnson and Fremont Counties show a larger percentage of property crimes brought against Big Horn Basin residents than shown previously. It is hard to say exactly why this would be so, but perhaps crime was being addressed somewhat more efficiently. The basin then had deputies from both Johnson and Fremont Counties, and a complete complement of justices of the peace and constables. The last year Fremont County and Johnson County made election declarations for the Big Horn Basin was 1894, and these showed the precincts of Embar, Gooseberry, Arland, Otto, Fenton, Alamo (formerly Sullivan's Ferry), Lovell, Wood River, Kirwin, Meeteetse, Marquette, and Chapman in Fremont County, and Shell Creek, Lower Shell, Paint Rock, Ten Sleep, Spring Creek, Red Bank, Bonanza, Torrey, and Warren in Johnson County.[17]

Even though more property crimes appeared in the records, there were still many cases involving violence. Jack Hollywood first came to the attention of law enforcement authorities in 1893, but he would reappear time and again, a bad penny turning up well into the twentieth century. By an Information dated January 11, 1893, it was charged that Hollywood did "beat and strike one Ella Owens [causing] grievous bodily harm by the use of a weapon, commonly known as a revolver." The file shows only the Information, and therefore the charge was obviously not prosecuted to conviction, but it is impossible to determine why it was not pursued further. This offense apparently occurred in Buffalo, but Hollywood was also well known in Ten Sleep. On February 25, 1895, he was charged with assault; James Fullerton, the Ten Sleep justice of the peace, wrote that Hollywood was caught "flagrante delicto" and that he has "borne a bad character for years."[18]

Hollywood then went to Hyattville, where he built a bar and was accused of having committed a rape on December 19, 1895. That prosecution was unsuccessful, and the victim retaliated. She was charged with arson in October 1896, for trying to burn down Hollywood's saloon. She pleaded guilty, but the record does not reveal her sentence.[19]

Hollywood then moved his bar to Thermopolis, and there he was charged with a January 1899 murder: He was supposed to have beaten the foreman of a local ranch over the head with a pistol, killing him. Again, he escaped justice. Finally, in September 1909, he committed one crime too many and the State of Wyoming put Jack Hollywood in the penitentiary. He shot and killed a man in his Thermopolis bar, was charged with first-degree murder, and was convicted of manslaughter. By 1909, change was accelerating in the Big Horn Basin, and after sixteen years of putting up with Hollywood, perhaps people finally felt they had outgrown his lawless antics.[20]

In March 1894, Bill Gallagher had a dispute with Belle Drewry regarding a bill of sale. Three men, Gallagher, William Wheaton, and "Blind Bill" Houlihan had gathered at Drewry's place, about five miles from Arland, downstream on Meeteetse Creek. Gallagher pulled a pistol and threatened first Drewry and then the two men, Wheaton and Houlihan. Gallagher kept the pistol on all three people for an hour, but then he sent Houlihan outside to obtain some horses, and when Houlihan failed to reappear, Gallagher took Wheaton out of the house at gunpoint. While the party had been in the house, however, Drewry had managed to slip a small pistol to Wheaton. When Gallagher was unable to find Houlihan, he brought Wheaton back to the house but then slipped and gave Wheaton an opportunity: Wheaton shot Gallagher in the head and killed him. Houlihan, finally returning to the scene, was infuriated that Wheaton had killed Gallagher, and a few days later, he came after Wheaton to avenge his friend.[21]

It is not clear exactly what happened then, but when Houlihan was distracted, Wheaton shot and killed him. Both Wheaton and Drewry were charged with murder, although Drewry was released after the preliminary hearing. Wheaton was tried (Will L. Simpson was the Fremont County attorney then) and claimed self-defense, but he was convicted of manslaughter and sentenced to eight years in the penitentiary.[22]

During the Wheaton trial proceedings, Rose Williams, who had moved her house of prostitution from Arland to a local ranch, was found dead along a road near Belle Drewry's home. There was speculation that Drewry had poisoned her. Only three years later, in 1897, Belle Drewry was killed under mysterious circumstances, after she had shot and killed the leader of a cowboy gang. This young woman, only thirty in 1897, was then interred in a hill overlooking Arland.[23]

In 1894, several attempts to prosecute livestock theft in the Big Horn Basin were not notably successful. Melvin Chapman and J. Brown were charged with killing a cow owned by the Bay State Ranch, a large ranch with its headquarters about a mile east of Ten Sleep. The case was dismissed, though, because it was based only on the testimony of one unreliable witness. On September 2, 1894, Earl D. Murray was accused in the Torrey Precinct of stealing a horse and saddle. The constable of Torrey, Henry Sherard, brought Murray in front of Charles D. Manderson, the justice of the peace, and Manderson heard evidence. Murray exercised poor judgment and testified; he admitted that he had stolen the horse but said he was induced to do so by two other men. Murray was sent to Buffalo for trial, in the custody of Constable Sherard. It is not clear how this case was finally resolved, but it would seem that a conviction should have been gained, given a virtual confession by the defendant.[24]

In another livestock case involving the Bay State Ranch, Melvin Chapman and Alfred Chapman were accused of killing cattle but were acquitted by a jury. In still another case involving the Bay State, Edward Blackman was accused of two counts of killing neat cattle. The file shows the issuance of subpoenas but no indication of either a trial or a dismissal. A charge involving livestock theft was always a hard one to make stick in Johnson County, but this might not have always been because juries resented large ranch owners. Juries of almost all eras have respected and faithfully applied the instruction that the accused must be proved guilty beyond a reasonable doubt. Given the hard chore of hauling defendants, witnesses, and evidence over the Big Horn Mountains by horseback, the quality of evidence presented to juries in Johnson County might not have been good. That the distance and trouble influenced prosecutor's decisions is shown in the case of *State v. Conway*. John Conway was charged with stealing livestock and had been bound and brought over for trial, but prosecutor T. P. Hill reported to the district court that the evidence against Conway was not strong. More than that, though, "The witnesses live in that portion of the County of Johnson County, known as the Big Horn Basin, and in the remotest portion thereof, which will necessitate their coming a distance of one hndred [sic] and twenty miles at great inconvenience and expense to themselves as to Johnson County." The prosecuting attorney requested that the case against Conway be dismissed.[25]

A conviction *was* obtained in the case of *State v. Woods,* in which Bert Woods pleaded guilty to stealing William A. Richards's saddle and bridle. George B. "Bear" McClellan, foreman of Richards's Red Bank Ranch (twenty-five miles south of Ten Sleep), was the complaining witness. Woods had made a poor choice of victim: Richards had been a Johnson County commissioner and had just been elected governor of the state of Wyoming.[26]

The poor judgment of another criminal defendant also resulted in a rare conviction. In August 1895, William J. Ewing was attacked at a crossing of a badlands stream that empties into the Big Horn River just north of what is now Worland. Ewing was traveling from Andersonville, which was located at the mouth of Owl Creek, about ten miles north of the southern rim of the Big Horn Basin. Ewing was carrying a great deal of cash, and the apparent motivation for the attack was robbery. As Ewing prepared to cross the streambed (which probably had no water but did require a slow, painstaking traverse down and up banks), a masked man ordered Ewing to throw up his arms and then fired at him, hitting Ewing in both arms. Ewing's horses bolted and carried him away from the robber and back to Andersonville. Soon after Ewing arrived, Albert "Slick" Nard rode into Andersonville. Something immediately gave him away, because Nard was accused of the crime against Ewing. When Nard's goods were examined, several clues tied him to the crime. He was taken to Buffalo, tried, and found guilty of assault with intent to commit murder and sentenced to fourteen years in the penitentiary.[27]

Whatever possessed Nard to ride into the very town in which his victim had just sought refuge is hard to fathom. Nard got his nickname, Slick, from cattle and horse rustling, but it appears that Slick was not very slick. His name was attached to the badlands stream where he staged his ambush, though, and to this day the little drainage a mile west of Worland is known by the euphonious title of Slick Creek (As spoken in Washakie County, the phrase rhymes).[28]

On January 5, 1895, the Wyoming Supreme Court finally rendered a decision and determined the fate of Big Horn County. They declared that constitutional provisions did not apply to valuation but did to population; therefore, because Big Horn County had claimed only 300 electors when seeking to organize the county, "the injunction prayed for will issue" (meaning that those challenging the creation of Big Horn County won the case). Though it may not appear so, this decision was a victory for Big Horn County. The biggest impediment to the organization of the county had always been valuation levels. If the constitutional levels had been required, it would have been well into the twentieth century before Big Horn County began life. The decision of the Wyoming Supreme Court removed that impediment and left only the requirement for a population of at least 1,500. The Big Horn Basin might not have had 1,500 people in 1892, but it certainly did by 1895, which meant that the way was open for creation of the county.[29]

The area had been growing, adding different kinds of people from those who had arrived in earlier years; farming families began to arrive. The land in the center of the Big Horn Basin is far too dry to support farming from rainfall alone, but those high mountains around the basin supply water in the form of streams rushing down from snowcapped peaks. These streams carry large volumes of water that can be diverted and spread upon the land. Land seemingly unable to grow anything but a sparse crop of sagebrush becomes remarkably fertile with the simple addition of water. Thus, settlers came in along the larger streams of the basin, dug irrigation ditches, and started growing alfalfa and grain. Along the Greybull River, the towns of Otto and Burlington were started by Mormons coming out of Utah. Large irrigation canals were dug near Cody, and an area north of what was to become Worland was settled by colonists from Germany. The Mormons arrived in larger numbers, with many families coming to the Big Horn Basin after 1893. In the spring of that year, William H. Packard, his wife, Cynthia, and their several children made the 400-mile wagon trip from Cache Valley, Utah, to a place a mile west of what is now Burlington, Wyoming. The Packard family was probably typical of a Mormon family of the day, though the account of this family's experiences—struggling constantly to eke out tiny economic gains, a new child born every year, followed by disease and death from all too common maladies such as scarlet fever, diphtheria, pneumonia, and typhoid fever—is a wrenching chronicle. Still, the Packards could be deemed more successful than most families, because Will Packard's ventures as rancher, farmer, and beekeeper were reasonably successful. One biographer said that Packard was "good at whatever he did," and his neighbors held him in such high esteem that they appointed him the first bishop of the Burlington Mormon Church. Will Packard had no way of knowing it in 1893, but in 1909, he would play a prominent role in a celebrated murder trial. Throughout the rest of the nineteenth century, Mormon families continued to come into the Big Horn Basin, a move that Leonard J. Arrington and Davis Bitton describe as, "the last important colonization in the traditional Mormon pattern."[30]

After the decision of the Wyoming Supreme Court, a new application was made to form Big Horn County, and by letter dated June 27, 1896, Governor William A. Richards issued commissions to newly appointed commissioners. That fall an election was held to determine a county seat and the first sheriff, county clerk, treasurer, and assessor of Big Horn County. It was a close election, with Basin City narrowly beating out Otto, though winning by a more substantial margin over Cody. Basin City was well situated to be the county seat, sitting on the banks of the Big Horn River, at about the geographic center of the Big Horn Basin, but its selection was still surprising. The town had not even existed until a few months before the election, when Winfield Scott Collins established it in a fit of pique over his inability to complete a purchase of land in Otto. Collins was an outspoken civil engineer and lawyer who was first admitted to the bar association in Springfield, Illinois, but who had been in the basin since at least 1887. Collins seems like a man who was greatly valued when he was on your side and detested when not: An Otto resident referred to him as "a shyster lawyer and a villain," but the people of the new county seat called him "the father of Basin City."[31]

The new county had hardly begun when events reminded residents that it was still full of tough customers and untamed people. Besides the killing of Belle Drewry in early 1897, there was a violent and deadly confrontation on September 10, 1897. Several cowboys working for the Pitchfork Ranch had a disagreement. One drunken cowboy, Henry Morse, was offended by a cook, Bob Jackson, and shot and killed him. Then Morse threatened other cowboys and fired at William West, only fifteen years old. Morse missed, however, and young West shot and killed him. A coroner's jury was quickly convened, and the jury rendered a verdict that killing Morse was justifiable, exonerating West.[32]

In 1900, the census was taken, and it showed interesting information about the new county, how the people of the Big Horn Basin had changed, and the ways in which they had not changed. Between 1895 and 1900, many more families had settled in the basin, bringing the 1900 population to 4,328 people. The basin still looked like a frontier population, though; 72 percent of people over eighteen were men, and only 28 percent were women. The men were mostly unmarried, but almost all of the women were married, except for a few older widows. The average age of the whole population was 24.6 years, a surprisingly low figure given the relatively small percentage of children.[33]

With the modest exceptions of Basin City and Cody, there is a remarkable uniformity of occupations listed in the census. For instance, in the Ten Sleep Precinct, sixty-seven men state their occupations, and all but three list "farmer" or "farm laborer." (Of the three nonconformists, two list "carpenter," and the third, Thomas Gorman, lists "machinist.") In none of the precincts in the Big Horn Basin does any man list his occupation as "rancher," and seldom does one list "cowboy." In today's parlance, though, most of the farmers would now be referred to as ranchers, and the great majority of the young men of the Big Horn Basin would be referred to as cowboys. If the definition of "farmer" extends only to one who raises crops for market, virtually no person in 1900 Big Horn Basin could be considered a farmer. It was nearly impossible to raise cash crops for market because, for almost all of the basin, no railroad was nearby. (The railroad arrived in Toluca, Montana, in 1900.) The only product that could be raised for cash was livestock, creatures that could be driven to a railroad or market. Crops were grown, especially by some of the newcomers, but apparently were consumed by the families living on the land and by their livestock. There were probably also small sales between neighboring ranches of items such as hay. Among those who listed themselves as farmers, the great majority did not own land. The census papers do show, however, many medium-sized ranches, businesses that employed two to five men, as well as a great many men not associated with a specific ranch, men who obtained seasonal work as it became available.[34]

One of the families arriving in the last few years of the nineteenth century was the McClellan family, Kenneth and Jennie McClellan and their children, who came to a place near Ten Sleep. It is not clear exactly when they arrived, but they were almost certainly there by 1898. We also do not know why Kenneth McClellan brought his family to the basin, but presumably there was work available. When they came to Wyoming, at least four children were still at home, and we know from the 1900 census, which showed that the McClellans had six children, that all six were living but only three were still at home in that year. One of their children, Maggie, probably left home in September 1898 when she married Tom Gorman.

McClellan's parents came from Scotland and apparently moved to Iowa, where Ken was born in 1846. His wife, Jennie, was born ten years later in Minnesota. They married in 1876, but where is unknown. The birthplaces of their children show that the family had moved around quite a bit. Their daughter Maggie was born in Nebraska; their daughter Annie in Colorado; son Kenneth back in Nebraska; and son John in Wyoming (in May 1898).[35] Paul Frison, in *When Grass Was Gold,* told an interesting story about Ken McClellan and his unknown brush with a violent death:

> There was a man living just below the mouth of Ten Sleep Creek on the No Wood named "McClellan." He was poor and had a large family. Eaton (Ed) told me the following story:
>
> "I was coming in one evening about sundown from out near Castle Gardens. The trail down the ridge was pretty sandy, and my horse wasn't making much noise. I came around the bend, and down in the bottom of the draw, old man McClellan was skinning a beef. He did not own a hoof of livestock. I reined my horse to one side; got off and, with my .30-30 rifle, sneaked up to about 100 yards of him. He was working like a beaver. Every now and then he would look around and then turn back and go on skinning the critter.
>
> "I took careful aim for his heart; had a perfect bead on him, but I kept thinking about his wife and five kids and just couldn't pull the trigger. I lay there and watched him for awhile; then slid back out of sight, put my gun back in the scabbard and rode down the other side of the ridge and went to the ranch. The poor s— of a b—— had a right to live, and he wasn't any worse than his neighbors. He never knew how close he came to being dry-gulched."[36]

Of course, a lot of single men were still coming to the area. Tom Gorman arrived not long after the formation of Big Horn County.

Gorman was born in New York in February 1870 and grew up in Penn-sylvania; as with the McClellans, not much is known about how or why he came to the Big Horn Basin near Ten Sleep. When he did arrive, though, he worked as a small ranchman and a freighter. (There were almost cer-tainly no jobs available in his declared occupation of machinist.)[37]

The years between 1898 and 1902 were peaceable years in the Big Horn Basin, and it was about time. But the murder of Tom Gorman shattered this brief time of peace in Big Horn County, and the criminal case of *State v. James Gorman* kept this little frontier county agitated for more than two years after Tom Gorman's death.

4

♦

The Trial

After the arrests of Jim and Maggie Gorman, the Wyoming press weighed in. The first newspaper stories about Tom Gorman's killing were hardly balanced. For instance, the *Cheyenne Daily Leader* carried a "special from Cody" stating that, "A horrible murder was committed near Basin, a short time since, and only became public yesterday. Tom Gorman, on Broken Back creek, about forty miles from here, discovered an intrigue between his wife and his younger brother, James Gorman. The victim endeavored to drive his brother away, when the pair turned upon him and killed him with clubs."[1]

The first article that appeared in the *Sheridan Enterprise* began with unabashed editorializing: "It's pretty difficulty [*sic*] to have the mind realize that a wife, bound by sacred ties, and a natural brother would be the parties to the murdering of a husband and brother, but unless all the circumstances surrounding the taking off of Tom Gorman are at fault, such is the case in the latest and most cruel murder in Big Horn county."

The article further declared, "It would appear that the deceased became convinced that unlawful relations were maintained between the guilty pair and frequent quarrels resulted. Mrs. Gorman and James finally decided to commit the foul deed that ended in taking the life of husband and brother, and fleeing together to distant parts." It closed with a startling pronouncement: "In addition to the above information has been received that the little daughter of the murdered man is also missing. When the man and woman hurriedly left the scene of their crime the little girl was taken with them but when arrested she was not to be found. The fear is entertained that she was pushed from the wagon and drowned in the Big Horn River."[2]

This theme was picked up by other newspapers. The *Natrona County Tribune* went so far as to report that Mrs. Tom Gorman and James Gorman were lynched when a committee asked them where Maggie's child was. Supposedly, Maggie told this group of people that it was none of their business, and she went on and abused the men in the group. Whereupon, "without further ceremony the couple were taken out and hanged." To the credit of the *Wyoming Dispatch*, a newspaper published in Cody, this paper took the *Natrona County Tribune* to task, saying: "There has been no lynching, nor will there be. The child above referred to is with its mother, and has been all the while. It is strange how so many erroneous reports similar to the above, originate in our country. It must be that some news paper correspondent is seeking notoriety."[3]

It is not clear where little Rose Gorman was at the time of the arrests. Perhaps she was with her mother "all the while," as the *Wyoming Dispatch* indicated, but none of the newspaper accounts mentions the little girl when telling of her mother's arrest. She might have been left with her grandparents, the McClellans. Wherever she was, she certainly had not been drowned, and later newspaper stories quietly mention the little girl being with her mother.[4]

Whether it was from the newspaper reports or general reputation, though, most people of the Big Horn Basin believed from the beginning that Maggie Gorman was just as guilty as Jim Gorman. They assumed that Jim and Maggie Gorman were lovers and that Maggie had a hand in her husband's death in some form. Tom Gorman was well liked; his brother was not; and Maggie was seen as too good-looking. Fred Bader seemed to express the attitude of the citizens of Big Horn County when he said that Tom was "homely, but a good, hard-working fellow and honest. Jim was good-looking, lazy, and dishonest"; he further declared that

Maggie was fickle and emotional. Such loaded perceptions certainly affect the analysis of an event, and these shared observations could have unfairly colored the judgment of Maggie Gorman's peers. Unfortunately, the historical chronicle is fragmented and ambiguous, making it impossible to know with reasonable certainty whether the community judgment of Maggie Gorman was based on accurate perceptions or distorting stereotypes.[5]

Regardless of whether the people of Big Horn County had fairly judged Jim Gorman and Maggie Gorman, the Big Horn County attorney, the same W. S. Collins who founded Basin City, had to address the concrete problem of prosecuting a murder. Collins was working on the case before September 1902, as shown by requests, to the Big Horn County commissioners in September, for reimbursement for expenses in the Gorman case.[6] Collins would have obtained a good idea of Jim Gorman's defense from a number of possible sources, most probably statements made by Jim at the time of arrest and during incarceration. By the time trial drew near, Collins surely knew that Jim Gorman was going to claim self-defense, asserting that his brother attacked him and was killed when Jim defended himself. Such a defense can be hard to overcome when the only witness describing an event is the accused person.

An interesting thing happened before the trial, however: Two attorneys, M. L. Blake, of Sheridan, and John P. Arnott, of Basin City, were retained on behalf of Maggie Gorman. There is some indication that Arnott had been hired in June, when arrests were first made. On the other hand, not until a week before the October 27 trial date did the district court appoint an attorney for Jim Gorman, when Gorman announced that "he has no funds with which to employ counsel." The obvious implication was that Maggie was unwilling to present a joint defense with Jim Gorman.[7]

Her later testimony shows that Maggie Gorman must have told her lawyers that she had nothing to do with the killing of her husband, that Jim Gorman was responsible, and that he forced her to go along after the killing. Maggie's lawyers surely passed this information on to the county attorney, probably with a proposal to turn state's evidence.[8]

Such a proposal would have meant heavy thinking for Collins. It seemed unlikely that Maggie Gorman was directly involved in the killing, but there were serious questions about whether she helped plan it or assisted Jim Gorman after it happened. On the other hand, if Maggie Gorman were a strong witness, her testimony might defeat any claim of self-defense by Jim Gorman. A decision to allow a defendant to turn state's evidence, and to provide a lenient deal in return, has to be made cautiously. The worst thing a prosecutor can do is to provide leniency to the person who proves to be the worse actor. Thus, the worse actor escapes punishment, and the remaining defendant is probably acquitted for being less culpable than the one exonerated.

If Collins did his homework, he interviewed Maggie Gorman at length. Nothing in the historical record indicates that Winfield Collins did interview her, but he most probably did, and, if so, this is what she would have told him: Jim Gorman had lived with Tom and Maggie at different intervals between 1900 and 1902. The brothers had quarreled several times, had each time made peace, but during the year before her husband's death, Maggie felt frightened and intimidated by Jim Gorman. One day she noticed her husband's absence and shortly thereafter saw a fire near the house. Then she had a conversation with Jim Gorman, and he said he had killed Tom and buried his body nearby. He told Maggie that he had stepped from behind a wagon as Tom came by and hit him with a hatchet, and that Tom had dropped without a sound. After Tom fell, Jim hit him again to make sure he was dead. Maggie had not revealed what she knew, because Jim had threatened to kill her and her child.[9]

Obviously, if a jury believed the testimony of Maggie Gorman, a self-defense claim by Jim Gorman would be out of the question, but it all hinged on her believability. The calculus of determining whether a jury will believe a witness is extremely complicated. Of course, the internal consistency of Maggie's story and its plausible relationship to other facts was highly important, but probably as important was the personality of the witness. Would this beautiful young woman charm an all-male jury or offend them? Did she project integrity? Did she have the fortitude and intelligence to fight off the inevitable hard cross-examination?

The county attorney apparently found Maggie Gorman's story persuasive, because he decided to enter into an agreement with her, whereby the charges against her would be dismissed if she would testify against Jim. The wisdom of that risky decision would soon be tested. The cases against Jim and Maggie Gorman were set for the 1902 October term of court, which meant that proceedings would begin the week of Monday, October 20, 1902.[10]

Since their June 14 initial appearances, all the people involved in the case had been preparing for, worrying about, and dreading the time of trial, and all too soon that time arrived. Lawyers, witnesses, jurors, and court personnel congregated in Basin City. One of those court personnel was the presiding district judge, Joseph L. Stotts. Stotts had practiced law in Sheridan, where he lived, before appointment to the bench as district judge in 1897; his court was very active.[11]

Judge Stotts had to travel from Sheridan to Basin, of course; in 1902, his trip began from a railroad in Sheridan, to Billings, Montana, and then south, continuing by rail. The Chicago, Burlington and Quincy Railroad had crept into the northern part of the Big Horn Basin, arriving in Cody from Toluca, Montana, in November 1901. The nearest railhead to Basin, though, was still a good fifty miles to the north, in Garland, and required a long day in a wagon or on horseback. In every county in Wyoming, cases were set for two different dates, during a spring term and a fall term, an arrangement that accommodated the arduousness of travel. In present-day Wyoming, terms are viewed as archaic relics, having little significance because communication and transportation are highly efficient, but in another day, they served a practical purpose. When Judge Stotts arrived in Basin for the fall term, he stayed there and worked through all pending cases before returning to Sheridan.[12]

On October 20, 1902, Maggie Gorman was arraigned upon an Information filed by Winfield S. Collins charging murder. She was present in court with her attorneys, Blake and Arnott, and she pleaded not guilty. Jim Gorman was also arraigned on charges of murder, and at this time, two Sheridan attorneys were appointed for him, E. E. (Edward Elmer) Enterline and, oddly, M. L. Blake. Blake was never a strong presence in the legal community in Wyoming, but E. E. Enterline was a major figure for more than half a century. In 1892, as a young attorney in Rock Springs, he filed suit against the biggest corporation in the state, the Union Pacific Railroad, and took the case to the Wyoming Supreme Court. He lost that case but persisted as an active and assertive attorney. During a span of more than fifty years, the name of E. E. Enterline is listed more than one hundred times as counsel in Wyoming Supreme Court cases. In 1898, he moved to Sheridan. He had no way of knowing it in 1902, but by 1910, he would form a partnership with Joseph Stotts in Sheridan; Stotts was already associated with another lawyer, a young man named Fred Blume. Enterline moved to Casper in the late 1920s and practiced law there until at least 1943. Between 1931 and 1933, he served as the president of the Wyoming State Bar Association.[13]

On October 21, Jim Gorman's attorneys made a motion for a separate trial, probably because they were aware that Maggie Gorman would assist the state against her brother-in-law; the motion was granted, and *State v. James Gorman* proceeded. The first order of business in the case was the selection of a jury. In any criminal case, the makeup of a jury is highly important, and to the prosecution, jury selection is the first step in a process intended to secure a conviction. When the charge is murder (mandating a death sentence under Wyoming law in 1902), this beginning proceeding is crucial. By state statute, the chairman of the county commissioners, the county treasurer, and the county clerk were charged to meet on the second Monday of each January and to make a list of persons to serve as trial jurors (placed in a series of four jury boxes); they were to select from the last assessment roll of the county and were to omit those persons "known by them to be incompetent or not qualified to serve as trial jurors."[14]

This arrangement is obviously different from the one used in the beginning of the twenty-first century, even more than may at first appear. The modern procedure is designed to produce a jury that is broadly reflective of the general makeup of the society. In Wyoming, assessment rolls are not used at all; the jury list is prepared from voter rolls, which are further expanded by the use of driver's license lists.[15]

Edward Elmer Enterline.
Courtesy the Colorado
Historical Society and the
Denver Post.

The applicable statute a century ago directed that people be listed on
the assessment rolls if they owned land, buildings, or personal property
such as livestock, "carriages and vehicles," "clocks, watches, jewelry, gold
and silver plate," furniture, musical instruments, farming utensils, and
corporate stock. The actual rolls show that the great majority of people
listed owned land and buildings, as well as a good amount of personal
property. Oddly, at least for Wyoming, women did not serve on juries. At
first, when women were granted suffrage in territorial Wyoming, they
did serve on juries, but this practice had died out.[16]

The panel that was to hear the case against Jim Gorman had been
selected just a few days prior to the beginning of the trial, from residences
that seemed to be evenly distributed around the Big Horn Basin. This

twenty-five–man panel did not look like most of the rest of the people in the county. It could fairly be called a collection of patriarchs, successful men who were leaders in the society. Almost three-quarters of the panel members were married, yet within Big Horn County, less than half that percentage of men were married. Less than half of the men in the 1900 census owned real property; the majority of panel members did. Further, the census forms show that among the two occupations listed most frequently (farmers and farm laborers, over 90 percent in many precincts), nearly twice as many men are listed as farm laborers than are listed as farmers, and yet only *one* member of the panel (of eighteen panel members who appear in the census) listed his occupation as farm laborer.[17]

Not one juror is an example of the most common kind of man found in the Big Horn Basin, the lone cowboy who eked out a living while working as a hand for different ranching outfits. That is the clear consequence of the Wyoming law in 1902, which provided for jurors to be selected from a list prepared by the county assessor. The Wyoming Supreme Court did not shrink from this result but declared, "It is a necessary qualification of a juryman that he must have been assessed upon the last assessment roll of the county, and no authority is conferred upon the jury commissioners to make a jury list except from the assessment roll."[18]

Though the use of assessment rolls for selecting a jury assured that any jury would be atypical, the selected jurors so closely followed a model that one suspects the overseeing officials exercised a further role, informally excluding those viewed as not having settled down or not being sufficiently responsible. In 1902, many Big Horn Basin citizens were deeply concerned about suppressing lawbreakers and would have welcomed a jury of stern patriarchs. If such a process of exclusion did take place, it would have been done not out of a Machiavellian impulse to manipulate justice, but out of an unspoken ethic that was widely shared by the majority of the population, and that was probably not even perceived as unusual. Indeed, when the defense attorneys started exercising challenges to the panel, they showed that their primary concern was not the apparently austere makeup of the jury, but more mundane considerations.

The first step taken was the drawing of twelve names, followed by examination of the prospective jurors by the attorneys to see if there were demonstrable grounds for disqualification, referred to as "cause." A man from Bonanza was challenged for cause and excused, though the record does not reveal the basis for the cause. Bonanza is only about fifteen miles down the Nowood River from Brokenback Creek, and perhaps this man had some personal involvement in the case. Other prospective jurors were challenged for cause, though again, there is nothing in the record to indicate why. The Big Horn Basin, with a population of about 5,000, was a small community, and people associated with the prosecution or the defense would frequently have a great deal of firsthand knowledge of the jurors. It was a social society; people did not huddle in their homes watching television. On Sunday afternoons, the favorite pastime was to go to other people's homes and visit, and more often than not, talk about other people they knew. Social events, such as dances, were central events in their lives. All the local newspapers from that time are filled with short notes about the visits everyone was making with everyone else. A prosecutor would have the advantage of a network of informants—county employees, sheriffs, deputies, and their families—who would report back about jurors, telling what kind of men they were, what kinds of associations they had, and often what comments they might have made about a case. The defense would also have a network: employees, friends, and relatives of the attorneys. Both sets of attorneys took ready advantage of this kind of information.[19]

After the challenges for cause were completed, peremptory challenges began, challenges not requiring the announcement of any reason for disqualification. The state was allowed ten challenges, and the defense, twelve. The state, however, used none of its challenges. Not so the defense, which used all but three of its challenges. Peremptory challenges flow from a hundred sources, some accurately directed at a hidden prejudice and some whimsical. In an individual situation, perhaps the glint in the eye of a prospective juror offended Enterline or perhaps he had heard a juror was a stern man; it is impossible to know why any specific challenge was made. As will be seen, though, some general patterns did emerge.[20]

The state kept waiving its challenges, taking the consistent position that it was quite happy with the jury exactly as it stood at any given time. With four challenges remaining, the jury boxes were exhausted, and Judge Stotts issued an "open venire" to Sheriff Hale (without apparent objection by the attorneys) so that the sheriff could obtain more jurors. It sounds like the sheriff was directed to go out and round up six men from wherever he could. This procedure seems questionable, but open venire is addressed in several Wyoming cases, including *Gunnell and Elder v. State,* in which the Wyoming Supreme Court accepts the practice, if not enthusiastically. As late as 1979, in *Peterson v. State,* an open venire was undertaken when a jury was short two jurors; the Wyoming Supreme Court once again accepted the practice.[21]

Sheriff Hale summoned six men; they were added to the jury box, and one was drawn as the last juror. The final jury members were C. C. Smith (Shell), John B. Gleaver (Meeteetse), Cornelius Workman (Lovell), A. J. Martin (Marquette), C. H. Watson (Sunshine), F. A. Whitney (Meeteetse), S. A. Watkins (Cody), W. E. Beck (Fenton), Dan Jimmerfield (Fenton), W. W. Leavitt (Shell), W. J. Chapman (Cody), and George Crosby (Lovell). Since the defense was the only party exercising peremptory challenges, the final look of the jury was very much the product of defense intentions. A map of the Big Horn Basin showing the residences of the jurors would be instructive. Such a map would show a distinctive pattern, as if someone were standing at Brokenback Creek and firing a shotgun to the west: There would be many little points in an arc a considerable distance away. The most important concern for the defense was obviously to keep people off the jury who had known the Gormans. The defense probably assumed that such people had liked Tom Gorman, or disliked Jim Gorman, or liked Maggie Gorman. Nothing indicates that the defense was otherwise offended by this final collection of patriarchs. They look very much like the initial panel; five out of the nine from our original nineteen exactly fit the model of a married man with children, owning his own home and ranch free and clear. One of these five, F. A. Whitney, became the foreman of the jury.

Seating the trial jury did not take long; the procedure was begun the morning of October 27 and completed within enough time that long opening statements were made and testimony begun the same day. Clarence A. Zaring, a Basin attorney who had been added to the prosecution team when Collins complained that he was "alone in this case and the defendant has two attorneys," gave the opening statement for the prosecution. (Zaring was a young man from Indiana, who was then part of the law firm Collins and Zaring.) Enterline gave a four-hour opening statement on behalf of Jim Gorman.[22]

Many newspapers carried stories about the Gorman trial, but almost every report was cursory, at least with respect to the evidence presented during the trial. This is particularly unfortunate because no transcript of the trial is available; nor are issues of the *Big Horn County Rustler,* the newspaper published in Basin and the one most likely to carry detailed information. Luckily, one contemporaneous newspaper article reported the trial in excellent detail. The November 10, 1902, *Cheyenne Daily Leader*'s story "Big Horn County's Terrible Tragedy" occupies two long columns, setting out the events of the three-day trial, and has every sign of having been written by a reporter who attended the trial and took careful notes. Indeed, the reporter, though not identified, was likely someone from one of the local newspapers, specially hired for this story.[23]

The first witness called was Sheriff Dudley Hale. Hale began his testimony on Monday, October 27, but it is not clear whether his testimony was concluded on Monday; a great deal of time could not have been spent hearing testimony that day. The purpose of Sheriff Hale's testimony was to set the scene, to provide the *corpus delicti*: proof of the fundamental fact that a crime has been committed. Hale used a diagram of the crime scene and told jurors of that spring day when he came to Tom and Maggie Gorman's home, learned of "certain suspicious conditions," and "traced the body of the deceased to its resting place." The *Cheyenne Daily Leader* reported that Hale's testimony "was listened to by all in the court room with breathless attention."

The second prosecution witness was even more closely heeded, because he provided sensational testimony. Hugh Collins testified that he had seen several quarrels between the Gorman brothers in which Maggie Gorman "interfered to prevent a tragic ending." Then he stated that on one occasion, apparently when he and Jim Gorman were walking to Basin, Gorman made some startling admissions. Tom Gorman had just taken a .30-30 Winchester rifle and chased Jim away from his home. Hugh Collins testified that Jim Gorman told him that "he had enjoyed illicit relations with Mrs. Maggie Gorman for about two years," that this was the reason Tom Gorman had got after him, and that Jim intended to return with a six-shooter and kill his brother. The *Cheyenne Daily Leader* reported that after Hugh Collins's direct testimony, "Mr. Enterline took him in hand for cross examination," that each of Collins's damaging statements was "rigidly dissected," but with little effect, and that "the prosecution felt that an important point had been secured in establishing a motive for the crime."

What should be made of this testimony? The prosecution had just forwarded evidence that on its face represented a damning indictment of Maggie Gorman, the most important witness for the prosecution, showing she had been engaging in adultery. The prosecution had to know, also, that Maggie Gorman would deny any such "illicit relations"; the testimony of Hugh Collins would appear to show her a liar. Yet the prosecution painted Collins's testimony as a great coup, emphasizing that it established a motive.

These thoughts surely came to the jurors' minds when the prosecution presented Maggie Gorman as their next witness. Until the prosecution called Maggie as a witness, members of the public had not known she was turning state's evidence. The announcement that Maggie Gorman would testify for the prosecution "caused a sensation in court, as she was charged jointly with the defendant with the crime, for which he was on trial."

From the moment she stepped into the courtroom, there was no question that Maggie Gorman refused to accede to the judgment of most of Big Horn County that she was a scarlet woman, complicit in the murder of her husband. At 11:30, the morning of October 28, 1902, Maggie appeared "entirely clad in black, and heavily veiled." There was a brief skirmish in which Enterline protested the acceptance of evidence from her, but to no avail: Maggie Gorman took the stand and began her testimony. The *Cheyenne Daily Leader* reported, "She was apparently as cool and self possessed as any person in the courtroom. She took off her heavy cloak, raised her black veil, and looked at the jury with an air of composure."[24]

Maggie first told how Jim Gorman had arrived in 1900 and that the brothers had had several quarrels, but that they had made peace. She said she first noticed her husband's absence on April 20, 1902. The next day, when she had gone looking for horses in the adjacent hills, she saw smoke. Shortly afterwards, she had a conversation with Jim Gorman in which he told her he had killed her husband and buried him in a washout.

The *Cheyenne Daily Leader* reported the dramatic climax of her testimony:

> She related the story of the murder as it had been told to her with a tearful modulation of her voice. "He told me," said she, "that Tom was coming from the corral, and that, as he came past the wagon, I (Jim) stepped from behind it and hit him a biff with a hatchet, and that he fell like a beef without a kick or a groan. He said that he hit him a second time to make sure that he was dead. He did not tell me what he had done with the body," she continued in answer to questions, "except to say that he had decided not to burn it because it would cause too much smoke and smell, and so had buried it."
>
> Mrs. Gorman continued and told the jury she had not revealed what she had learned because Jim Gorman had threatened to kill her and her child "if she said a word to anyone about the crime." In early June, she started to Montana with Gorman "under his threat to kill her if she did not." The hatchet used to commit the murder was shown to Maggie and she identified it.

Here the *Daily Leader*'s presentation of Maggie Gorman's testimony stops. Unfortunately, neither the *Daily Leader* nor any other newspaper reported Enterline's cross-examination. Perhaps Enterline chose to ask no questions at all, which seems highly unlikely, but if so, that striking moment surely would have been reported. The *Daily Leader*'s article is dainty regarding any references to sexual relations between Jim and Maggie Gorman. Besides Hugh Collins's direct testimony, the article reports nothing regarding cross-examination on this subject. (Enterline surely addressed it, at least indirectly, in his cross-examination of Hugh.) Nor does the article say anything about the prosecuting attorneys' positions on whether their chief witness against Jim Gorman was a liar and an adulteress.

Despite the lack of assistance from the historical record, we can surmise what the position of the prosecuting attorneys had to be. They had to state that Hugh Collins had told the truth when he said Jim Gorman had declared he had "illicit relations" with Maggie Gorman, but that did not mean it was true. Young men sometimes may exaggerate their sexual conquests, especially regarding an exceptionally attractive woman such as Maggie Gorman. The only thing Hugh Collins's testimony shows for sure is that Jim Gorman strongly desired Maggie Gorman, which certainly provides motive to kill her husband, who had driven him away under humiliating circumstances.

Shortly after the testimony of Maggie Gorman, the prosecution completed its case in chief and rested. Jim Gorman immediately took the stand in his own defense. His story, in the most important elements, was sharply different from Maggie's. Jim testified that he was born in Allegheny, Pennsylvania; he came to the Big Horn country in 1900 "at the solicitation of his brother," who promised him a partnership in his business interests. He lived with his brother and his brother's wife at intervals up to the time of the killing. He stated that he and his brother quarreled frequently. The first quarrel was over the colors of the British flag, Tom saying it was only red and white, and Jim maintaining it was red, white, and blue. This disagreement escalated to the point that Tom ordered Jim off the place at rifle point. Jim testified that he later returned at his brother's request.

Jim Gorman stated that the next quarrel was caused by Mrs. Gorman, and that his brother had threatened his life with a .30-30 Winchester. He said that Tom followed him out the door, throwing a beer bottle at him as he left, and then made him put down a saddle "upon peril of his life." Jim admitted that he came to Basin on foot with Hugh Collins but denied that he said anything regarding improper relations with Maggie Gorman or that he threatened his brother's life. He stayed two weeks in Basin but then spent the following six weeks with Kenneth McClellan, Maggie Gorman's father. Jim testified about his movements the day of the killing and said that he had returned to his brother's property to get a horse. The *Cheyenne Daily Leader* reported that "his testimony was given with a frankness that was impressive."

Enterline then tossed Jim Gorman a slow and easy pitch: "Tell us what happened on April 20, 1902. Tell the story of that day to the jury." The *Daily Leader* set out Jim Gorman's response in careful detail:

"In company with my brother Tom, we began building a wool rack," said the witness. "We worked together on it for some time and he left me and went into the house and stayed a long time. About 2 o'clock in the afternoon Tom came out where I was working, and asked me if I was going home. Why don't you stay and marry Anna McClellan, he said, applying an obscene name to her. I told him that I did not want to marry anyone, and that he had no business to talk about Maggie's sister as he did, as he had sisters at home in Pennsylvania. Tom got very mad and left me and went back to the house. I went on with my work. Shortly after our talk about Anna McClellan he came back, and grabbed a broken singletree [and] said to me, 'Now get down on your knees and say your prayers, you s— of a b——,' and he struck me a blow on the side of the head which glanced over my left shoulder. I picked up a shovel and threw it at him. He kept on coming at me, hitting me all over the body with the singletree. In my excitement I grabbed a hatchet and struck him, I don't know how many times. He fell and I dropped the hatchet and went to the corral, intending to go away. Shortly after that I came back to where Tom lay and found he was dead. Went to the house and saw Mrs. Gorman; told her I had had a fight with Tom and killed him, and that I was

going to give myself up. 'Don't do it,' she said, 'they'll hang us both.'
She advised me to bury the body, which I did. I dragged it to the
washout, laid it in, and caved the sides down for dirt to cover it with.
Next morning, I discovered a fire on the grave, but I did not build it.
Mrs. Gorman said that a fire would destroy all signs of fresh dug
earth."

The cross-examination of Jim Gorman is not reported, but the response
of Maggie Gorman certainly is. The trial went into an evening session,
and at 7:30 that night, Maggie was recalled for rebuttal. The *Cheyenne
Daily Leader* reported that "she denied point blank several statements
made by the defense." The exact statements are not identified but can be
easily inferred by the inconsistencies in the two versions. Maggie Gorman
most likely denied that Jim Gorman had reported a fight requiring self-
defense, that she had told him not to give himself up, and that she had
advised him to bury the body or had suggested or started a fire.

Surprisingly, Maggie Gorman's evening testimony completed all the
evidence offered in the case. The next morning, at 8:00, the case resumed,
but both sides had rested, and the jury heard no further testimony.
Instead, the judge and the lawyers addressed jury instructions. In Wyoming, the jury is instructed first, and then arguments are given. In a first-
degree murder case, the most important instruction is a general verdict
form, which includes lesser offenses. The jury is told to determine first
whether a defendant is guilty of murder in the first degree; if they find
the defendant not guilty of murder in the first degree, then they consider
the lesser offense of murder in the second degree. If they find the defendant not guilty of second-degree murder, they are to consider the lesser
charge of manslaughter. This instruction was no doubt given in the
Gorman case and is given today.[25]

There is also little doubt that each of the attorneys spent a long time
arguing from this instruction, although the contemporaneous newspaper
articles do not provide the details of the arguments. Zaring began for the
state "with a short address, in which he reviewed the facts and deduced
conclusions from them." Enterline then gave the principal argument on

behalf of Jim Gorman, and he spoke for two and one-half hours. He was followed by Blake, who, in return, was followed by Winfield Collins. Although no report of the content of the arguments exists, they can be inferred.[26]

The prosecution no doubt argued strongly for a first-degree murder conviction, saying that the evidence showed that Jim Gorman killed his brother purposely and with premeditated malice, as required by the first-degree murder statute. Jim Gorman's statements to Hugh Collins, the prosecution would have argued, strongly show that Jim Gorman had been planning to kill his brother for months, and the testimony of Maggie Gorman shows that Jim ambushed his brother and, rather than acting in self-defense, hit him a second time to finish him off. The defense, on the other hand, no doubt argued that neither Hugh Collins nor Maggie Gorman was credible, that Jim Gorman's account was believable, and that he was justified in using deadly force because he reasonably believed that his brother Tom intended to take his life or inflict great bodily harm upon him.[27]

After the arguments, the jury was put in the charge of the bailiff and retired to their room for deliberation. All other participants just waited. Time moves very slowly for those waiting for the return of a jury. In *State v. James Gorman*, though, the wait was not extensive. The jurors returned to the courtroom at 8 P.M., having deliberated for four and one-half hours.

The announcement of a verdict is a formal event; the defendant must be present, and the official participants in the trial—the judge, attorneys, bailiff, and clerk of court—also appear. Jim Gorman was brought into the courtroom, and when all the players were gathered, the verdict was read: "We the jury duly empanelled and sworn in the above entitled cause do find the defendant guilty of manslaughter."[28]

5

♦

The Second Trial

The manslaughter conviction looked like a defense victory. After all, if a killing that was "one of the most atrocious [crimes] in the history of Big Horn County" produced only one twenty-year prison term, it would seem that the defense came out pretty well. That is exactly how the prosecution saw it, and with good reason. The jury, in order to convict of manslaughter, had to do little more than accept Jim Gorman's testimony but believe he had misperceived his peril during the fight with his brother, that the younger Gorman probably was not really in danger of losing his life or suffering great bodily harm. To acquit Jim Gorman of first-degree and second-degree murder, it seemed they had to wholly reject Maggie Gorman's testimony.[1]

The remarkable thing is that the defense did not view this verdict as a victory at all. The defense asked for a new trial! Members of the prosecution, feeling they would do better in another trial, readily agreed; the verdict was set aside, and a new trial was set for the spring term of 1903. Regarding this event, Judge Stotts is supposed to have said, "Next time we will have a good jury, and we will hang the s— of a b———." Such a comment seems unlikely, but it does illustrate the strong feeling that the Jim Gorman jury had been far too lenient. In fact, though none of those involved in the prosecution and defense apparently knew it, at least one member of this jury was predisposed to leniency.[2]

Cornelius Workman was sorely troubled when he was called to jury duty in the Gorman case. Workman was bothered that he would be sitting on a capital case, because he did not believe in the taking of another human life, even by the state. He was member of the Church of Jesus Christ of Latter Day Saints, and he discussed his great conflict with his bishop (in the Mormon Church, the bishop is normally a layperson who acts as the minister of a congregation). Apparently, he reconciled his feelings, and the matter was not addressed in the questioning of prospective jury members, because Workman became a member of the jury. His feelings, though, would have led him to avoid ever having to confront the dilemma of finding a man guilty of a crime that carried the death penalty. During the jury's deliberation, Workman probably interpreted the prosecution's case skeptically and readily chose a compromise verdict of manslaughter. His attitude was probably not reflective of his religion; indeed, even in the twenty-first century, many prosecutors like Mormon jurors, feeling that they are, in general, an orderly people, not averse to insisting that citizens follow the rules.[3]

Cornelius Workman might not have been the only jury member bothered by the death penalty, though, considering the jury reached its verdict quickly, so quickly that it is unlikely a strong debate occurred between those wanting to convict Jim Gorman of a more serious count of homicide and those accepting manslaughter. The results from jury trials in the region in the previous twenty years would indicate, also, that all-male juries sometimes held a "boys will be boys" attitude, and perhaps this perspective arose during the jury's deliberations, a view that this crime was merely a spat between brothers that got out of hand. All this is speculative, but one thing is sure, a patriarchal jury of successful men did not always act the way stern patriarchs were supposed to act. Whatever the reasons for the jury's verdict, the verdict and the motion for new trial meant Jim Gorman would remain in the Big Horn County jail, and almost no formal proceedings would take place in the case until the spring term of 1903. There was one significant event shortly after the trial.

On October 30, 1902, the day after the manslaughter verdict came in, the prosecuting attorney filed a *nolle prosequi,* dismissing all charges against Maggie Gorman. Maggie Gorman was staying near Ten Sleep (perhaps this was required as part of the agreement for dismissal of charges), as shown by a November 15, 1902, article in the *Sheridan Enterprise.* The article noted that Maggie Gorman was in one of the Basin hotels earlier in the week, "with her fatherless and bright infant daughter." The story further stated: "She was studiously shunned by her sex. Verily, the way of the transgressor is hard. Mrs. Gorman, it is understood[,] will remain on Tensleep this winter, not far from the scene of the awful tragedy in which she is supposed to have borne a conspicuous part."[4]

The wait between the end of October 1902 and April 20, 1903, was a long one. The motion for a new trial had seemingly been made in haste, and now members of the defense had a long opportunity to consider their quick action and, perhaps, to repent at their leisure. What neither side may have known in the last days of October was that the granting of this motion invoked a legal question that was one of the closest and most vigorously disputed issues in American jurisprudence. Gradually, though, as April 20 approached and both sides prepared for the new trial, that reality must have come into sharper and sharper focus, together with the grim realization that the resolution of the question carried heavy consequences.[5]

By the time of the Gorman case and the fateful motion for a new trial, at least twenty-two American jurisdictions had considered the question of whether a criminal defendant, upon his own successful motion for a new trial, could be retried for a greater crime after being convicted only of a lesser included crime. Eleven states, Alabama, Florida, Iowa, Illinois, Louisiana, Michigan, Oregon, Tennessee, Virginia, and West Virginia, had ruled that no such trial could be held. The highest appellate courts in these states believed that these cases invoked the doctrine of double jeopardy; that is, the prohibition against a defendant being tried twice for the same offense. They reasoned that the acquittal of greater offenses (such as first- and second-degree murder) meant that the defendant completed the trial process and jeopardy attached, and that the defendant could not again be placed in peril of life or limb with respect to an offense for which he had been exonerated. On the other hand, eleven other states, Georgia, Indiana, Kansas, Kentucky, Missouri, Nebraska, New York, North Carolina, Ohio, Utah, and Vermont, had ruled that a defendant could be charged with the more serious crimes. These states declared that the defendant's voluntary action in seeking a new trial represented a waiver of any double jeopardy claim.[6]

Both camps had compelling reasons for their decisions. Those courts ruling in favor of defendants could demonstrate the unfairness of any other decision to criminal defendants. A new trial that could result in a much greater punishment, including even a death penalty, might well deter a defendant, no matter how innocent, from once again placing his life in peril.

Those courts ruling in favor of the prosecution could demonstrate the unfairness of any other decision to the state. Because of constitutional double jeopardy provisions, the state is prevented from appealing any determination against it (such as an acquittal of first- or second-degree murder), no matter how erroneous its basis, yet a defendant is free to seek a new trial on the conviction obtained on a lesser charge. When the motion for a new trial was made in the case of Jim Gorman, it is unlikely that either side knew that upon an appeal to the Wyoming Supreme Court, each side could present the decisions from exactly eleven state courts in support of its position. Typically, when faced with making a motion such as Jim Gorman's motion for a new trial, an attorney relies on his own knowledge of the law and on research he can complete within a couple of days. Legal research sources were limited in northern Wyoming in 1902, however; at the time of making the motion to dismiss, Enterline would have known that no controlling decision had been made in Wyoming (that is, not one by the Wyoming Supreme Court directly relating to the issue), that there were cases in several states declaring a defendant could not be retried for greater offenses, and that there were cases in several states asserting otherwise. Since there was no controlling precedent from Wyoming, it was difficult to know exactly how a district judge might rule; the question would be resolved on whichever line of cases the district court found persuasive. Enterline's initial research might well have given him an inaccurate picture of the state of the law, because of his inability to scan the entire landscape of relevant decisions.

Any good attorney, however, and Enterline certainly fit in this category, knows that the results of legal proceedings are unpredictable and that there is a distinct chance that a legal ruling will go against him, with possible disastrous consequences to his client. At the same time, that same good attorney would have to conclude that Jim Gorman would probably again be convicted of manslaughter. Even if a new jury fully accepted Jim Gorman's fight story and believed that he was in great danger, a hatchet in his brother's head did not appear to be the most appropriate recourse. (One obvious alternative was simply to run.) Thus, the motion to dismiss had a limited chance of producing a more favorable result and a distinct chance of producing a disastrous result. It has to be concluded that this motion was ill considered.

Based on E. E. Enterline's record as an attorney, though, it seems unlikely he would have recommended such a motion, even if his research had painted a skewed picture. On the other hand, past events had shown, and future events would confirm, that Jim Gorman was a willful and immature young man, and such a personality frequently makes decisions based on self-centered righteous indignation. Therefore, the decision to move for a new trial might well have been made against the recommendation of Jim Gorman's attorney. The client makes the final decision, and ultimately, the attorney can only advise. When a client makes an ill-advised decision, the attorney can only swallow his misgivings and proceed. Nothing in the record indicates that the motion for a new trial was made against counsel's recommendation, but there would not be any record of this. The last thing in the world Enterline could or should have done was to protect his own reputation by announcing something like, "My client has made a poor decision, against my advice, to try to obtain a complete acquittal." An attorney must always keep in confidence the information his client has given him; Enterline's obligation remained solely to Jim

Gorman, and he had to continue to use his best efforts to represent his client successfully.

Further complicating this legal quandary was the fact that many of the players had changed by April 1903, thus adding new variables to the new trial. In 1902, an election year, a new county attorney, John P. Arnott, had been elected. Arnott had assisted the defense in the first case, however, representing Maggie Gorman, and therefore, because "the public interest requires the appointment of some attorney to conduct the prosecution thereof," Hilliard S. Ridgely, of Cody, was appointed to prosecute Jim Gorman. Ridgely had just arrived in Cody, Wyoming, that year, supposedly to act as "Colonel Cody's attorney." He was an experienced attorney, having already served as the Lincoln County, Nebraska (North Platte), county attorney. Ridgely was another lawyer of substance, and during his career, he handled many important cases. The prosecution had obtained some strong talent.[7]

In addition, Jim Gorman made an application, supported by affidavit, for a change of judge, and Judge Stotts granted it. On April 25, 1903, an order was entered designating "the Honorable Charles E. Carpenter, Judge of the Second Judicial District of Wyoming," to try and to determine the case. Judge Carpenter had a connection to the Big Horn Basin in that the far northern part of his district included Fremont County, with a narrow strip in the south of the Basin, which was part of the Second Judicial District. Carpenter had just stood for election in 1902, and the people of Thermopolis, among others, had voted for him.[8]

Charles E. Carpenter was a stout, handsome man of forty-seven. He looked as a judge in 1903 ought to look: serious eyes over the obligatory mustache. An article in the October 24, 1902, *Thermopolis Record* described him as he might want (perhaps he wrote it himself): "he is a man of mature years and judgment, yet is in the full vigor of early middle life." The same article hastened to note, "Socially, the judge is a pleasant man and has made many friends."

Indeed, Carpenter did have some weighty qualifications, starting with his graduation from one of the best law schools in the country, the University of Michigan, at a time when a large number of practicing attorneys had not attended law school at all. He came to Laramie in 1881, when every place in the territory of Wyoming was young and raw (it is not known why he chose this rugged outpost), and then began the practice of law. For a time he was the Albany county attorney, and he served in the Wyoming legislature. He seemed to be what a Victorian gentleman should be, above reproach in his private life and habits, and to match reasonably what was proclaimed of him, "a man who is peculiarly fitted by nature, by education and by many years of active practice in the profession of law, to occupy the bench of an important court."[9]

The biggest change of all, of course, was to come from the jury, twelve completely new men; but before that process ever began, the looming crucial question had to be resolved, the one that would determine what crimes a jury could even consider when pondering the guilt or innocence of Jim Gorman.

The acting county attorney, Ridgely, apparently filed new papers (the information) against Jim Gorman, charging him with first-degree murder. The court file is unfortunately not available to confirm the exact procedural steps taken, but entries in the district court journal provide a good guide to what was done. The journal, though, only summarizes what was done without setting out the contents of pleadings; it is particularly disappointing that the full text of the parties' pleadings and briefs are not available.

Enterline attacked the Information by filing a pleading referred to as a "plea in bar." He probably recited the favorable decision of every appellate court he could find that had rendered a decision supporting his position. The prosecution responded by filing a demurrer, a paper saying that even if all the facts asserted by the defendant were correct, he must still lose. Again, we can safely assume that the prosecution forwarded at least most of the many cases supporting its position. One newspaper noted that in addition to the crime being one of the most revolting in the history of Wyoming, "it is interesting to the bench and bar because of the legal question involved," and noted that the defense was raising, for the first time in the history of Wyoming jurisprudence, the question of former jeopardy.[10]

On April 27, 1903, oral arguments were held before Judge Carpenter. The *Cheyenne Daily Leader* again covered the trial; not as thoroughly or as well as the previous trial, but it did mention these arguments. Of the arguments on behalf of Jim Gorman, the *Daily Leader* said: "The attorneys for the defense made a strong fight for their client, arguing that having once been convicted of manslaughter, Gorman, by this conviction, had been acquitted of murder in the first and second degrees, and therefore could not be placed in jeopardy on his own motion, for any crime greater than that of which he was convicted." Judge Carpenter was not convinced, however, and he ruled in favor of the prosecution, declaring that Gorman, when he asked for a new trial, had waived any constitutional rights and "stood in the same relation to the court as if no former trial had been held."[11]

The critical legal question having been resolved, at least until the Wyoming Supreme Court could render a decision, the trial proceeded. Jim Gorman was arraigned the same day, being read the information and asked how he wished to plead; of course, he pleaded not guilty. As with the first trial, M. L. Blake assisted E. E. Enterline; C. A. Zaring assisted H. S. Ridgely. All parties announced they were ready to proceed, and the process of empaneling the jury was begun. Apparently, this was well under way, but not complete, when the noon hour arrived on April 27. It had been a busy morning, with the hearing on the defendant's plea in bar, the arraignment, and the beginning of jury selection.[12]

As in the first trial, the jury was selected from an original panel. These jurors looked very much like the jurors in the first trial. Thirteen of these men are found in the 1900 census, and eight of these thirteen exactly fit the model found in the first trial, of a married man with children, declaring himself to be a farmer on the farm (with house) that he owns free and clear.

When the jury selection proceeded, though, there were apparently many successful challenges for cause, because Judge Carpenter ordered that a new group of sixteen prospective jurors be named. These additional jurors were still not sufficient, and, as with the first trial, an open venire had to be issued. The sheriff of Big Horn County (then J. J. Fenton) was commanded to go out and find ten more jurors. He did so, but the process offended Enterline, who at this point must have been acutely aware of how much peril his client faced, and who must have felt strongly, as he surely did in the first trial (and as virtually all defense counsel do in capital cases), that he was fighting to save his client's life; he made a motion to "quash the array," which means to declare the jury selection invalid; in this case, to start over with a new panel. The motion was denied. The long process of empaneling this jury continued, even through an evening session, and the court recessed until Wednesday, April 29. On that Wednesday morning, the court had to first recess while the sheriff went out and found more prospective jurors. After that was done, and they were all questioned, there were *still* not enough panel members. Why there was so much difficulty in selecting qualified jurors would be interesting to know, but there is no record available to enlighten us. Perhaps Enterline was able to establish that in light of the first trial, many prospective jurors held unshakable opinions of guilt. There was no doubt a lot of talk about the first trial, and the apparent, strong consensus was that Jim Gorman had literally gotten away with murder, but we have no way of knowing exactly why one juror after another was excused.[13]

A new open venire was issued, and the sheriff once again sallied forth to summon twelve qualified jurors; the court stood in recess until 2 P.M. When 2 P.M. arrived, however, a new matter had arisen, as recorded in the district court journal: "the sad news had been brought to him [Judge Carpenter] of the sudden death of our beloved Governor, Honorable DeForest Richards, and with feeling [he] gave expression to the sentiment that all who knew our Governor, regardless of party affiliations, appreciated his high moral character, integrity and ability both as a man and an officer of this Commonwealth, and held him in high esteem." The judge went on and declared that in honor of Governor Richards's memory, the court would stand adjourned until the next morning, and E. E. Lonabaugh, Carl L. Sackett, and M. L. Blake were appointed to a committee to prepare a tribute "to be spread upon the Journal of the Court."[14]

When court resumed the next morning, Sheriff Fenton presented twelve new jurors, and Enterline made another motion to quash the array. One plausible reason for these motions was that there had just been a major challenge to the jury-selection system in Wyoming, and Enterline surely knew it. In the case of *State v. Bolln,* decided in September 1902, the Wyoming attorney general had made a motion before the Laramie County District Court to quash the array. The district court did not want to deal with the issue and referred the whole question to the Wyoming Supreme Court. The Wyoming Supreme Court rendered an opinion in which it found that some parts of the system were constitutional, but it was critical of open venires (indicating they should be used sparingly and only if certain strict requirements were met) and left a lot of questions hanging. Enterline must have felt that given the messy jury-selection proceedings in this second trial in *State v. Gorman,* there were fertile grounds for establishing an error on appeal. His motion was again denied, but the defense now had one more basis on which to challenge any conviction.[15]

Peremptory challenges were exercised, but in this trial, that process is not described in the district court journal. A jury was finally selected, however, and this jury was comparable to the first jury in that almost all the jurors were owners of substantial property. It was different, though, in that more of the jurors were of the Mormon faith, probably a majority. The foreman of the jury would turn out to be Ora Sommers, a man from Otto who listed himself in the census as a "lumberman," and who was likely Mormon. The known residences of the jurors show the pattern from the first jury, wherein men from areas close to Brokenback Creek were excluded, although one juror, William Lewis, might have been an exception to that rule.[16]

The evidentiary part of the trial finally got under way on the afternoon of Wednesday, April 29. The second trial was unfortunately not reported as thoroughly as the first had been. Perhaps newspapers felt that the trial would just be a repetition of the earlier proceeding; but a trial is performance art, and how a witness, attorney, or judge will play a scene at any given time can vary to a surprising extent. Records do show that the beginning witness for the state was the coroner, Dr. Carter, and that Maggie Gorman again testified. The only newspaper article with any detail, from the *Cheyenne Daily Leader,* is a disappointment. Some of the headings give a flavor of the article: "Termination of Sensational Trial at Basin City—Wife of Murdered Man and Paramour Turned State's Evidence against Her Quondam Lover." Most of the article just provides a jazzed-up history of the case and makes a few generalizations: "The trial was a sensational one, the conviction . . . being secured through the confession of the murdered man's wife, who turned state's evidence against her lover upon the promise that she would be released and not prosecuted for participation in the crime." There is no detailed and accurate recitation of testimony as there was in the article about the first trial; indeed, there is no indication at all that a reporter actually attended the trial. Virtually every statement in the article could have been obtained second-hand from some source such as one of the prosecuting attorneys, and, apparently, every statement was.[17]

Once the trial began, court and counsel went at it diligently; on Wednesday, April 29, the court did not adjourn until 6:00 P.M., and at 7:30 that evening, the trial resumed; they were back in the courtroom at 8:30 the next morning. They proceeded to hear witnesses through that morning, but during the afternoon of April 30, the trial was interrupted again over the death of Governor Richards. The jurors in the Gorman case first came into the courtroom and sat in the jury box. Then the presence of the defendant and his counsel was acknowledged. Judge Carpenter assumed the bench but then gave way to Judge Stotts, who announced a tribute to Governor Richards: "This Court having been notified that the Funeral of Our Beloved Governor is to be held at the hour of Two O'clock P.M. of this date. It is hereby ordered that this Court be and is hereby adjourned until 2:30 P.M. of this 30th day of April, 1903." A committee of lawyers was appointed to draft resolutions, and these resolutions were spread "upon the Journal." Recitations cited how DeForest Richards had spent the best years of his matured life developing "great business industries" as a private citizen and then used his talents and efforts as a legislator and as chief executive, and how he was profoundly respected because of his "unsullied reputation" and his "lofty ideals and aspirations." The tribute closes with something like a peroration:

Now, therefore, Be it Resolved, that we join with the people of Wyoming in mourning the great and irreparable loss they have suffered in
the death of Governor DeForest Richards and extend to his sorrowing
family our heartfelt sympathy, And, as a mark of our sincere respects
for his memory, these resolutions be spread upon the records of the
April term of the District Court of Big Horn County, now in session,
and a copy thereof be mailed to his bereaved family.[18]

It was signed by eight attorneys. Many recent Wyoming governors
have been well liked, but it is hard to feature such elaborate ceremonies
to mourn any of them had he died, interrupting a capital murder trial to
declare such strong public grief. Richards had been popular enough to
earn a second term, but beyond that, there is nothing in the historical
record showing unusual public devotion to this governor. Apparently, in
Wyoming in 1903, however, Governor DeForest Richards was well known
to the members of the bar and genuinely liked.

There was still a murder trial to complete, however, and the trial
resumed. No evening session was held that day, though, perhaps because
all witnesses had been heard and a convenient stopping point had been
reached. The proceedings did not begin again until the next morning,
Friday, May 1, 1903, when the attorneys presented jury instructions.
These must have been a repeat of the instructions in the earlier trial; thus,
these proceedings probably did not take long. It appears that final
arguments began at 10:00 A.M. and, as with the first trial, were lengthy.
The themes sounded by each side were probably those sounded in the
first trial. The evidence in support of each point might have been stronger
or weaker than in the first trial, but the basic positions would not have
changed. No doubt the prosecution again argued that the testimony of
Maggie Gorman and Hugh Collins demonstrated premeditation on the
part of Jim Gorman, and no doubt the defense again argued that Jim
Gorman's testimony was the most believable and that he was justified in
using deadly force in defense of his life.[19]

The arguments were finally concluded at 5:15 that afternoon, and the
jury began to deliberate. Once again, the anxious wait for a verdict began.

In this second trial, the wait was longer, but not by much. After five hours, the jurors sent a note to the judge that they had reached a verdict and were ready to return.[20]

Once again, the elaborate ceremony for the return of a verdict was played out. It was very late that Friday evening when all the parties— the judge, the jury, the attorneys, the clerk of court, and the defendant— were gathered. Some of these people might have felt the weariness brought on by the hour; the attorneys and the defendant surely did not. Indeed, the adrenaline surge is so strong at such times that sleep becomes impossible for hours afterward.

Each of the jurymen filed into the courtroom, each had his name called, and each answered to his name. The foreman presented the verdict to Judge Carpenter. He read it and gave it to the clerk of court, who finally read the decision. This is what those in the courtroom that very late evening heard: "We, the Jury duly empanelled and Sworn in the above entitled Cause, do find the defendant Guilty of Murder in the First Degree as Charged in The information."[21]

Jim Gorman must have been stunned. Perhaps his attorneys were, too. There are obligations and expectations, though, and people numbly follow through on these; Gorman was taken by the sheriff "to await the pleasure of this Court," but there was no mystery in that. The "pleasure" of the court had already been commanded by statute. As the *Cheyenne Daily Leader* observed, Jim Gorman must now "pay the extreme penalty of the law."[22]

The *Daily Leader* also observed that Gorman was the fourth man currently under sentence of death in Wyoming, the other three being Tom Horn, "the notorious cattle detective convicted of killing Willie Nickell, a 14 year-old boy at Iron Mountain, on July 18, 1901"; a man named James Keffer, for murdering a stock tender near Rawlins; and Joseph P. Walters, "convicted of murdering Mrs. Agnes Hoover on the streets of Thermopolis on September 7, 1901, because she refused to marry him." Walters was already in the Big Horn County jail when Gorman was arrested in June 1902, and he and Gorman must have known each other well. The *Daily Leader* went on to note that every one of these cases was on appeal to the Wyoming Supreme Court, but that the Walters case was the only one "under consideration," apparently meaning that although briefs had been submitted and oral argument made in the Walters case, no decision had yet been made.[23]

The next day, Gorman's attorneys made motions to protect his appeal, including a motion for a new trial and a motion in arrest of judgment, but both were denied. Judge Carpenter proceeded to sentencing. He asked Jim Gorman whether he had anything to say about why judgment should not be passed upon him, and Gorman answered that he had nothing to say (what could he have said?). Whereupon, Judge Carpenter pronounced sentence:

> It is therefore Ordered, Considered, Adjudged and Decreed by the Court that, you the said James W. Gorman, defendant, be taken by the Sheriff of Big Horn County, State of Wyoming and there to be confined until the twenty-sixth day of June, A.D. 1903 [when] you [will] be taken by the sheriff of said Big Horn County, Wyoming, to an enclosure in the immediate vicinity of said jail prepared for that purpose as provided by law, And by said Sheriff therein hanged by the neck until you are dead.

A notice of intention to appeal to the Wyoming Supreme Court was also filed on that day, and so the sentence and judgment (and the execution thereon) was suspended until the first day of the following term, and the slow workings of an appeal begun.[24]

6

♦

Joseph Walters

E. E. Enterline could at least feel positive about the appeal. Bad as the result from the jury had been, the game was not over. On the question of retrying Jim Gorman for first-degree murder, Enterline could legitimately reason that his client had a 50 percent chance of winning; and that chance was augmented by the possibility that the supreme court would be offended by the jury-selection method. Thus, Enterline had two legitimate grounds of appeal. Most criminal appeals are hopeless from the beginning, proceedings that would be deemed frivolous if they were appeals of noncriminal cases, but not so Jim Gorman's appeal.

Gorman's hopes must have been buoyed by the appeal of his cellmate, Joseph P. Walters, wherein Enterline had forced the Wyoming attorney general to admit that the prosecution had committed error before the trial court. Joseph Walters had shot and killed Agnes Hoover on September 7, 1901. She was the widow of John Hoover, a prosperous Otto businessman who had died in January 1901, leaving her with a substantial estate, as well as the care of two young sons and a stepdaughter.[1]

That summer, Mr. Walters, a clothing salesman, spent time in the Otto area. He was a smallish, white-haired man of fifty, a man with an evident history of abusing alcohol, but who looked "more like a kindly grandfather than a murderer." He became enamored of Mrs. Hoover, to the point of proposing marriage, but she was not interested. A friend of hers, Alice Massey, a keeper of an Otto hotel, found a gun under a pillow in Walters's room and warned her about him. The Hoover family and the Massey family decided to take a trip to Thermopolis, apparently with the hope that if Hoover left the Otto area, Walters would go away.[2]

They went to a place near the large hot springs at Thermopolis but on the east side of the Big Horn River (so that they remained just inside Big Horn County), where they camped in tents for two weeks. Unfortunately, Walters learned where Hoover had gone and followed her there. He confronted her in the presence of her six-year-old son and again asked her if she would marry him. When she vigorously refused, Walters grabbed her arm, said, "We will both die now," and shot both her and himself. Hoover was killed instantly, but Walters's injuries were not serious. He was immediately arrested and returned to Basin. Agnes Hoover's body was returned to Otto in the same wagon that had brought camping equipment to Thermopolis. She was buried in Otto next to her husband, the site of "the tallest Woodman of America stone in the cemetery."[3]

Although Walters was confined in the Basin jail for murder, no attorney was appointed for him until the beginning of the October term, on October 21, 1901. On that date, B. R. McCabe, a young and relatively inexperienced attorney, was finally appointed, and on October 22, M. B. Camplin was appointed to assist in the defense. But then on October 23, Camplin was called away "to attend to other matters," and he asked E. E. Enterline to present a motion for continuance. Enterline agreed to do so, subject to the condition that he would proceed solely for the purpose of seeking a continuance. On October 23, two additional attorneys, William S. Metz and John P. Arnott, were appointed to assist the state. The state was now represented by four attorneys, including two who had "been engaged in the practice of law . . . for a number of years."[4]

The motion for continuance was heard on October 26, 1901, and the only attorney who appeared on behalf of the defendant was McCabe, who by then had also submitted an affidavit in support of a continuance until the following spring term, an extension of about six months. McCabe's affidavit showed that he had interviewed the defendant and believed

Walters "was irresponsible for the act set forth in the information"; that
the alleged homicide took place seventy miles south of the county seat, in
an area without railroad service; that it was necessary to go there and
interview potential witnesses; that great prejudice existed against the
defendant and he could not get a fair trial in this fall term; and that the
defendant was of no assistance because he "states he has no recollection as
to his conduct." McCabe added that he "was wholly unprepared to try
the cause at said term, and that he was engaged in the trial of other causes
at said term." All of these statements were probably accurate, but the
motion for continuance was quickly denied and trial upon the charge of
first-degree murder was set for October 30, just four days later.[5]

At some time before the trial, Dr. Julius Schuelke, a physician, had
interviewed Walters. Walters told him that he was "greatly disturbed"
because Mrs. Hoover had not wished to see him, but in addition he
claimed that "he had been weakened for weeks and weeks, during the
time that he was associated with this lady, by constant drains of semen,
and that his mind had become unhinged."[6]

When the day of the trial arrived, McCabe renewed his motion for
continuance and submitted a more detailed affidavit, showing, among
other things, that for a portion of time after the order setting the trial, he
was "engaged in the trial of another cause pending in the court for which
he had been retained and employed a long time prior to the commencement" of the term. This makes sense, because attorneys were then retained
to try cases to be heard upon the commencement of a new term. Had the
murder of Agnes Hoover never occurred, McCabe would have been
thoroughly occupied at the beginning of the fall term. McCabe stated
further that in order to prepare for the trial of this murder case, he would
have to travel at least 250 miles and stop at least a day at five different places
to investigate and subpoena witnesses. The state countered this affidavit
with its own, stating that McCabe "thoroughly understood the cause and
that the County Attorney had subpoenaed all the witnesses for both the
State and the defendant." The motion for continuance was again denied.[7]

When the trial proceeded, the result was no surprise. The state presented a compelling case, and the defense had very little to forward. The

testimony of three doctors was presented, and McCabe asked only perfunctory questions on cross-examination. Walters was found guilty and
sentenced to be hanged on December 16, 1901.[8]

Walters appealed, and in his appeal, he was represented by Enterline,
who wrote a strong brief to the Wyoming Supreme Court, setting out in
persuasive detail why a continuance should have been granted, but also
demonstrating a significant error in the trial. The jury in *State v. Walters*
had been instructed that the defendant could be found guilty of first-
degree murder if he formed the intent to kill "at the time the shot was
fired." In another case just decided by the Wyoming Supreme Court, an
instruction with this phrase had been addressed. In *Ross v. State,* the
supreme court made the cogent observation that this instruction was
improper in a first-degree murder case, because if such a statement were
correct, the distinction between first- and second-degree murder would
be abolished. First-degree murder in Wyoming required premeditation
(and still does), a time and an opportunity for deliberate thought. Clearly,
if premeditation was formed at the instant of firing a shot, there could
have been no time and opportunity for deliberation. In the Ross case,
however, the defendant had been convicted of only second-degree
murder, and therefore the supreme court declared that the error was
harmless. The pronouncements in *Ross* represented what lawyers refer
to as "dictum," that is, a statement of law unnecessary to resolve a case
before the court, and thus one carrying less weight in a subsequent
appeal. Still, *Ross* had been decided only two years earlier, and two of
the three judges who had decided *Ross*—Jesse Knight and Charles N.
Potter—were still on the supreme court; Enterline had good reason to be
optimistic that when the Wyoming Supreme Court actually addressed a
case of first-degree murder in which the criticized instruction was given,
the court would follow through on its earlier pronouncements. This
asserted error probably represented the best chance for reversal. The
complaint about the refusal to grant a continuance might well draw
some sympathy from members of the supreme court, but standing
alone, it would probably not have resulted in what the defense sought,
a reversal and new trial.[9]

In the brief, Enterline also effectively demonstrated that the defense of insanity required "great research and careful study," and with time to prepare, thorough examination could have been made on "nervous diseases," and (reflecting the state of psychiatric knowledge in 1902), it could have been shown that "insanity is frequently caused by self-abuse or sexual excesses. In fact [examination] could have brought out that the asylums are full of the male sex as a result of sexual excesses."[10]

Within the files of the Wyoming attorney general is a fascinating set of letters between Enterline and the man who was then the attorney general of Wyoming, J. A. Van Orsdel. The letters show that they were old friends, or at least they acted like old friends, as they exchanged candid observations and humor. Enterline wrote Van Orsdel on July 16, 1902, telling him that he was mailing the brief in the Walters case under separate cover, and that if Van Orsdel needed additional time to respond, "I will be pleased to stipulate with you for further time. My client is not anxious to be hanged during this hot weather." On July 30, 1902, Enterline again wrote Van Orsdel ("Dear Friend Van") and again offered to accommodate an extension of time, saying, "I am not afraid that the judgment will be affirmed, but am afraid that a new trial might result the same, so am not in a hurry." In other words, Enterline is candidly telling Van Orsdel that he thinks the conviction will be reversed, but that Walters will probably be again sentenced to hang.[11]

On August 13, 1902, Enterline again writes "Friend Van," but this time teases him about a Big Horn County dispute involving water rights: "What in the d——l have you been doing in Big Horn County? I notice that Metz has been interviewed at Basin, and announced that you are way off on some legal questions affecting water rights." Enterline makes an observation regarding Metz that is surprising given their later association: "I don't take much stock in a lawyer's opinion who is being interviewed for the purpose of advertising the fact that he has been retained in a case. I confess that I haven't the same good opinion of Metz's ability as a lawyer as some of our courts seem to have."

Enterline goes on to make some remarkably frank admissions to opposing counsel in a capital case: "I'll admit that the record in the Walters case shows up bad against him, but then he had no defense. He stands a good chance though of getting a new trial on the mistakes of the prosecution. I suppose that you'll argue as you did in the Roberts case that it looks as if the defense tried to get error in the record." Enterline made some more unflattering references to Metz:

> I'll even upon on my friend [?] Metz in that case. He tried his best to get Judge Stotts to appoint me to assist in the defense the day the case was called for trial, but Judge Stotts wouldn't do it. After I saw the instructions that he prepared I knew that there was a good chance of reversal[,] especially when I noticed[,] as I did as soon I heard the instructions read[,] that the court was giving the same instruction that Corn criticized in the Ross case. It was a popular case to prosecute, and Metz of course wanted to be on that side. And he wanted me on the other. I knew he would be retained to take the case to the Supreme Court, and I managed to see that the record was kept in shape so that it would be determined in the Supreme Court on its merits.[12]

Enterline wrote Van Orsdel again on August 25, 1902, and this time he expressed more confidence in a favorable resolution of the case for Walters: "I do not think that Walters will ever reach the halter. I can make a good defense next time—I mean a better one than was offered by the learned counsel who defended. In fact he had no defense."[13]

The briefing schedule in the early part of the twentieth century was leisurely, and the attorney general did not file his brief until January 15, 1903. In the meantime, he had been in contact with Metz, who had apparently been the primary trial counsel in the Walters case. Metz addressed the problem instruction given in *State v. Walters*. He told Attorney General Van Orsdel that he thought the language in the challenged instruction in *Walters* was different from that in *Ross,* but he acknowledged, "this is a very close proposition." A lawyer who makes this kind of admission may mean it, but the admission also may signal that the lawyer is in trouble and wants to hedge. Metz went on to insist on the justice of the conviction of Walters: "There is absolutely *no evidence* of any defence of any character to this maliciously cruel murder, . . . there is absolutely *no evidence* of any insanity."[14]

When the state filed its brief in response to Enterline's opening brief, it reflected Metz's input, at least to an extent. The attorney general obviously believed that giving the *Ross* instruction, the one allowing premeditation at the moment a shot was fired, was a weak point for the prosecution. He admitted that the instruction given was in error, apparently feeling he had no choice. Attorney General Van Orsdel was not about to agree to a reversal of the trial court's decision, however. After his admission of error in the instruction, Van Orsdel then went on to assert that the jury could not have been misled by the erroneous instruction, because the wording was different from that of the *Ross* instruction (as Metz had pointed out to Van Orsdel). Van Orsdel noted that the word "purposely" had been used in the *Walters* instruction but not in *Ross,* and he asserted that this made all the difference. From a hundred years' distance, it is hard to see how the word "purposely" salvaged the overall problem with the defective instruction, one that allowed premeditation to occur the instant a shot was fired. Second-degree murder requires only that the crime be committed "purposely," and thus the commission of a "purposeful" homicide says nothing about premeditation and cannot establish first-degree murder.[15]

In addition, the state argued that it had been proper not to grant a continuance, because it was incumbent upon the defendant's lawyer to specify the names and residences of each of the witnesses he would have called, the facts expected to be proved by these witnesses, and their materiality, and to ensure that the facts cannot be proved by any other witness. To poor McCabe, who had not been given the time to conduct even the most perfunctory of investigations, this position of the State of Wyoming must have seemed like outright sophistry. How could he conceivably have stated detailed information about witnesses when he had been denied the opportunity to find and interview them?[16]

For that matter, to almost any modern attorney, this refusal to grant a continuance presents a shocking example of unfairness. By the standards of 1902, the position of the State of Wyoming was apparently not beyond the pale, but even in that day and time, a court would consider fundamental considerations of fairness. If an attorney is not given any real opportunity to investigate the offense with which his client is charged, there frequently will be no possibility of producing a defense, even if the client has a strong and meritorious one.

On March 30, 1903, the attorney general wrote Enterline ("My dear Enterline"). One of the purposes of the letter was to discuss oral argument of the *Walters* case before the supreme court, but the primary subject was Van Orsdel's application to be appointed as the United States district judge for Wyoming: "I am in receipt of your letter of March 27 assuring me of your endorsement of my candidacy for a place on the U. S. District bench if the vacancy occurs. I wish to thank you for your kind support in this matter." A day later, Van Orsdel wrote Enterline and told him that the Wyoming Supreme Court had set oral argument in *Walters* and another case for April 13; Enterline wired back that "April 13 will suit me."[17]

Van Orsdel might have been Enterline's friend, but in his reply brief, Enterline was hard on the state. He pointed out that "Unfortunately for the Attorney General," he (Van Orsdel) had discussed a statutory provision other than the one under which the defendant sought a continuance, and that the attorney general had "wholly failed to even comment upon the provisions of [the actual provision relied upon]." Enterline further commented that the attorney general was also in error regarding his assertions that there was no showing of insanity or of drunkenness, and Enterline showed there had been quite a bit of such evidence. He then noted that the attorney general had confessed error on two of the instructions but had sought to avoid these errors "on the theory that the evidence warrants the conviction of the defendant and that this Court should not disturb the verdict." Enterline responded: "Such a doctrine is monstrous and can not be supported by authority."[18]

Oral argument was, in fact, heard before the supreme court on April 13, 1903. Normally, in an argument before an appellate court, the judges' questions show how they are leaning. Indeed, a knowledgeable observer of a court can usually predict the outcome of the appeal after listening to the arguments. Van Orsdel and Enterline probably knew, after April 13,

1903, whether the supreme court was likely to follow through with what
had been stated in *Ross v. State,* or would look for some reason to evade
the declarations made in that case. It would not be long, however, before
speculation would be unnecessary; the supreme court's decision was
expected by the week of August 3. When Enterline returned to Basin
City, as he did in late April 1903 to retry Jim Gorman's case, he surely
visited Joseph Walters in the Big Horn County jail. Enterline likely told
Walters either that he was optimistic his (Walters's) conviction would be
reversed, or that he (Enterline) was not optimistic and that Walters
should consider making his last arrangements. In the end, though, this
interview, whether joyous or somber, told nothing of Joseph Walters's
fate. Something else was stirring in Big Horn County, something ugly
and quintessentially American.[19]

7

◆

Judge Lynch Appears

The first ominous rumblings were heard in June, a few days before June 26, 1903, when Jim Gorman had first been scheduled to be hanged. For some reason, people in and around Basin City perceived that the Wyoming Supreme Court had granted Gorman a new trial. As noted earlier, however, when Judge Carpenter pronounced sentence on Jim Gorman (May 3), he also noted Gorman's appeal and suspended the execution of his sentence until the first day of the following term. Thus, in June, the date for the hanging had long since been set for October. There is no record showing any action by the supreme court, although some action must have been taken. A new trial was certainly not granted, but perhaps a routine order was entered, suspending the execution beyond the October term, until the supreme court could complete its review. Regardless of the accuracy of the information on the street, though, some members of the local population were genuinely upset. As a local newspaper reported, "Great indignation was expressed at that time over the court's action and it was reported that Judge Lynch was threatening to take the matter up." A later commentator observed, "It was felt that justice was being thwarted and gradually this feeling became alarming."[1]

This "alarming feeling" did not abate, and on Wednesday night, July 15, 1903, Sheriff Fenton received word that "a party of determined citizens from Shell and Paint Rock were coming to Basin to lynch Gorman and Walters." In the late nineteenth and early twentieth century, a time when many peace officers had the experience of facing a lynching party, some of them just stepped aside when a mob demanded a prisoner. Fenton, however, was not the kind of lawman to meekly turn his prisoners over to a lynch mob. He was described as a fearless man, "of medium height, stockily built, with a keen gray eye and a firm jaw." The sheriff decided that the best way to protect his prisoners was to get them away from Basin, out of harm's way, so Fenton, his undersheriff, Felix Alston, and another deputy took Walters and Gorman out of the jail to "a canon several miles from town."[2]

It is difficult to determine the exact location of this "canon," because it was variously described. Different newspapers referred to it as being "about two miles from town," "a narrow defile in the mountains several miles from town," "seven miles north of Basin," and "the gulch back of the jail." Just south of what is now Greybull, Wyoming, though, there are some high rock bluffs that might be the place where Sheriff Fenton took Gorman and Walters. This place, below tan sandstone cliffs, and with heavy riparian vegetation, seems to fit some later newspaper descriptions of a desperate flight to freedom by Jim Gorman.[3]

As the sheriff and his deputies were establishing what they hoped to be a zone of safety for the two men convicted of murder, Jim Gorman bolted into the dark night and swam the Big Horn River to escape. Newspaper reports asserted that Gorman was "a powerful man" and that he broke off handcuffs and disappeared in the darkness, despite several shots being fired "at his retreating form." Gorman was slender, only five foot eight and 150 pounds, and therefore he could not fairly be described as "a powerful man," but newspapers of that time were always ready to attribute fearsome powers to those convicted of crimes.[4]

Of course, Gorman's escape caused an uproar. The news of the escape was immediately sent back to Basin, and a number of mounted men started to pursue Gorman. One newspaper reported that "those who have gone after him openly declared their intention of saving the county further expense if they got within sight of him."[5]

During the night, Jim Gorman headed toward the Big Horn Mountains, with its rugged terrain and heavy timber. He was facing a long trek of some twenty miles just to get to the beginning of the Big Horns, but the mountains were Gorman's best chance to make his escape good. After getting across the Big Horn River, Gorman would have first headed downstream about a half mile, past the bluffs, and then climbed the hills coming down to the river from the east. When he reached the top of these hills, though, he would have made a frightening discovery. To the east, there is no cover. This remarkably dry, sparse area does not even support sagebrush, and the terrain does not have a great deal of relief; a lone man can be spotted easily from a long distance. To the north, however, Shell Creek proceeds due east toward the Big Horn Mountains, and along the stream, there is a riparian area full of cottonwood, sumac, and willow. Even in the middle of the night, Gorman must have been drawn to Shell Creek, with its heavy cover and broad avenue to the mountains, but Shell Creek also held peril. It was well settled even in 1903, with ranch houses all the way up the creek, holding many people and dogs. Gorman probably walked as directly east as he could, avoiding ranch houses, but trying to stay close to the timber along Shell Creek.

He was headed toward the small town of Shell, Wyoming, a place that sits only two or three miles from the base of the Big Horn Mountains. This is an area of great beauty, the site of dramatic canyons and formations. As dawn comes, the sun reveals starkly beautiful examples of fault block handiwork. When the dawn came on July 16, 1903 (and on July 16, dawn comes very early), however, Jim Gorman's attention would not have been upon the scenery, but on the fact that soon the rising sun would reveal a walking figure from miles away. He had to find a place where he could be safe during the coming day. Not until Shell Creek issues from the mountains, though, is there the slightest cover, except along the creek itself. Only near the mouth of Shell Creek Canyon are there any cedars, and even there the cedars are very sparse. Just to the north of the canyon, there might have been a few cedar patches offering good cover, but everywhere else, there are just salt-and-pepper patterns scattered lightly upon foothills.

The Big Horn Mountains, one place of safety, would have strongly beckoned, with the opportunity to get in the rugged Shell Creek Canyon and start moving up to timber; but twenty miles is not traversed quickly on foot, and Gorman surely needed most of the night just to get near Shell. Any walk up the canyon would be strenuous, and lodgepole pine and Douglas fir do not appear until 6,000 to 7,000 feet (Shell lies at about 4,200 feet), meaning no cover for several miles up from the mouth of the canyon. The probability is that during the early morning of Thursday, July 16, 1903, Jim Gorman found some place of safety near Shell, Wyoming—whether in the Shell Creek timber, or just inside Shell Canyon, or in the heaviest cedar he could find—and holed up for the day. His hiding place was likely near where the body of Jim White, the Buffalo hunter murdered in 1881, lay buried.

Horsemen were looking hard for Gorman—one report stated that he was "followed all day Thursday"—but it is unlikely this was literally true. Still, Gorman was probably very aware of pursuers. He needed to sleep that Thursday but almost certainly found it impossible to do.[6] When night fell, Gorman headed up the mountain, working his way at night through steep and broken country, trying to get to the heavy cover of a pine forest, and he probably reached such a safe place before dawn on Friday. Again, reports claim he was followed all day Friday, and, again, he probably had great difficulty getting the sleep he desperately needed. When night fell that Friday, however, he once again started climbing upward. By this time, Gorman was about fifty miles from the place he had escaped and had just about exhausted his energy and his will.

After Gorman's recapture, the *Wyoming Tribune* wrote a story that made it seem as if Gorman's pursuers had been hot on his heels all the way up the mountain, finally cornering him and clubbing him into submission. This does not ring true, though, and several other reports are inconsistent with it.[7] The truth is probably more mundane, that Gorman reached the end of his endurance and had to have food. When he stumbled across a camp high in the Big Horns, on upper Shell Creek, he went into it and asked for food. Jim Gorman's bad luck continued: One of the men in the camp, C. C. Smith, had been a juror in the first trial and immediately recognized him. (This coincidence was not overlooked; much later it was noted, "Thus does fate sometimes have its way with men.") About 1 A.M., Saturday, July 18, Smith and Hal Sweeney captured Gorman and returned him to Basin; he was unarmed and offered no resistance.[8]

By the time Gorman was recaptured, however, the community had become "entirely against Gorman" and "greatly excited."[9] One newspaper reported that Gorman's captors had to elude a mob just to bring him back to jail in Basin, and another reported that a roundabout course was taken back to Basin because of fear of meeting a mob. Gorman was safely returned to the jail, though, where he was reunited with Walters, who had not attempted to escape. That evening, saloons in Basin City, Shell, and Hyattville were jammed with drinking men, all talking about the murders committed by Walters and Gorman and of Gorman's attempted escape; one newspaper observed that "by nightfall, the restlessness had become general."[10]

Sheriff Fenton had been right: The safest place for Walters and Gorman was away from the jail. But Gorman, by his impetuous action, had made his protector, Fenton, look like a fool and had made it impossible for Fenton to move his prisoners from the jail again. Worse, Fenton felt he had to leave Basin and go sixty miles south, to Thermopolis. In February, Ben Minnick, a very young sheepman (barely twenty), had been murdered near Black Mountain, about twenty miles east of Thermopolis. His brother, William Minnick, had pastured sheep in an area within an 1897 deadline declared by cattlemen; that is, an area within which cattlemen declared no sheep were to come. As a result, men came gunning for William Minnick. A man found the young and trusting Ben Minnick, who invited the stranger into his sheepwagon; when Minnick turned away, the man shot him in the back. His assailant then realized his error and apologized to Ben, saying that he had the wrong man, that he had intended to kill Ben's brother. It did Ben little good; his spinal cord had been severed, and he died that evening.[11]

The public was greatly angered by this killing, but despite working on the case for months, Sheriff Fenton had not yet made an arrest. Then in July 1903, a break came in the case. Jim McCloud (Driftwood Jim) was taken to the Thermopolis jail in connection with a charge of horse stealing. Fenton believed him to be implicated in the Minnick case, and wanted to bring him to the Big Horn County jail. On Saturday, July 19, probably shortly after he learned that Jim Gorman had been recaptured, Sheriff Fenton and Deputy A. L. Stone rode down to Thermopolis to arrest McCloud for the murder of Ben Minnick. After securing McCloud, Fenton and some men he had apparently deputized in Thermopolis proceeded to leave, but they were then confronted by armed men. The intent of these armed men is not at all clear, whether they were friends of McCloud, come to "deliver" him (in the parlance of the day, this meant free him from captivity), or friends of Ben Minnick, who wanted to lynch McCloud. Further, it is not even clear what kind of confrontation occurred. Different newspaper stories speak of seemingly unconnected events, writing about an attempt to leave Thermopolis, an incident on a bridge, and a retreat to a hotel. After the incident, the local newspaper, the *Thermopolis Record*, published a long article, the unsubtle thrust of which was that everything had been blown out of proportion.[12]

Whatever the true state of affairs, Sheriff Fenton was convinced that he and his men were in peril. He wired the governor to send militia, used primitive telephone systems to try to notify his deputies to bring posses from different parts of the Big Horn Basin, and prepared to hold on until reinforcements arrived. He would certainly not be returning to Basin that Saturday evening, which meant the Big Horn County jail was not well guarded.[13]

A jailer, George Mead, had remained in Basin, and his station was near the jail cells, which were within the small courthouse. Only one other man was in the courthouse the night of July 19, 2003—Christopher Earl Price, then twenty-six years old. Price had come to Wyoming as a boy, when his family had moved to the Big Horn Basin from Missouri, and had lived in Embar (a ranch area west of Thermopolis), Thermopolis, and Shell. He had then moved to Basin, where he worked as deputy county clerk. Housing was apparently short in Basin City, and Earl (as he was called) slept in the clerk's office at night on a cot that was kept rolled up under the counter during the day. Earl was a friendly and well-liked young man, but he must have been somber during that July; just a month before, his fiancée, Maude Hoover, had died.[14]

Since Price was already in the small courthouse, he was appointed a deputy sheriff to assist George Mead. These men surely knew there was a good chance of a raid on the jail during the night, and they must have been extremely apprehensive, but nothing happened during the evening hours of July 19. By midnight, all was quiet in Basin City, this tiny county seat of Big Horn County, Wyoming.[15]

Just seven years from its founding, the population of Basin was only about 200 in 1903, but for such a small town, it held a surprising number of public establishments. There were three general stores, two drug stores, one newspaper, a bank, four saloons, a church, a Masonic lodge, two hotels, the county courthouse, and, probably, a couple of houses of prostitution; four of the residences were frame dwellings and another was native stone, but most homes were still log cabins or dugouts. The streets were not paved, but some wooden walks had been constructed. The town sat just above the Big Horn River.[16] A man named John M. Tillard operated a ferry, and he lived in a cabin on the east side of the river, just downstream from the site of the ferry.[17]

At about 1 A.M., Tillard was rudely awakened by a group of armed men. A six-shooter was poked under his nose, and he was told he was needed at the ferry. A very frightened Tillard quickly dressed and, in the company of masked men, made his way to the ferry, where he found thirty to forty men. They left their horses tied on the east side of the river, but the weight of the men alone threatened to swamp the ferry. The trip was made safely, though, and one of the men stayed at the ferry to guard Tillard, while the remainder "started off on a rapid walk around the town to the county jail." It was reported that when other men in Basin heard the mob and realized what was happening, they "joined in the stampede for the jail."[18]

In addition to the jail, the Big Horn County Courthouse held four offices, those of the assessor, county clerk, county treasurer, and sheriff. The main street in Basin, then as now, ran north and south, but the courthouse was to the west, north of the present courthouse, which was

The Big Horn County Courthouse in 1909, with militia. This was also the county courthouse in July 1903, at the time of the lynching. Courtesy the Colorado Society and the *Denver Post*.

not built until 1917. The old courthouse was a brick structure, none
too large for the several offices within it. It faced south, and a person
approaching it encountered two front entrances; the one on the right led
to the county treasurer's office, and the one on the left to the county clerk's
office. There was a vault in the back of the county clerk's office (to the
north), and the sheriff's office was behind the county treasurer's office;
the jail sat behind both the county clerk's vault and the sheriff's office.
The entrance to the sheriff's office opened to the east.[19]

The men in the mob quickly reached the Big Horn County Courthouse. Their actions were covered extensively by many papers throughout
Wyoming, but inconsistencies abound in the reports, starting with conflicting reports of exactly what happened when the mob arrived at the
jail. Two newspapers, the *Cheyenne Daily Leader* (in a story announced as
"Special to Daily Leader") and the *Wyoming Tribune* (a "Special to the
Tribune") stated that the men in the mob just started shooting into the
courthouse, firing "a fusillade of shots through the windows." In this
version, a bullet wounded Mead, passing through his arm and killing
Price, hitting him in the heart.[20]

A second contemporaneous version reported that the mob first banged
on the door of the sheriff's office; then Mead declared he would not give
up his prisoners and fired over the heads of the members of the mob,
whereupon "a promiscuous fire was opened into the place." In neither
version was there any question that Earl Price was shot to death shortly
after the mob arrived. George Mead was probably the only source for the
second story, and perhaps this version was colored by Mead's wish to
avoid criticism; as it was, one newspaper seemed to fault Mead for
timidity. The fire into the courthouse was certainly enough to intimidate;
it was estimated that "considerably over 100 shots were fired into the
office."[21] Mead "got out of the way as quickly as he could."[22]

When the mob had come west through the streets of Basin, they had
seized a telephone pole, and now they made good use of it, battering
down the outer doors of the jail, exposing the jail cell itself, and rushing
in.[23] Walters and Gorman reportedly "begged and pleaded for mercy"
and "cowered down in the corners of their cells in fear and trembling."[24]

The July 21, 1903, *Laramie Boomerang* story ("Gorman and Walters Shot") went beyond this, elaborately describing the reactions of Walters and Gorman, stating, among other things, that "the criminals were plainly seen cringing in one corner of a death trap like animals possessed of a deadly fear," "they groveled in the corner of the cage, rattling the bars in their frenzy and chattering for mercy," and "the wild terror of the doomed murderers was terrible to behold." The prisoners were no doubt very frightened and instinctively shied away from the mob, but the reporter, who was almost certainly *not* at the scene, seems to be adding his own enthusiasm for the event.

The mob intended to pull the prisoners out of the cell and kill them the traditional way in a lynching, by strangling them with a rope. But the mob was frustrated by the jail cell and could not get the door open. As they milled around in the courthouse, someone was sent to a nearby blacksmith shop for tools, and "for some time an effort was made to beat down the doors of the cells."[25] Sledgehammers were used, and those hammers slamming into the jail doors resonated in the night, terrible sounds never forgotten by many of those who lived near the jail. Many people were listening that night, people who could probably not help but listen, but who would have vastly preferred not to be hearing this gruesome event.[26]

That evening there had been a late meeting of the Basin Freemasons. This was a notable meeting, well attended, at which the grand master of the Grand Lodge of Wyoming was the special guest, and the meeting did not break up until almost midnight, when men drifted back to their homes and the grand master returned to his lodging for the night at the Mountain View Hotel, only a short distance from the courthouse. The shooting that soon erupted ensured that their evening's sleep, if it had begun at all, was short lived. It seemed as if everyone within the Mountain View Hotel got up to see the ruckus. Other people who resided close by, such as C. A. Zaring, were also awakened by the shooting; even the owners of the Antlers Hotel, an establishment at least a block farther from the courthouse than was the Mountain View, were awakened.[27]

The new owner of the Mountain View, E. C. Fisher, believed the grand master might be able to stop all this, and Fisher went up to his room and spoke to him. The grand master was none other than Chief Justice Charles N. Potter, of the Wyoming Supreme Court, a man who had just heard the appeal in the case of *State v. Walters,* and who undoubtedly knew what the supreme court had decided about the fate of Joseph P. Walters. Potter's response to Fisher was that he did not think it would do any good. Justice Potter was most likely correct, but it would have made for wonderful theater if the good judge had gone to the jail and tried to justify his court's careful, logical, and well-balanced resolution to a mob incensed by such calm and rational processes and determined to sweep them aside.

Not all onlookers were appalled by what was happening; some saw it as an exciting event. Many of the voices of the mob were clearly heard in the night, and within the lobby of the Mountain View Hotel, a young man apparently supplied a running commentary, naming several of the men as their voices were heard. When Tom Olney reminded him that he might be called as a witness, the young man named no more.[28]

Inside the jail, the mob was not making any headway against the steel of the cell doors, and at some point in the process, it became apparent they were not going to be able to get in. Perhaps this was voiced so that the prisoners heard it, because Walters was supposed to have done an amazing thing that night. Most contemporaneous reports just state that the mob reached a point at which they decided to start shooting at the prisoners, but there is at least one contemporaneous report (and several later ones) that Walters came up to the jail door and told the mob something like, "Don't break the jail down[,] boys. I know you want me here and you may as well kill me here as to take me outside." Then, supposedly, someone in the mob immediately placed a gun next to Walters's head and blew his brains out.[29]

Jim Gorman was not so accommodating. Again, though, reports are inconsistent about what happened that night at the Big Horn County jail. The contemporaneous newspaper accounts just report that after the mob was unable to break into the cell, the members started shooting at Walters and Gorman, after telling a horse thief who was also in the cell to get to one side.[30] The odd thing, though, is that all reports acknowledge that Gorman did not die immediately, but much later that morning. Some of the stories state that "volley after volley" was poured into the bodies of Walters and Gorman, but three say that Gorman was hit by only five bullets, and another says that Gorman was shot once in the head and three times in the body.[31]

"Volley after volley" makes no sense. Thirty or forty men firing from point-blank range would have killed Jim Gorman outright, and there would have been many more than five wounds. This may be one of those unusual circumstances in which contemporaneous reports are less accurate than later ones are, when the ability to more fully interview witnesses allows for a complete story. Some of the later accounts mention Jim Gorman hiding under his cell cot, which apparently provided some protection.[32]

Even more to the point, later accounts tell the story of John Guffy, the alleged horse thief, who had just been arrested, evidently by mistake, and who found himself in the middle of a maelstrom. Supposedly, he was ordered by the mob to pull Gorman from under the cot. Saban indicates, probably based on the statement of Dr. Carter, that Guffy was interviewed later, and that he said, "As fast as I could drag him out, he crawled back again." Such a report would explain why Gorman was not immediately killed, and why he might have been hit only four or five times.[33]

After the shooting of Walters and Gorman, the leader of the mob, a "tall and powerfully built man of middle age," gave the command to "fall in," and "all recognized his voice."[34] By then a lot of people in Basin had been aroused, and when the mob marched out of town, "the people of Basin was all up standing in the street."[35] There was virtually no opposition to these men as they left, although Dr. C. M. Gillam supposedly offered to open fire on them with a rifle but was "dissuaded," and the town marshal, Bert Brigam, emptied a .32 revolver into the darkness after the mob had almost returned down the hill to the ferry by the Big Horn River, a distance of at least four or five hundred yards.[36] There was even speculation that a member of the mob had been shot, but this was apparently not true.[37] A few men cautiously rode out from Basin in the general direction the mob took, actions evidently taken considerably after the event was over; there were no signs of the mob, and these men soon returned.[38]

After the mob was gone, people in the town gradually moved to the courthouse. The scene they found was "frightful," with a jail that was "a wreck," showing the scars of multiple bullets. George Mead was treated for the bullet wound in his arm, which was not serious, and Jim Gorman was taken to Dr. Carter's office; he died at about 7 A.M. Earl Price's body was taken to an inner room in the courthouse, where it was viewed that same day by members of a coroner's jury.[39] The next day the jury submitted a report, which echoed the infamous language found in coroner's reports all over the United States following the work of a lynch mob, that the deceased had met his death "at the hands of parties unknown." The report stated that Price, Gorman, and Walters had all come "to their deaths at the hands of a mob, the members of which are unknown to the jury."[40]

Folklore arises from an event such as the killing of Jim Gorman. People get excited about such a dramatic happening, and they talk about it, in the process adding to the story. In this case, embellishments arose through the years, as people made the story better and construed it to fit their preconceptions. One story goes as follows: When Dr. Carter examined Jim Gorman, he determined that Gorman's wounds were fatal, told him so, and then asked Jim if he had anything he wanted to say. Jim Gorman replied, "I haven't given up anything yet and I'm not going to start now."[41] Gorman did indicate, though, that he was innocent and knew who really did the deed. Then he asked, "Where's Maggie?" and was told that Maggie was gone, that she had received a paper with a rope drawn on it and the words "24 hours" and had departed to a stage stop thirty miles south of Basin, which was owned by C. H. Worland. The story goes on to add that when Maggie Gorman was told of the death of Jim Gorman, the only thing she said was, "Did he say anything?"[42]

Of the above statements, the only ones with contemporaneous support are some of those attributed to Jim Gorman. The *Thermopolis Record* reported on July 25, 1903, that Gorman maintained his innocence of the murder of his brother, that he knew who did the deed, but he had never "squealed" on anyone in his life and would not do so now. Dr. Carter, in an autobiography written some time in the late 1920s or early 1930s, also verifies that Jim Gorman made statements to this effect, except that he does not say that Gorman told him he knew who did the deed.

The statements about Jim Gorman's asking about Maggie Gorman, and Maggie having just received a note with a noose and "24 hours" printed on it, are corroborated by Dr. Carter, but Maggie Gorman was already in Worland at the time of the lynching, and her supposed comment upon hearing of Jim's death ("Did he say anything?") does not have any support in the contemporaneous historical record. It appears, without attribution, in papers written from thirty-three to seventy-five years after the fact, and has every earmark of one of those apocryphal tales that arise from people embellishing an exciting event.[43]

Neil J. Anderson, the proprietor of the Antlers Hotel in 1903, provides reasonably reliable information about Maggie Gorman. Anderson's statement shows that at the time of the lynching, Maggie Gorman was working in what would become the town of Worland, and that not long after Jim Gorman was lynched, she received notice that she should leave the country or she would go the same way as Jim had. Anderson told how one evening Charles Worland (better known as Dad Worland) came to Anderson's hotel and wanted rooms for himself and Maggie Gorman. Maggie Gorman was heeding the warning she had received, and Worland was taking her to Garland, which was then the nearest railroad point. He did so, and she got on the train and disappeared into the mists of history.[44]

Other examples of tales associated with the Gormans include a story in *Old West* that claims that "years later" Maggie Gorman told a different story than what she had related on the witness stand. Supposedly, Tom returned from a freighting trip, found Jim in the house with Maggie, and attacked Jim. The fight spilled into the yard, where Tom knocked Jim down and was about to kill him. Maggie ran out with a hatchet and struck Tom on the head, "dealing the death blow."[45]

Given what we know of the trials, this story is absurd. If something like this had happened, the easiest thing in the world for Maggie Gorman would have been to back up Jim Gorman's story about killing his brother in self-defense. That would have protected both her and Jim; but, of course, she did nothing like that. She took the stand, and her testimony was completely hostile to Jim Gorman; she related what Jim Gorman had told her, which clearly demonstrated first-degree murder. If Maggie had been the true culprit, Jim Gorman certainly would have given away Maggie's secret after she swore that he had killed her husband in a premeditated manner. The story is highly implausible for another reason: Why would Maggie Gorman ever broadcast another entirely different version of events, one that was highly incriminating? Furthermore, Maggie Gorman was not in the Big Horn Basin "years later." One wonders to whom and how she told "a different story," and how it got back to the Big Horn Basin. In *Sagebrush and Roses,* Carla Neves Loveland cites an account by John W. Loveland, which attributes this story to Frank James, the deputy sheriff who first arrested Jim and Maggie Gorman; perhaps this is the source of the *Old West* story. It is especially implausible, however, that Maggie Gorman would say such a thing to a peace officer.[46]

As Basin City cleaned up on the Sunday morning after the raid on the jail, one of the first of many chores was to notify Earl Price's parents of his death. This sad duty fell to former sheriff, then deputy Dudley Hale. Early that day, July 20, Hale rode to Welling, a tiny community about ten miles south of Basin, to telephone Price's parents in Owl Creek. At that time, telephone service from the south had not reached Basin; a line had been strung north from Thermopolis, but it reached only to Welling. At Welling, though, Hale received a call from Sheriff Fenton, who told Hale of his plight in Thermopolis and instructed him to send help.[47]

Hale must have told Sheriff Fenton that there had been a disastrous raid on the Big Horn County jail, but the first order of business was to rescue the sheriff. Deputy Hale immediately came back to Basin, informed Captain C. C. Price of the militia that the sheriff needed assistance in Thermopolis, and separately organized a posse to go to Thermopolis. Forty men from the Basin light artillery saddled up the evening of July 20 and, armed with "Winchesters, Krags and Springfield rifles" rode south through the night, fighting a terrible dust storm, but arriving in Thermopolis the next morning.[48] Twenty-five more men came to Thermopolis from Basin, Cody, and Meeteetse. The Basin men were led by Dudley Hale; the Cody men, by W. J. Chapman; and the Meeteetse men, by Jeff Nichols.[49]

Of course, when all of this hit newspapers in the rest of Wyoming, great alarm was expressed. The same edition of the *Laramie Boomerang* that carried the first story about the lynching also carried the Thermopolis story, announcing, "Sheriff Wires for Militia." The *Boomerang* commented: "Lawlessness reigns supreme in this part of the country," and stated that, "The imprisonment of the sheriff, coming directly on top of the murder at Basin, has completely destroyed law and order in this section of the country."

The presence of some sixty-five armed men certainly ensured that the lawless element would be suppressed in Thermopolis, but there was still the question of how imperiled the sheriff and his men had really been. Although one newspaper reported that "the presence of troops caused a decided abatement of the mutterings of the crowds of indignant citizens who wanted to lynch Jim McCloud, . . . and also caused the small coterie of McCloud's friends who have been threatening to take McCloud from the officers, to leave town," the local Thermopolis paper scoffed at the whole endeavor.[50] The *Thermopolis Record* carried a heading that read: "A Serio-Comic Affair in which the Comic Largely Predominated." It declared that when all the men arrived in Thermopolis, "they realized they'd been called on a wild goose chase." The article fills more than a long column, but two of its paragraphs should provide a good taste of its tenor:

> While there were some rumors in the air there was nothing, so far as we could learn, on which to base any fears of an attempt at rescue. Some of McCloud's friends had been seen in earnest conversation, some one sent an unsigned letter of warning to the sheriff, the posse saw three or four horseman riding through the sage brush at night— these things called for more men, and they came in plenty. . . . It was

said that Admiral Dewey was on his way up the river with his fleet, but if so he stopped somewhere below town.

Sheriff Fenton and his men are nice men personally and treated everyone well while in our neighborhood, but we cannot get away from the conclusion that there was a deplorable lack of judgment used in handling the whole matter. The sheriff's office had made a sorry batch of their own affairs at home—had left the jail practically unguarded in the face of the fact that they had reliable information that a mob was coming—and the result was that a most exemplary citizen and two prisoners, whom it was the sheriff's official duty to protect, lost their lives. That affair had to be squared in some way, and a grand-stand play was made in the McCloud case to divert the attention of the people.[51]

The article makes a provocative point when it asks why the jail was left "practically unguarded," but the statement that this Thermopolis event was intended to divert attention from the lynching is wrong and unfair. When Fenton decided to remain in Thermopolis and to start calling for help, no raid had occurred, and the sheriff did not know that a raid was about to occur. He was probably first informed that the jail had been attacked when he reached Dudley Hale the next morning. One item reported by David John Wasden, however, is consistent with the *Thermopolis Record*'s point of view: "When the National Guard arrived they found Deputy Sheriff Garland riding around in a buggy with two girls."[52]

Regardless of how the *Record* perceived the situation, however, the sheriff and those who would extricate him still believed there was great danger. The *Laramie Boomerang* reported, "There is a feeling, however, that the trouble is not over and that Sheriff Fenton and his escort will be led into an ambuscade on the road between Thermopolis and Basin. . . . Sheriff Fenton is preparing for such an emergency and if he is interfered with there will be a bloody battle and many of the friends of McCloud will learn too late that they cannot violate the laws with impunity."[53]

On Wednesday, July 22, the entire group of some sixty-five men headed back to Basin. A strict order of march was established to protect against ambush. The Meeteetse posse rode in front, apparently to provide a buffer between the posse and a group in a wagon that included Jim McCloud, who was handcuffed to Sheriff Fenton and to a deputy. A rear guard of twenty men rode 300 yards behind. Whenever "the cavalcade" rode through broken or wooded country, scouts were sent out 500 yards on either side.

All these men arrived in Basin City at about 10 P.M. and were warmly greeted. The people of Basin certainly felt their sheriff had been in peril, and a large crowd "sent up cheer after cheer" for "the nervy officer, who had given defiance to a country full of hostile cowmen by his sixty-mile ride from Thermopolis yesterday."[54] McCloud was reported to be sullen, and he was placed in the jail with a heavy guard without and within, apparently occasioned by rumors that an attempt might be made to lynch McCloud.[55]

Despite all the agitation and activity surrounding McCloud, the evidence was never strong enough to charge him with Ben Minnick's murder, although he was eventually convicted of other charges out of Cheyenne and served time.[56] That week, Joseph Walters was buried in Basin; Earl Price, in Thermopolis; and the body of Jim Gorman was shipped back to his home in Pennsylvania. In the same week, a reporter from the *Sheridan Post* went to the office of E. E. Enterline, who must have been shocked by the lynching of two of his clients and no doubt wanted people to understand that these men he had represented were not monsters. The Sheridan newspaper published a story that stated, "The other day the Post man saw a letter written by Gorman's father to attorney E. E. Enterline, in which he begged the attorney to do all he could to save his boy. The elder Gorman is a poor man and is heart broken over his son's crime." The senior Gorman surely was sick at heart over his son's crime, but much deeper sorrow had to come from watching two of his sons leave for the wilds of Wyoming, and then learning of the sordid death of each one.[57]

8

◆

Lynching in America

The attack on the Big Horn County jail on July 20, 1903, was a singularly ugly event, but it did not occur in a vacuum. Westerners of that time liked to think they had completely reinvented themselves in their new world and that their attitudes were entirely new, owing very little to the tamer parts of the nation. Of course, that was untrue. The people in the Big Horn Basin in the nineteenth and early twentieth centuries were merely Americans placed on a different stage and confronted with a different set of challenges, and they carried with them all the experiences of their former lives. No matter how profoundly different the western stage, people of the West could not escape an American perspective; they were captive to its good and its ill. When the mob hit the Big Horn County jail, it was not just an event of the Big Horn Basin or of Wyoming, nor just of the West; it was an American event. For all the good of the American experience, there is another side, a side of rowdy, almost gratuitous, violence; it is a consistent, undeniable theme throughout our history. And one of the most distinctly American manifestations of that wide, rowdy streak was lynching.

Lynching was almost exclusively an American phenomenon, virtually unheard of anywhere else in the world. James Elbert Cutler referred to it as "our country's national crime." Instances of mob action, including lynchings, went back a long way in American history. One of the worst examples of mob action was the treatment of a group that made up a substantial percentage of citizens in the Big Horn Basin in 1903: the Mormons. In the 1830s and 1840s, Mormons were harassed in virtually every place they stayed; they suffered virulent mob attacks in Missouri (Missouri Governor Lilburn W. Boggs put out an extermination order in 1838), and in 1844, the leader of the Mormons, Joseph Smith, was lynched in the Carthage, Illinois, jail, in a manner similar to the fate of Jim Gorman. These attacks finally drove fifteen to twenty thousand people of the Mormon faith to Utah.[1]

Later in the nineteenth century, lynching—that is, the seizure and killing of a person by a group without lawful authority, most commonly by hanging—became commonplace throughout much of the United States. From 1882 to 1951, there were lynching deaths every year. The worst time was during the late nineteenth century, when more than one hundred people were lynched almost every year (in 1892, 230, the deadliest year), but the practice steadily dropped off until by 1936, the numbers were down to single figures. The problem was most acute in the southeastern United States, where black people were frequently lynched for offenses ranging from murder to being "uppity." Of the 4,743 people lynched in the United States, almost 73 percent were African Americans, and the old confederate states of Virginia, North Carolina, South Carolina, Georgia, Florida, Alabama, Mississippi, Tennessee, Louisiana, Texas, and Arkansas were responsible for more than 3,500 of these deaths. Three states alone, Texas, Mississippi, and Georgia account for 34 percent of the deaths, and of those, only about one out of seven of the people lynched were white.

For different reasons, the nineteenth-century frontier also suffered a relatively high number of lynchings. For example, in Wyoming (thirty-five), Montana (eighty-four), and Colorado (forty-three), despite their small populations, many more people were lynched in each state than in New York (two), Pennsylvania (eight), New Jersey (two), Connecticut (zero), and Massachusetts (zero) *combined*.[2]

On the frontier, citizens faced the practical problem of a weak and ineffective civil government, not sufficiently established to provide security and to punish wrongdoers. Thus, people frequently felt, admittedly with good cause, that they had to resort to "summary proceedings" to protect themselves. This weakness of government was made all the more alarming because of the presence of large numbers of wrongdoers. The frontier drew hooligans, ranging from rough-and-ready cowboys, gamblers, and prostitutes to outright thieves and murderers. For instance, a criminal class seems to have been drawn to the Montana gold fields in the early 1860s, and a crowd of malefactors appeared at each new town in Wyoming as the Union Pacific Railroad came through and established new towns that were hell on wheels. These were the times when formal committees of vigilance arose.[3]

The example of the Montana Vigilantes is particularly informative here. In the early 1860s, gold was discovered in what was to become southwestern Montana, and miners flooded in. At that time, there were no railroads across the United States, and southwestern Montana was as remote an area as could be found in the country. Effectively, it had no civil organization. The miners recognized their strong need for law enforcement, however, and on May 24, 1863, the town of Bannack elected town officials, including a sheriff, Henry Plummer. It was not learned until much later that the new sheriff secretly led a gang of robbers, thieves, and murderers. The region was plagued with crime, and when Plummer's chief deputy killed several men in November 1863, the miners had had enough. Vigilante groups were organized, and they went after the criminals. They acted openly, electing officers, keeping records, and holding trials, and went about their business in daylight without masks. They arrested and hanged more than thirty men. As the vigilantes carried out their grim tasks, they learned of the deep criminal involvement of the sheriff, and he became one of their victims. The remaining desperados cleared out, and the crime wave stopped.[4]

Thomas J. Dimsdale, an Englishman who found himself in the gold-fields of Montana in the 1860s, wrote a treatise about the actions of the vigilantes. He begins his defense of their actions by stating, "It is not possible that a high state of civilization and progress can be maintained unless the tenure of life and property is secure; and it follows that the first efforts of a people in a new country for the inauguration of the reign of peace, the sure precursor of prosperity and stability, should be directed to the accomplishment of this object."

Dimsdale perceived that Americans took the following part of the Declaration of Independence very seriously, "Governments are instituted among Men, deriving their just powers from the consent of the governed, That whenever any Form of Government becomes destructive of these ends, it is the Right of the People to alter or to abolish, and to institute new Government," and he caught well the attitude of many American men in the nineteenth century when he wrote that if courts fail, "the people, the republic that created them, can do their work for them." Throughout the United States in the nineteenth and early twentieth century, men frequently did the work of the courts and "altered and abolished government" when they took the law into their own hands and carried out lynchings.

Dimsdale demonstrates the extreme conditions in the mining camps that he believed created the need for vigilantes, and he closes his treatise with something like a peroration:

> Is it lawful for citizens to slay robbers or murderers, when they catch them; or ought they to wait for policemen, where there are none, or put them in penitentiaries not yet erected?
>
> Gladly, indeed, we feel sure, would the Vigilantes cease from their labor, and joyfully would they hail the advent of power, civil or military, to take their place; but till this is furnished by Government, society must be preserved from demoralization and anarchy; murder, arson and robbery must be prevented or punished, and road agents must die. . . . where justice is powerless as well as blind, the strong arm of the mountaineer must wield her sword; for "self-preservation is the first law of nature."[5]

The interesting thing is that the men who led vigilantes, in Montana and elsewhere, were not the dregs of society, as was frequently true of lynch mobs, but were the leaders. This was claimed to be true in Wyoming during the late 1860s, the only period in which regular vigilante groups were formed. Wyoming's experience was similar to Montana's in that large numbers of men suddenly converged on places that were completely empty seemingly moments before.[6]

Wyoming was created as a political entity by the Union Pacific Railroad; the tracks arrived in the brand new town of Cheyenne on November 13, 1867. The *Wyoming Eagle*, in 1930, described what happened when Cheyenne suddenly became a "metropolis of the frontier": "Unbridled license soon made its very name notorious everywhere, until there came into being a band of Vigilantes like to those of earlier days in California. Quietly and in keeping with the spirit of the West, which was never one of braggadocio, these sturdy men transformed Cheyenne, and did it in less than a year."[7]

In 1868, five or six men were lynched in and around Cheyenne by the Cheyenne Vigilance Committee. Generally, the men who were hanged could be described as rowdy toughs who drank and misbehaved, doing such things as shooting into a dance hall and saloon full of people, shooting and wounding other men in a fracas, shooting and killing a partner (the man who committed this offense, Charles Martin, was acquitted by the courts and threatened revenge upon the chief witness against him), and stealing mules. It did not appear that the vigilantes in Cheyenne operated as openly as the Montana vigilantes did, nor that the offenses for which they imposed capital punishment were as serious. Still, their actions did produce a salutary effect on the hoodlums in Cheyenne. Then again, the bad people might just have moved down the line to Laramie when the railroad moved west over the Laramie Mountains. Laramie is where the next committee of vigilantes arose, when "gamblers, cut-throats and prostitutes" arrived, along with "respectable merchants, railroaders, wives and mothers." In Laramie, there was a pitched gun battle after which several men were hanged. After Laramie, though, only one other formal committee of vigilance was formed along the Union Pacific Railroad.[8]

As the Union Pacific neared Bear River City, in far southwestern Wyoming, the town found itself split into two factions. The first, the group first established (just barely), consisted of "the respectable element," and the second was "the usual crowd of gamblers, prostitutes and ruffians." The first group was besieged by robberies and assaults, and they formed a group of vigilantes, headed by the chief tie drivers from the railroad; they invited "all decent male citizens" to join their group. The vigilantes selected three of the worst offenders: Jimmy Powers, a "notorious thief"; Jack O'Neill, who had just assaulted, robbed, and disfigured a man; and James Reed, who was supposed to be guilty of assault and robbery. On November 10, 1868, all three were seized, taken to a spot by a nearby town, and hanged close to the railroad tracks; a notice was pinned on their coats: "Warning to the road agents."[9]

Unlike the response in other frontier towns, however, these events did not intimidate the toughs but infuriated them. There were riots and raids, in a sequence of events that sounds like war. The vigilantes took several men to a jail just completed, but 250 men then came into town, stormed the jail, and freed the arrested men. This mob set fire to the jail and went charging over to the offices of a local newspaper, apparently to lynch the editor, who had been vociferous in his criticism of the lawlessness in Bear River and the need to do something about it. The editor was warned, though, and escaped, but his press and equipment were destroyed. A big gun battle developed between the vigilantes and the men in the mob, not ending until shortly before cavalry came into the town the next morning to find fourteen men shot and killed and thirty-five wounded. Bear River, just a month old, was a wreck. The Union Pacific then finished it off when it declined to put a switch there, and the town was deserted just a few months after it began.[10]

Lynchings were perpetrated throughout Wyoming during the remainder of the nineteenth century, although none was carried out by a previously organized vigilante committee. These lynchings were the work of more or less spontaneous actions of a mob, formed for a brief time to address a perceived outrage. On October 31, 1878, two men were lynched: Billy Mansfield and Archie McLaughlin, who were being taken to Deadwood, South Dakota, on charges of highway robbery. The stage-coach between Cheyenne and Deadwood had been plagued by robberies and murders, and Mansfield and McLaughlin were supposed to be a part of this criminal activity. The notorious George Parrott (Big Nose George) and his partner, Dutch Charlie, killed two deputy sheriffs in Carbon County, Wyoming. Dutch Charlie was captured by a posse near Rock Creek, east of Rawlins, and then transported by train to Rawlins. On January 6, 1879, a mob found Dutch Charlie hiding in the baggage car, dragged him out of the train, and hanged him on the crossbeam of a telegraph pole. Big Nose George was not arrested until August 1880, and he was convicted of first-degree murder in December. In March 1881, he attempted escape, assaulting the jailer. He was unsuccessful, though, and remained trapped in the jail. Word spread, and a large number of citizens broke into the jail, took Parrott down to the railroad tracks, and, as with his partner, throttled him with a rope over a telegraph pole. Big Nose George's final fate was particularly gruesome, because a local doctor (John Osborne, who later became governor of Wyoming) used some of George's skin to make a pair of shoes, and various of Parrott's bones were employed for other uses, such as for a doorstop.[11]

Lynchings continued in Wyoming, usually, but not always, for serious crimes such as murder. Henry Mosier was lynched in Cheyenne on September 17, 1883, for murder; the killing of Mosier was brutal, but he was lamented only by his dog. William Maloney was hanged on May 19, 1884, by his co-workers from a crew hired to do work along a tributary of Sybille Creek (near what is now Wheatland). Maloney had shot down George Metcalfe, a fellow employee, in cold blood, which resulted in Maloney's seizure and subsequent hanging from a cottonwood tree.[12]

The infamous Rock Springs Massacre occurred on September 2, 1885, when white miners attacked Chinese workers who had been brought in as strikebreakers. This event was more a riot than a lynching, but the results were even deadlier: Twenty-eight Chinese people were killed, fifteen others were wounded, and hundreds were driven from the town; an immense amount of property was destroyed. Remarkably, Chinese labor was so unpopular that indictments could not even be brought in against these rioters.[13]

Ella Watson and Jim Averell were lynched on July 20, 1889, ostensibly for cattle theft, but a persuasive case has been made that their real crime was that they were a thorn in the side to large ranchers, making homestead claims in the middle of the ranchers' ranges.[14] These killings were just a prelude to two killings in 1891 of suspected rustlers in Johnson County, and to the Johnson County Invasion of 1892, in which two more men were killed. The deaths in 1891 were old-fashioned assassinations, whereas the two in 1892 might appropriately be called lynchings, although the victims were shot rather than hanged. In June 1891, Tom Waggoner of Newcastle was pulled from his home by three men and was found days later, hanged on a branch of a cottonwood tree. This was apparently a lynching, but the motivation was a mystery. Helena Huntington Smith makes a plausible argument that Waggoner was the keeper of a large herd of stolen horses, and that the local ranch people probably did him in, but the evidence in favor of this supposition is slim. Malcolm Campbell, the sheriff of Converse County during the Johnson County War, accused rustlers of doing the deed.[15]

For about the next ten years, there was a lull in the steady drumbeat of mob killings in Wyoming, but then the activity picked up. In Casper, Charles Francis Woodard had murdered the sheriff of Natrona County during a jailbreak, and he was tried and sentenced to be hanged on March 28, 1902. An appeal was filed, however, and the Wyoming Supreme Court granted a stay of execution, pending a resolution of the appeal. As with the Gorman case, this action incensed the public. Woodard was pulled from the jail, and the mob used the gallows that had already been constructed in the jail yard to hang Woodard. No one from the mob was arrested. Just over a year later, "Diamond Slim" Clifton was charged with murder in Weston County; he was placed in the county jail, awaiting trial for the murder of a well-liked young couple. On May 23, 1903, a mob of thirty-five cowboys besieged the jail; at first, the sheriff resisted them, but then, supposedly realizing that he had no choice, he ordered a deputy to unlock the cell containing Clifton. Clifton was taken to a high railroad bridge near Newcastle and hanged. "Hanged" is perhaps not the right word, because the long fall decapitated Clifton. There is no indication that any official action was taken against any of the mob. Even before the 1903 attack on the Big Horn County jail, far more people had been lynched in Wyoming than had been legally executed.[16]

9

A Big Horn County Grand Jury

The killings of Gorman, Walters, and Price were the topic of many
public comments in Wyoming. The Biennial Report of the Attorney
General to the Governor of Wyoming contains a matter of fact paragraph
that glossed over the horror of that early morning of July 20, 1903:

> At the time of my last report the following criminal cases were pending
> before Supreme Court of this state, but had not yet been decided:
>
> Walters v. State of Wyoming; proceedings in error from the District
> Court of Big Horn County. In this case the plaintiff in error had been
> convicted of murder in the first degree and sentenced to be hung.
> After the case was argued before the Supreme Court, and before the
> court had rendered its decision, the plaintiff in error was killed in the
> county jail at Basin by a mob. On motion of the Attorney General, the
> case was dismissed by the court without further action.[1]

There is no hint in this dry, factual recitation that the attorney general
found this event to be shocking and appalling. He probably did not. As
previously discussed, within the state of Wyoming, as in many places in
the United States, lynching was commonplace. These ugly events probably
did not upset most citizens in a profound way; a large number approved
of the practice.

Wyoming newspapers generally disapproved of the happenings of July 20, but with significant reservations. An editorial in the *Sheridan Post* stated:

> The better people of Wyoming deeply deplore the unlawful act which took place in Basin Sunday morning, resulting in the killing of two convicted murderers and a guard, who died at his post of duty. Following up the lynching of Chas. Woodard at Casper a year or more ago and the mobbing of Clifton at Newcastle a short time ago, this Basin affair brings up anew the question, what occasions these unlawful acts? Do a certain number of our citizens lack confidence in the courts as a means of justice? Do the courts act too slowly and are the people too impatient? Perhaps all of these questions might be answered in the affirmative. . . . the only way to prevent and wipe out this moblaw spirit is to change the laws so that the courts may act without any unnecessary delays, and to emanate a strong public opinion against such lawlessness. The members of mobs who unlawfully kill should be dealt with severely.[2]

Certainly, the men in the mobs who killed Woodard and Clifton had not been dealt with severely. The unavoidable fact is that even among many of "the better people of Wyoming," there was a favorable attitude toward lynching. An example of this feeling is found in a July 25, 1903, article published in the *Laramie Boomerang* that quotes a "prominent Wyoming lawyer," with apparent approval:

> The indifferent and utter carelessness of the judges is the third reason why justice is retarded in Wyoming. Any old excuse presented by a lawyer for not having his case ready is taken without a murmur, and the case is postponed. This can be done any number of times, until years have passed without justice being done and crime punished.
>
> This man Walters, who was murdered at Basin by the mob, had been in jail three years—or longer. . . . He would likely have been there just as much longer, and then been set free. But the people had not forgotten his crime, and administered justice themselves.[3]

It is beside the point that the observations of the "prominent Wyoming lawyer" regarding postponing cases are exactly opposite of what happened in the Walters case, and that he had other facts wrong. This lawyer was quoted because he faithfully reflected what people already believed about the justice system and wanted to hear.

The *Sheridan Post* editorial cited above was actually one of the stronger statements against the lynching of Gorman and Walters. Other newspapers openly justified it and only deplored the death of Earl Price. For example, the *Casper Derrick* wrote that "while there is little regret expressed over the killing of Gorman and Walters, the sad death of Price is deeply regretted. . . . The county authorities will do everything possible to learn the identity of the men who murdered him and bring them to justice." The *Thermopolis Record* made an even stronger statement regarding the killings of Walters and Gorman. One of their headlines on July 25, 1903, read, "Earl Price Falls a Victim of a Mob at Basin, Who Also Take the Worthless Lives of Murderers Gorman and Walters." The chief thrust in the body of the article was the terrible calamity of the killing of Price, and it criticized the lynching because it was carried out incompetently, when "Earl was instantly killed by some fools in the mob who fired a volley at the guards as soon as they made their appearance." This theme was also sounded in the *Wyoming Tribune* on July 21, 1903; the *Tribune* lamented that when the mob shot Price, they showed themselves to be "poorly organized and poorly captained." It seems never to have occurred to any of these people that the dignity and majesty of the law in Wyoming might have been offended when a mob slaughtered two prisoners in the care of the state.[4]

In the days after July 20, 1903, the politicians chimed in. When the *Cheyenne Daily Leader* asked Governor Fenimore Chatterton what he was going to do about the Basin lynching, he replied, "You can say that I will call upon the prosecuting attorney of Big Horn County to take prompt action in this matter and bring to justice the slayers of Price." He followed this declaration of the obvious with a telegram to the Big Horn County commissioners, proclaiming that "a foul murder was not only committed, but the dignity of the law was assailed, the reputation of the state blackened, and the safety of all citizens threatened." The governor continued, "I deem it my duty to call upon you, and all your peace officers, and the good citizens of your county to use every endeavor to bring the guilty persons to justice. The county owes it to itself and the state to take quick and decisive action. Expense should not be considered."[5]

The text of this telegram was released to the state's newspapers. Then the governor issued letters in which he made similar declarations, reflecting, among other things, his apparent beliefs that there had been only one murder and that the county should not flinch at the expense. Governor Chatterton tendered no financial assistance from the state to Big Horn County, though, and then, as now, the counties bore virtually the entire cost of criminal prosecution. The governor did offer to send the attorney general to the Big Horn Basin to share his experience in the Tom Horn case. Chatterton apparently knew his audience well, because state newspapers approved of his declarations. One even ran a large headline blaring that, "Governor Chatterton Is Opposed to Lynching and Is Not Afraid to Say So."[6]

Chatterton's posturing might have looked good in Cheyenne, but it provided little practical benefit in Basin City. Despite the lack of meaningful assistance from the state, however, the Big Horn County authorities appeared determined to do something about the lynching.[7] It was an event about which a large number of the citizens of Big Horn County knew a great deal, but they were reluctant to talk. The authorities still diligently went about the investigation, and they developed evidence warranting the calling of a grand jury in October. They managed to procure a confession from W. H. Smith, one of the participants on July 20, 1903. Smith supposedly gave the authorities the names of thirty-five members of the mob, and it caused quite a stir. On the eve of the meeting of the grand jury, a newspaper story declared that "it is feared there will be another lynching party and that the man who made the confession will be strung up."[8]

Smith was placed in the jail, and several deputies were employed to protect him "from those who are threatening vengeance upon him." It was a tense time, as shown by further excerpts from the *Daily Leader* story: "The grand jury . . . is meeting here this afternoon, but it is declared that they are in great measure intimidated and may not have the courage to bring in indictments against all of the thirty-five men implicated by the confession which Smith made to the district attorney. Governor Chatterton and the local authorities, however, are determined that the members of the mob shall be punished."[9]

On October 22, 1903, the authorities began the business of empaneling a grand jury. One of the names drawn was that of Marvin B. Rhodes (although he was then excused by the court), who later wrote extensively about the events in Basin in the early years of the twentieth century. Twelve men were selected to sit on the grand jury, and none of these men was prominent. D. N. Hale, listed as one of the jurors, is apparently Dudley Hale, the sheriff's deputy who had been in the middle of the tumultuous events just three months before. It is surprising that a law enforcement officer served on the grand jury, but two of the men were from Basin and surely had a lot of firsthand information about the raid on the jail. Perhaps a rule of necessity was applied here.[10]

The grand jury proceeded to hear testimony, some sixteen different witnesses from Shell, as well as two brothers named Smith (presumably including W. H. Smith) and one Willis Ditmer who was "compelled to accompany the party" the night of the lynching. After hearing the evidence, the grand jury issued indictments against eight men, an event remarkable enough to be noted by Cutler in his classic treatise about lynch law in the United States. Cutler observed that only within the previous three or four years before publication of his book (1905) had there been determined efforts in a few places to arrest and punish members of a lynch mob, and he cited seven examples in the United States, including the Wyoming indictments.[11]

The grand jury showed courage in proceeding as they did, but they were not without support. It was reported that "ranchmen of the Greybull country" raised $1,000 to assist in the prosecution of those in the mob who attacked the Big Horn jail on July 20.[12] It was also reported that there were two distinct factions in Big Horn County, those who were determined that the members of the lynch mob should be punished and those who wanted "to whitewash the affair."[13]

The identity of those indicted was not revealed to the press, but that did not prevent speculation. The newspapers noted that the sheriff had left town with arrest warrants and was headed in the direction of Otto. Several men were mentioned as having been indicted, most of them supposedly from Otto. The men actually mentioned in news stories, though, were not from Otto, but were from Ten Sleep, Shell, and Hyattville, and the newspapers never did get their identities right.[14]

Court records list the eight men indicted: James G. Tatlock (of Shell), apparently the first man against whom an indictment was issued, on October 26, 1903, followed by George Saban (Shell). Indicted on October 27 and 28 were Daniel Lee Morse (an older man from Shell who had worked as a cowboy in his youth), Colin F. McKenzie (a shopkeeper from Shell), Ralph Mercer (a stockman from Hyattville), and Tyancum T. Taylor, Walter Feuder, and Orville Hardee (of unknown origin).[15]

The indictment of George Saban caused the most comment in the newspapers, because he was the most prominent of the men indicted. Saban was held in "high esteem" and was a "man of means" with many friends. It was asserted that he was a leader of the mob and, on other occasions, *the* leader. Saban was most likely the "tall and powerfully built man of middle age" whose voice was widely identified when he gave the order to "fall in."[16]

George Saban comes down to us as a fascinating and contradictory character, a man of intelligence and drive, who harbored beneath a wholly likeable exterior an Old Testament capacity for vengeance. He was born in Maine in October 1873, and his family moved to Nebraska when he was eight years old. When Saban was only fifteen or sixteen, he left home, went to the Black Hills, where he worked as a cowboy, and then rode over the Big Horn Mountains from Sheridan to the Shell valley. He must have shown exceptional qualities early on; he started working for Colonel J. L. Torrey, and after only a few years, when Saban was still in his early twenties, Torrey put him in charge of his horse ranch on the upper end of Horse Creek, and made George part owner. Saban married Bertha Whaley in 1897, and when Harry Sweeny, the 1900 census enumerator, found George and Bertha on June 1, 1900, they already had a child (the first of six) and could tell Sweeny that they owned their home and a farm free and clear. George listed his occupation as "wool grower."[17]

Saban appears time and again in local historical accounts. People talk about him at length; they were obviously drawn to him. He was described as a born leader, but he certainly was not an extroverted person; he never drank, swore, used tobacco, or even carried a gun. Saban was so athletic and such a skilled cowboy that Joe Magill, an early newspaperman, wrote a poem inspired by Saban's horsemanship, entitled "Saban of Shell." At one point, an old friend of his, Felix Alston, tried to list all the distinctive characteristics of George Saban. He said that Saban was a "Big, dark, complexioned man, Brown Eyes, walks very erect," that he was 5'10 1/4" tall and weighed between 185 and 200 pounds, that he had a "loud, hearty, peculiar attractive laugh," was a good cow puncher, that he shot and roped left-handed and was "very attentive to the ladies."[18]

There was something in Saban, though, that seemed to make him crave war or things akin to it. Shortly after his marriage, he dropped everything and went off to Florida with Colonel Torrey's Rough Riders, a contingent that was supposed to fight in Cuba but never got there. And the raid on the jail was not the only time George Saban's name was mentioned in connection with armed and irregular raids. There were several sheep raids out of Shell in the first few years of the 1900s, and despite his early career as a sheep owner, Saban was almost surely part of these raids.[19]

After Saban was arrested for the murders of Joseph Walters, James Gorman, and Earl Price, he quickly posted $10,000 bond ($5,000 for the charge of killing Price, and $2,500 each for Walters and Gorman) and was released. The men who were indicted forwarded an aggressive defense. They hired good lawyers, W. S. Metz and E. E. Lonabaugh from Sheridan, who vigorously defended their clients. The indictment against Tatlock was not issued until October 26, but just a day later, on October 27, his lawyers filed a motion that they be allowed "to examine minutes of the grand jury as to the evidence relating to the charge set forth in the indictments."[20]

Arguments were heard the same day, and, of course, the prosecution vigorously resisted this request. The prosecution's witnesses were surely frightened and reluctant, even as they testified before the grand jury, a proceeding at which neither the defendants nor any of their representatives were present. Perhaps the witnesses were induced to talk on the representation that their testimony was secret, as is normally the case with grand jury testimony. The last thing Arnott and Ridgely (the prosecuting attorneys) would have wanted was for George Saban to pour over transcripts of the grand jury testimony. Judge Stotts could surely perceive all this and probably felt that the intent of the motion was more to intimidate witnesses than to obtain information, but although he refused to allow the defendants the evidence before the grand jury, he did order that the prosecution release the names of all the witnesses who testified. He might have done this because most of the names were already known, as the prosecution had endorsed its witnesses on the indictments.[21]

Papers speculated that Tatlock would turn state's evidence because he had "several times confessed to being a member of the mob," and he was "considerable of a boaster."[22] In Cheyenne, the *Daily Leader* crowed that the "the prominent stockmen who have been indicted for being members of the mob . . . will begin to think that times have changed in Wyoming."[23] When the April term neared, however, Tatlock had not turned state's evidence, and the defendants' attorneys were as assertive as ever.

On March 29, 1904, they obtained a commission to examine seven witnesses in Sheridan. These men were apparently not from the Big Horn Basin; perhaps they were alibi witnesses. Tatlock and Saban, who were expected to be the first men tried, challenged the jury panel, saying that the clerk of court failed to "thoroughly shake" the jury box. Sheriff Fenton countered, saying that the clerk "thoroughly shook the said jury box, revolving the said jury box around at least three times." Whether properly shaken or not, though, there was a "peculiar outcome" in the first selection of a new panel of jurors, in that some seventeen of the men first selected were from the Mormon community of Burlington, and Judge Stotts apparently ordered the selection of a new panel.[24]

The spring term of court in 1904 aroused a great deal of interest, in part because of the mob case, but also because of a suit for absolute divorce filed by William F. Cody. (The *Wyoming Tribune* speculated that Judge Stotts would probably be disqualified because of his friendship with Colonel Cody.) The case against Tatlock was to commence on April 25, but when the day arrived, the prosecution made a surprise move, announcing that the cases of Tatlock and Saban would be moved to the foot of the docket, and Daniel Lee Morse would be the first one tried.[25]

Daniel Lee Morse was described as "a man of upwards of 60 years, hale and hearty and said to be of a genial disposition and honorable. He came to Wyoming from Texas, where he is said to have gained an envious position for valorous work in the confederate army." It was further noted that "nearly all state witnesses are Morse's best friends, men in whom he had implicit confidence[,] and their evidence will be reluctantly given." Indeed, Morse had so many friends, fears were expressed that his friends would raid the jail and rescue him.[26]

The jury was rapidly selected, and the trial proceeded the morning of April 27, 1904. Unfortunately, the comments of the newspapers proved prophetic; the prosecution's case never got off the ground. In the district court journal is a terse description of the entire trial: "Witnesses for state sworn and case proceeded. After hearing several witnesses for the state[,] the State rests and makes motion that case be dismissed and jury instructed to render verdict of not guilty." The *Cheyenne Daily Leader,* under the headline "Dan Lee Morse Goes Scott Free," stated, "The prosecution dropped the case owing to its inability to get witnesses to testify and the court instructed the jury to find for the defendant." The *Sheridan Post* presented the event somewhat differently, noting that, "the defense succeeded in impeaching the chief witness for the state [never identified], whereupon the attorneys for the defense made a motion that the jury be instructed to return a verdict of not guilty. Judge Stotts sustained the motion." Regardless of exactly how it came about, the result was the same. Dan Lee Morse was acquitted of all charges, and the prosecuting attorney decided that it was not worthwhile to proceed with the trials of the other defendants. All the charges were dismissed against all defendants.[27]

The lynching and the complete inability to punish those responsible were terribly distressing events for those who wanted conflict within the Big Horn Basin to be resolved in a peaceful way, with the rule of law as the dominant force in the society. One of the most upsetting realizations must have been that the new county, with its local sheriff, jail, and courts, had not been enough to realize this goal. The society was still immature, and it was hard to know when this would change.

There was one positive result from the whole sorry episode. Senator Jake Schwoob, from Cody, introduced legislation to have prisoners who had been sentenced to death taken quickly from local jails, away from possible lynch mobs. It was passed by the Wyoming legislature, and after 1905, prisoners subject to the death penalty were transported to Rawlins, there to await execution.[28]

10

Sheep and Cattle

Even before the lynching of Jim Gorman and J. P. Walters, the Big Horn Basin had been plagued by a different and distinctive form of vigilantism, raids on sheep camps. One historian described the assault on sheep as "a type of extra legal justice peculiar to the conditions and times in which it took place."[1]

The "conditions and times" began with the fact that virtually all of the Big Horn Basin was public domain, an open range available to all. When the great cattle ranches were first formed, they carried out their operations on very little private land. Maybe a half section around a ranch headquarters would be patented, but the thousands and thousands of acres upon which cattle grazed were not and could not be.[2]

At first, this had little significance, but then later, into the 1880s and the 1890s, competitors for the land arrived. The cattlemen had come to the Basin first, and they vigorously defended what they perceived as their established use of the land. For several years after they arrived, the story was put abroad that nothing could grow in the Big Horn Basin, that farming was all but impossible, and that the land was good only for cattle grazing.[3]

It did not take long for people to see through this myth, and soon (especially after the 1886–1887 winter) settlers began to take homesteads on the better streams, such as Shell Creek, the Greybull River, and the Nowood River. The ranchers did not like losing their best cattle ground along the streams, but the force of law was clearly on the side of the homesteaders. As to upland grazing ground, though, the law was not so clear. In fact, there were no rules or regulations of any kind; the land could be used by the first person to come upon and exploit it. People are uncomfortable in such a lawless void, and they fill the emptiness, even if their inventions have no basis in reality. The cattlemen spoke of "range rights," "accustomed ranges," "rights secured by prior discovery and utilization," and "possessory rights due to occupation," but none of these concepts had any force in law. Thus, when sheepmen began to bring their sheep onto public grazing land, cattlemen had no legal protection at all for their crucial seasonal pastures. At the same time, the grazing habits of sheep (eating much more closely to the base of a plant than cattle do) were such that a range grazed by sheep was ruined for cattle until another season.[4]

Thus, the coming of sheep to the country represented a major threat to cattlemen, and they were not the type of people to accept passively what they perceived as the ruination of their range. The Big Horn Basin followed the pattern that had been set throughout the western United States when sheep and cattle interests clashed. First, there were warnings to sheep owners to keep out, followed by the setting of deadlines, and then seemingly inevitable violence by the cattlemen.[5]

As early as 1897, a deadline was set along the Nowood River, extending, generally, from Hyattville to Nowood (forty miles south of Ten Sleep). Representatives from the cattle interests, including George B. "Bear George" McClellan and Joe Emge, met with some sheepmen in Lost Cabin and established a specific line, extending from the head of Kirby Creek north to the mouth of Paintrock Creek (near Hyattville), from there to the summit of the Big Horn Mountains, directly back to Ten Sleep, then south along the base of the Big Horn Mountains to a point near Lone Tree Creek (near Nowood), and then back to the point of beginning.[6]

The sheepmen might have agreed to the establishment of a deadline, perhaps to head off worse violence, but they were probably not happy with it. Sheepmen felt they had as much right as the cattlemen did to use the public domain, and they resented deadlines. Their attitude was expressed by Edward Norris Wentworth: "The method could scarcely be termed a 'division,' but rather the arbitrary setting aside of lands for the exclusive use of cattle."[7]

This line, whether arbitrary or not, was taken very seriously by cattlemen; they policed and enforced the line. In September 1897, apparently shortly after the deadline was set, some sheepmen came across the line, and shots were fired into their tents. The Ben Minnick case is another example of cattlemen hitting hard when a sheepman was not careful enough to honor the 1897 line.[8]

Even in the absence of a declared deadline, however, friction developed. In 1902, along the Wood River in the western part of the basin, two bands of sheep were herded together and pushed over a steep incline. About the same time, three cowboys, including a man named Herbert Brink, pushed a sheepwagon over a knoll and watched it go end over end into a coulee.[9]

In the first few years of the twentieth century, the violence against sheepmen and their property seemed to accelerate. On June 4, 1904, the *Thermopolis Record* reported that Lincoln A. Morrison, a prominent sheepman, had been shot and killed without warning while at his sheep camp near Kirby Creek. The report was mistaken, however. Though he was shot and seriously wounded, Morrison did not die; indeed, he lived until 1967. No one was ever arrested or prosecuted for this crime.[10]

There were two particularly vicious attacks near Shell Creek. In the summer of 1905, Louis A. Gantz moved a large herd through the Big Horn Basin. Local cattlemen felt that he was moving too slowly, and that his sheep were eating all the grass. On August 24, 1905, his herd was camped on Shell Creek when ten masked men assaulted the encampment. They shot, clubbed, and dynamited the herd, killing or injuring some 4,000 sheep. Two horses were shot and killed, and sheepwagons with harnesses and provisions were burned. The raiders tied sheepdogs to the wagons and burned these essential animals to death, along with the wagons. Again, there were no arrests, although it was felt that Shell cattlemen had carried out the raid. George Saban was almost certainly part of this raid.[11]

In 1907, a man named J. L. Lynn brought a big herd of sheep into the Shell area, some 10,000 to 15,000 head. He established a headquarters near where Shell Creek enters the Big Horn River, as well as a summer pasture area near Trapper Creek, a small stream that runs into Shell Creek near the base of the Big Horn Mountains.[12] Lynn employed gunmen to protect his sheep, and he aggressively moved his herd around. Of course, the local cattlemen were incensed by Lynn's actions; as one of them put it, "His sheep would just sweep an area like a horde of locusts."[13] In early May, the cattlemen learned that Lynn had left a herd of about 3,000 sheep on Trapper Creek, tended by only two herders. This was an opportunity they had been waiting for, and every cowman in the area, except Arthur Flitner, came together for a raid. They descended on the camp and forced the two sheepherders to stand in the ice cold waters of Trapper Creek, while the cowboys destroyed the herd of sheep. They again used dynamite and apparently killed almost every animal in the herd by forcing them over an incline. It was stated that the identity of the raiders was common knowledge in the area, but no arrests were made, and one historian asserted that law enforcement officers did not conduct a vigorous investigation.[14]

During the entire time these sheep raids occurred in the Big Horn Basin, numerous sheep raids also occurred throughout Wyoming. They were so frequent that when only one or two hundred sheep were killed, the event is only casually mentioned in the historical record. By 1909, at least six men and thousands upon thousands of sheep had been killed in Wyoming during sheep raids. Untold amounts of property had been destroyed, including horses, wagons, tack, supplies, and those wonderfully trained and irreplaceable dogs. No cowboy had ever been convicted of a crime committed during a sheep raid. The closest anyone came to a successful prosecution of such crimes was in 1909 in Crook County. Several raids had been carried out against the S. A. Guthrie Company during 1908, in which a great deal of property was damaged, and Guthrie resolved to do something about them. He was aided by the Wyoming

Woolgrowers Association, which had been formed in 1905 and moved quickly to suppress sheep raids, not least by hiring a remarkable range detective, Joe LeFors. Guthrie retained two Sheridan attorneys, lawyers he apparently perceived as the best in the area, E. E. Enterline and W. S. Metz, and he offered their services to Crook County to assist in the prosecution of charges arising out of those 1908 sheep raids. It was a bitter struggle, as cattle interests also threw in money to help their side of the case. During hearings, armed cowboys descended upon Sundance and tried to intimidate witnesses. When the criminal charges came to trial in April 1909, lawyers for both sides proceeded to examine prospective jurors and went through some two hundred without forming a jury. The case was then compromised, however, by an agreement to drop all criminal charges but to assess large civil penalties against the nine defendants. The defendants also agreed that the S. A. Guthrie Sheep Company could use the range without disturbance.[15]

While ugly guerrilla warfare raged among livestock men, the rest of the Big Horn Basin forged into the twentieth century. Until the first few years of this new century, the dry center of the Big Horn Basin, through which the biggest stream flowed, the Big Horn River, was sparsely populated; so, too, along the Stinking Water (the Shoshone), another good-sized stream flowing through the basin. Then large irrigation projects were undertaken: The Hanover and Big Horn Canals opened thousands of acres to cultivation and created Worland (and augmented Basin, thirty miles north); the Garland Canal was the genesis of Powell; and the Sidon and Elk Canals were responsible for large population growth around Lovell.[16]

The railroad followed quickly; indeed, those who promoted the irrigation projects actively courted the railroad, knowing that only a railroad could provide a ready market for the sale of crops from all the newly irrigated acres. Charles Fremont Robertson, who was the prime mover behind the Hanover Canal and later the first mayor of Worland, made a crucial visit to the headquarters of the Burlington Railroad in Omaha in 1905. Robertson and David T. Pulliam succeeded in persuading the railroad company to build to Worland, but at an exorbitant

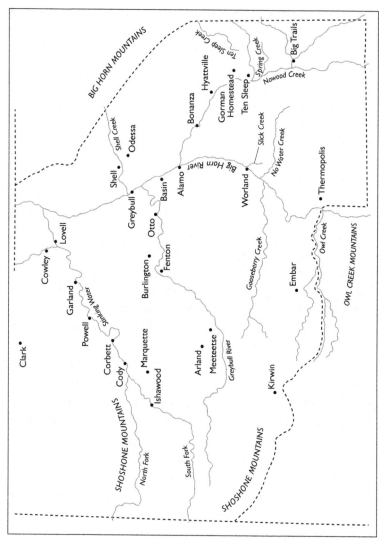

Big Horn Basin,
1909

price. The cost of bringing the railroad to Worland was that the town would be moved from the west side of the Big Horn River to the east side of the river, and the Lincoln Land Company, a wholly owned subsidiary of the railroad, would receive a half interest in two sections of land upon which the new town of Worland would be built.[17] Worland gulped but accepted the deal. During the dead of the frigid winter of 1905–1906, most of the town was moved across the frozen Big Horn River, a move that has gained the status of legend.[18]

A similar arrangement was sought for land south of Basin City, land to be used for the location of a division point, but no deal could be reached. As a result, the railroad formed a new town in 1906, just eight miles north of Basin, which it named Greybull, and Greybull became the site of the roundhouse for the Burlington Railroad. The railroad moved south quickly, arriving in Worland on July 10, 1906, and about twenty miles south of Worland in 1907, near coalfields at Gebo.[19]

The railroad changed everything. Suddenly, most residents of the Big Horn Basin were closely connected to the industrial might of their country. Transportation, to almost any place in the country, became a matter of a few relatively comfortable days. Goods could flow in and out without limit. It was an immense change from what had been just twenty-seven years before.

The population within the Big Horn Basin boomed to 13,795 by 1910, more than three times the number in 1900.[20] The people coming in were different from those already in the basin. Instead of being primarily ranch men, the newcomers were crop farmers and those having all the different occupations to be found in towns, such as doctors, lawyers, merchants, and teachers.[21] Many more families came to take advantage of the new farming opportunities; the Burlington Railroad created an immigration bureau to promote the settlement of families in the Big Horn Basin. The population growth was large enough that soon there was talk of making new counties within the Big Horn Basin.[22]

Not long after the town of Worland was founded in 1906, C. F. Robertson started lobbying the legislature to establish a county around Worland. At first he was unsuccessful, but in 1909 the Wyoming legislature enacted two bills, one creating Park County in the northwestern part of the basin, and the other, Hot Springs County (a name subsequently changed to Washakie County to honor the great Shoshone chief who had died in 1900). This latter county took in a large area in the southern part of the basin, from Wind River Canyon through Thermopolis to a line 4.5 miles north of Worland. The boosters of Worland were unhappy with this bill but were resigned to its passage. Then Governor Bryant B. Brooks did a surprising thing. Although he approved the Park County bill, he refused to sign the bill for Washakie County, citing serious questions about whether the new county arrangements met constitutional requirements for minimum valuations. The upshot was that Big Horn County would remain intact at least until 1911, when Park County would split off, and further county division would not take place until 1913. Thus, for eleven years into the twentieth century, the center for the enforcement of laws would remain in Basin City, resting in the care of officials elected by people throughout the Big Horn Basin.[23]

In 1908, the voters elected Felix Alston as sheriff of Big Horn County and Percy W. Metz as county attorney. Alston had been a deputy with the sheriff's office for some years before his election. He was involved in incidents such as the unsuccessful investigation of the raid on Louis Gantz and the attempt to move Walters and Gorman away from the jail (when Gorman escaped). He was a slender man, not overly imposing physically, and he had been supported by cattlemen in his run for sheriff, who perceived him as friendly to their interests.[24]

Percy Metz was the son of William Metz, the Sheridan attorney. He had followed his father into the practice of law and was a member of his father's firm, with his office in Basin. Percy was an engaging and likable young man, but in 1908, he was green, having just entered the bar two years before. His father supported him when he ran for county attorney, even pledging that he would help his son without charge if he encountered cases beyond his experience.[25]

In March 1909, two men, Joe Allemand and Joe Emge, gathered a large herd of sheep near Worland and proceeded to drive them east, directly toward the 1897 deadline. Their actions were the first in a chain

Percy W. Metz. Courtesy
the Colorado Historical
Society and the *Denver
Post.*

of events that would seize and engage Alston and Percy Metz for the rest
of their lives. Young Percy, at twenty-five, had no way of knowing it, but
well into his seventies, he would be telling fascinated audiences what
happened in 1909 near a small tributary of the Nowood River, on a little
stream called Spring Creek.

11

◆

The Spring Creek Raid

Joe Allemand and Joe Emge were an odd pair to challenge the deadline. It was odd that they had become partners and odd that either one decided to push sheep so aggressively. They had very different personalities. Allemand was an easy-going, well-liked man; he was born in France but had come to the United States before 1890, when he was about twenty-one. About 1900, he married a girl from Big Trails, Adeline Smith, and they had two boys. They lived on Spring Creek, near the base of the Big Horn Mountains, and Allemand had avoided conflict with the local cattlemen by ranging his sheep to the east, back over the mountain toward Buffalo. It was rumored, though, that he was having financial trouble and was trying to persuade his more prosperous neighbor on Spring Creek, Joe Emge, to come in with him in the sheep business.[1]

Emge, a forty-six–year-old bachelor, had been a cattleman, and a very intemperate one, who was supposed to have participated in raids against sheepmen and had once built a fence ten miles long between Spring Creek and Otter Creek to keep all sheep off the mountain. He was combative and excitable, the kind of man who made enemies. Emge finally agreed with Allemand, deciding that he was going to change sides and start running sheep, but he did not do so graciously. Some of Emge's friends tried to dissuade him, to the point of warning him, but Emge had made

The Allemand family. Courtesy Washakie Museum.

up his mind and stubbornly refused to reconsider. He is supposed to have said, "There are some fellows I want to get even with."[2]

Emge and Allemand might have been an odd couple, but they were serious about bringing sheep into the Upper Nowood, as the area south of Ten Sleep and upstream on the Nowood River was known, country that was the very heart of the land encompassed by the deadline. In February, they jointly purchased a 400-acre ranch from Charles E. Shaw at the mouth of Ten Sleep Creek, just southwest of the town, and it appears they went into quite a bit of debt to do it. In March, they bought two bands comprising 4,600 sheep and prepared to take them from Worland to Ten Sleep, a trip of about thirty miles over dry, desolate, and eroded country known locally as badlands. They employed three herders, Pete Cafferal (an older man from France, who also served as the camp cook), Jules Lazier (Allemand's nephew, also from France, in the United States for a brief visit), and Charles David "Bounce" Helmer (a young man from Big Trails, who was seventeen or eighteen).[3]

On March 28, 1909, Emge and Allemand started driving their sheep eastward. The two Joes were well aware there might be trouble; Emge is supposed to have stated that there was an "over $10,000 reward for my scalp." They were well armed, including a .35 Remington automatic, a .351 automatic, and a .30-40.[4] Emge and Allemand proceeded cautiously, expecting trouble. The trip across the badlands and up to Spring Creek took about five days, and Joe Emge got very little sleep during that time. On April 2, 1909, the sheep herd and all its keepers arrived at a place near where Spring Creek flows into the Nowood, about seven miles south of Ten Sleep. They thought they had arrived safely. Emge declared that he was almost home and could finally get some sleep.[5]

The site of the camp was about a quarter of a mile upstream from a ranch house, one that had been owned by the Greet family but was just then being vacated for a new owner, Porter Lamb. Fred and Frank Greet, twin young men in their early twenties, had spent most of April 2 at the site of their new ranch, about ten miles farther south on the Nowood, and had just returned to Spring Creek; that evening was supposed to be their last night at their old ranch. The Greet brothers were surprised to find Emge and Allemand near the ranch, but they were on good terms with their Spring Creek neighbors, and, at Joe Emge's invitation, had supper at a sheepwagon with Emge, Allemand, and Lazier.[6]

The Greets returned to their place at about 8:30 P.M. They left Emge, Allemand, and Lazier at the sheepwagon, which was located on the north side of Spring Creek. About a quarter of a mile south, on the south side of Spring Creek, there was another camp, with a sheepwagon, a supply wagon, and a buggy; this is where Bounce Helmer and Pete Cafferal were located. The large sheep herd was scattered all around the wagons. The Greets were staying in their old ranch house, and Porter Lamb and his brother-in-law, John Meredith, stayed in a tent close to the house. All of these men had gone to bed and fallen asleep that evening when, at about 10:30 P.M., they were sharply awakened by gunshots. Fred Greet and Porter Lamb would later testify that they first heard a series of rapid shots and believed they came from an automatic rifle. They heard shooting for about forty-five minutes, and then the sheepwagon at the north camp (the wagons to the north later became known collectively as "the north wagon," and those to the south, the "south wagon") started burning. About this time, Lamb and the Greet brothers, who had all been watching from places in the ranch house, came outside, to the east of the Greet cabin, to see better what was happening. Frank Greet heard someone say, "throw up your hands, throw up your hands." He then heard two shots fired almost immediately and saw two men walking up to the wagon. Then a shot was fired over the heads of those at the Greet cabin, and all the men retreated to places inside the house; Porter Lamb dragged his bed out of the tent and into the cabin, remarking that a tent did not provide much protection.[7]

The shooting continued for about another hour, and then all was silent. The men in the Greet cabin were afraid to come out because there might be a man about the house, and they assumed that all the sheepmen had been killed. They spent a tormented night, with one man or another always looking out the window; no one got much sleep. Shortly after dawn, the men went over to the sheep camp, and they found a horrible spectacle. To the south, the sheepwagon, supply wagon, and buggy had completely burned, leaving only blackened metal; around these wagons were dead and injured sheep and two dead dogs, all of which had been shot. The north sheepwagon had been completely consumed by fire, but the buckboard was intact, except for the tongue, which had been burned off. Inside what had been the wagon were two bodies, both hideously burned. About fifteen feet from the front of the sheepwagon lay the body of Joe Allemand. Allemand was lying on his back, and he had been shot.[8]

There was a telephone at the Greet ranch house, but the men had been too frightened to use it during the night. When they tried to use it that morning, they discovered that the line had been cut. They found the cut, though, repaired it, and about 8:30 that morning placed a call to Walter Fiscus at the hardware store in Ten Sleep. Fiscus, in turn, called Sheriff Alston in Basin, although he was not able to get through until 9:50. Alston immediately contacted Percy Metz and arranged to travel to the scene. He also called his deputy in Ten Sleep, Al Morton, and told him to go to Spring Creek immediately and make sure people did not disturb the area.

Fiscus called Dr. George W. Walker in Hyattville and requested that he come to Spring Creek.[9]

All parties quickly headed to Spring Creek that Saturday morning. Morton would have arrived first, in about an hour, and then Dr. Walker. Somewhere between 6 P.M. and 7 P.M. that day, Metz and Alston drove a buckboard over a low-lying hill and watched the Spring Creek Valley suddenly unfold before them to the southeast, stretching for three or four miles to the base of the Big Horn Mountains. The ugly scenes at the north and south wagons immediately presented themselves.

There was enough daylight for Alston to do a preliminary investigation. Allemand's body had not been moved, and Alston found a shovel close to it, which had been stuck in the ground. Two dead dogs were close by, and two woolly puppies, still alive, were curled up against Allemand's body. In the wagon, Alston found a small lump of gold under the head of one of the bodies (Emge had had a mouthful of gold fillings), and lying beneath that same body was a .35 automatic. Both bodies were burned so badly that they were "just a burned body and the trunk," and both of them held the same posture, the heads "reared straight back and almost standing straight up." It was never mentioned in any of the later proceedings, but the odor must have been frightful. The body under which the gold was found was put in a box and taken back to the house, and a tarpaulin was thrown over the other body and what remained of the sheepwagon. A cellar door brought from the Greet house was used to carry Allemand's body back to the house.[10]

That evening, Dr. Walker examined Joe Allemand's body. He found that a bullet wound had entered the rib cage from the left side and was necessarily fatal. The bullet had gone through Allemand's body, come out on the right side, and struck his right forearm, breaking the ulna. The doctor found the bullet embedded in Allemand's arm. He also found a second wound, a tearing wound that had ranged along the collarbone. Dr. Walker was unsure of the origin of the wound, but it would not have been a fatal injury.[11]

Alston and Metz were reasonably sure that this awful event had been a sheep raid, carried out by the local cattlemen. Of course, they knew that

Joe Allemand had been killed, and they believed the burned bodies were Emge and Lazier. They had no idea, however, what had become of Bounce Helmer and Pete Cafferal. They did not know who had participated in the raid, nor even how many raiders there were. Lamb and the Greet brothers were aware only that several men had been involved.

The next morning, Alston awoke to find that it had snowed during the night. He had hoped to examine the area around the wagons early that morning, but this examination would have to be postponed until the snow melted off. While he waited for the day to warm, Alston saw to it that the last body was removed to the house; he found a French medal underneath it. He and his deputies also found what they believed to be another gold tooth, as well as two other rifles, with all their wooden parts burned off. Even before the snow had melted, another significant thing happened: Bounce Helmer and Pete Cafferal showed up.[12]

Metz interviewed Helmer, who was a very frightened young man that morning. Bounce had been awakened by shooting and had sprung up and run through the sagebrush to get away, but then he had been intercepted by two cowboys, who took him and Cafferal prisoners. After a short while, they were led to an area just below the base of the hill on which the north wagons set. Bounce heard someone say, "Light that wagon," and "Put a light on that wagon, or we'll riddle it with bullets." Then he heard someone count to three and start shooting rapidly into the wagon, as with an automatic. Shortly after, someone said, "Get them hands up," and Bounce then heard two shots.[13]

Bounce and Pete Cafferal were then taken across the creek, back to the area of the south wagons. Bounce watched a man throw harnesses and collars into the fire and saw six to eight men around the wagons. The raiders finally decided to turn Bounce and Pete loose after telling them to get away from there. Bounce assured them, "If you will turn us loose, by God, I won't come back." The herders had headed south, toward the home of Ade Goodrich, Bounce's mother, two miles beyond Otter Creek, but before they had gone too far, Bounce had to sit down and pull cactus thorns from his feet; they had become embedded when Bounce fled after he first heard shooting.[14]

Percy Metz knew what an important witness Bounce Helmer was, a survivor of the raid who had not only been in the middle of the whole event, but who was familiar with all the cowboys in the area, and when he interviewed Bounce, Metz took him behind closed doors. What the county attorney most wanted to know was the identity of the raiders, but here Metz was disappointed and frustrated; Helmer told him he did not know who any of the cowboys were because they were all wearing masks. He insisted he had told Metz everything he knew.[15]

The snow finally melted, and Alston led a large group of men to the north wagon. On the south and the east sides of the wagon, people had been kept away, and Alston was able to identify eight sites where men had fired guns. At each site, he found at least two spent cartridges, and the cartridges included twenty .25–35 rifle brasses, three to five from a .30–30 rifle, two .45 pistol shells, and at least eight shells from a .35 automatic. The men were also able to track horses that had ridden to the sheep camps. They found a trail coming from the south, one they concluded the raiders had made when they first came near the camps. They also found the place where the men veered from the trail to a spot upstream on Spring Creek, where the raiders had tied their horses. Alston concluded there had been eight men, possibly more, and after the raid they had ridden back to the county road and returned to the south.[16]

It was obvious that more evidence was needed, and that Felix Alston must remain in the Upper Nowood to continue his investigation. Percy Metz drove the buckboard back to the county seat on Monday, April 5. Word of the raid had spread like wildfire throughout the Big Horn Basin, and when he arrived back in Basin City, Metz found an aroused citizenry, avid for more information.[17]

12

The Reaction

The murders of Emge, Allemand, and Lazier were deeply disturbing to many Big Horn County citizens. Just three days after the raid on Spring Creek, Peter Enders, the Big Horn County clerk, wrote a passionate letter to Governor Brooks. After reciting the facts as he understood them, Enders stated:

> This is the Sixth raid made on sheepmen in this section and the Fourth life that has been taken[;] absolutely nothing has been done heretofore . . . the miscreants [being] emboldened by the apathy and inefficiency of the officers in charge together with the deplorable fact that many of our citizens are intimidated from giving criminating information to the authorities, has brought about a state of affairs intolerable beyond imagination.
>
> This case beggars description[;] decent people here are getting discouraged[.] We need the whole might of the State Administration supplemented by the best detective talent available.
>
> It is not the greatest difficulty to know who are the guilty parties, it is a question of going right after the proposition and getting evidence sufficient to convict.

Let it become known that the State is making a determined effort to bring the guilty parties to justice[;] the good people here will give every assistance within their power. . . . While the eyes of the world are watching the outcome I pray to God that Wyoming justice will be vindicated.[1]

Wyoming newspapers soon joined in and loudly decried what had happened on Spring Creek. The *Cheyenne Daily Leader* was the first newspaper to go to print after the raid, and its opinion was unambiguously announced in sub-headlines: "In All the Sanguinary History of the Range Dispute in Wyoming Has Occurred No More Atrocious and Cowardly Crime than the Assassination of Joseph and Allemand Emge and Joe Lazier [*sic*]. . . . All Big Horn County is Horrified by the Outrage and Bitter is the Anathematizing of the Murderers."[2]

It might be expected that a paper from faraway Cheyenne would not hesitate to express a strong opinion, but when the local newspapers came to print, they also condemned the raid in no uncertain terms. The *Worland Grit* wrote of the "blackest crime in Wyoming's stirring history" and of the "hideous and incoherent" rumors that first filtered into Worland. Basin City then had two newspapers, and both of them responded strongly. The *Big Horn County Rustler* opened its April 9, 1909, article about the raid by declaring, "One of the most deplorable affairs in the history of the Big Horn Basin occurred on last Friday night at the mouth of Spring Creek," and closed by stating, "The trouble comes as a result of the old struggle over the range, a struggle which has been waged fiercely at times in every section of the west, but which it was hoped had ceased to demand its toll of blood."[3]

The story in the *Basin Republican* contained a stirring pronouncement at its conclusion:

The dreadful tragedy is to be deplored for many reasons. It puts another dark spot on the fair name of Wyoming and causes the outside world to gasp in horror at such bloodthirsty and fiendish atrocities. It will have a serious effect on those who were contemplating coming from the east to locate in the Basin and make this their home. Every lawabiding citizen of the county—and despite the fact of the awful tragedy narrated above nearly every resident of Big Horn County is a lawabiding, peaceable citizen—condemns the horrible outrage and wants to see the guilty parties brought to justice.[4]

Wyoming's sheepmen were especially outraged, and woolgrowers' associations immediately stepped forward and offered something that mattered very much here: cash. The Big Horn County Woolgrowers Association forwarded a $1,000 reward, the Wyoming Woolgrowers matched it, and the National Woolgrowers offered $2,000. In addition, J. A. Delfelder, the president of the Wyoming Woolgrowers, sent an appeal to members of the executive committee of the association for monies to support the prosecution.[5]

Of course, Big Horn County had the responsibility to investigate vigorously and prosecute the Spring Creek crimes, but the unfortunate reality was that prosecutions of complicated crimes were expensive, Wyoming counties had very limited resources, and the State of Wyoming forwarded no money for criminal prosecution. A county is merely an artificial entity, however, a unit created by a state to discharge the state's responsibility, and one of the most fundamental of state responsibilities is the prosecution of crime. To the extent that the State of Wyoming failed to provide adequate resources for a county to prosecute a crime, the state failed in a fundamental obligation to its citizens.[6] Johnson County had learned a hard lesson when the State of Wyoming provided no help toward the prosecution of the invaders, at least not when Johnson County needed it (the state legislature did appropriate some monies years after the invasion, when it did not help at all). Therefore, the monies to be gathered by the woolgrowers were important here, a big step toward assuring that the prosecution of the Spring Creek Raid would not go the way of the 1892 prosecution in Johnson County.[7]

Delfelder's letter to the woolgrowers' executive committee shows the depth of sheepmen's feelings about the raid. He began his letter by stating, "I beg to call your attention to the atrocious assassination of Allemand, Lasier and Emge on the night of April 2nd in Big Horn County by a band of inhuman and murderous raiders." Then Delfelder made declarations that ensured that these sheep raid cases would become symbolic, and celebrated, struggles:

> The time is at hand to call a halt on this willful defiance of the laws; ... I am confident that there could be no better time or occasion for making a test case than in this Spring Creek raid. It should not be considered a local matter, for if we succeed in bringing these murderers to justice it will have a salutary effect in all parts of the range country for years to come. ... It is impossible for the local authorities to cope with this matter and therefore we must offer a suitable reward to induce competent men to become interested and conduct the prosecution.[8]

The actual amount of reward money was more than the $4,000 offered by woolgrowers, because Joe Allemand's brother from Buffalo, Jacque, forwarded another $1,000, and the State of Wyoming, through the actions of Governor Brooks, $500. The total, $5,500, was a huge sum in 1909; it could buy a fine home or a ranch.[9]

At first, it seemed that virtually every person in Big Horn County had been enraged by the triple killing and intended to stop this kind of lawlessness. Still, all those associated with the prosecution knew the history of previous attempts in Wyoming to punish groups of men taking the law into their own hands. The expected woolgrowers' money was encouraging, but no one knew how much difference it would actually make. Johnson County's 1892 travails had occurred only seventeen years before, that worst possible example of a county overwhelmed by an obligation it could not discharge, and in the end having to watch impotently as arrogant wrongdoers thumbed their noses at the law. Even fresher was the debacle of the trial of Dan Lee Morse. All knew that no cowboy raiding a sheep camp had ever been convicted in the state of Wyoming. Despite public misgivings, though, in the first few weeks after the raid, as the prosecution gained momentum, it seemed that the dismal record of the past was no longer operative. Many things had evidently changed, even since 1903. Transportation and communication had improved considerably. The railroad now almost reached through the Big Horn Basin, and automobiles were appearing. Telephone wires strung along the Nowood had meant that a deputy sheriff could be sent to the site of the raid in time to protect the crime scene, and all other authorities could be summoned to the scene relatively quickly.

The money pledged by the woolgrowers was immediately put to use. When Percy Metz returned to Basin, he met with the Big Horn County commissioners and recommended that special counsel be appointed, admitting that he did not have the experience to prosecute the crimes associated with the raid. During the week of April 18, the Big Horn County commissioners met and resolved to hire W. S. Metz (Percy's father) and E. E. Enterline as special prosecutors. They were not from the Big Horn Basin, though, and it was felt that a local attorney was important. Billy Simpson, last seen in Lander as the county attorney, had moved to Cody and was also hired as a special prosecutor. Billy was about the only attorney in the basin who had not been retained by cattlemen, probably because he had done a great deal of work for sheepmen. Given the woolgrowers' money, the county commission was generous, providing $2,500 each to Metz and Enterline and $1,000 to Simpson.[10]

The initial investigation went somewhat better than expected (although not quite as well as the public was led to believe), and it resulted in two arrests. When Alston completed his investigation at the site of the raid, he proceeded south, deeper into the Upper Nowood. A heavy burden weighed upon Alston, and he might not have noticed the scenery, but the Upper Nowood country through which he rode in April 1909 would have been splendid. The Upper Nowood is well watered, and a traveler encounters one pretty little stream after another while passing buttes, bluffs, and canyons. The first such stream Alston reached was Otter Creek, about five miles south of Spring Creek, and there Alston visited and spoke with many people. In 1909, the population of the Upper Nowood was very small, only about 200 people, and those people knew a great deal about the lives of their neighbors. There were many staunch cattlemen in the Upper Nowood, but also many people who quietly disagreed with violent raids on sheep camps and who were quite willing to speak to Alston, if only off the record. Of course, a cataclysmic event such as the Spring Creek Raid inspires huge amounts of speculation, and thus Alston surely encountered people who wanted to play detective and were more than willing to tell him of their insights.[11]

Alston was able to quickly build a list of suspects. Several ranchmen and cowboys had been seen in the Spring Creek and Otter Creek areas on April 2, 1909, men whose actions did not fit within the normal flow of ranch activities. People living on the lower part of Otter Creek had noted men riding to various places around the ranch of William Keyes (pronounced "Kize"). The local stage driver and a trapper had also seen men riding in the area. Felix Alston quickly identified seven or eight men who were in place to commit the raid during the evening of April 2. These included Milton A. Alexander, a rancher who lived about five miles farther upstream on the Nowood from Otter Creek; William Keyes and Charles Faris, who ran small cattle operations from their lands on Otter Creek; Ed Eaton, a cowboy from Ten Sleep who had been trying to build a herd; Herbert Brink, Tommy Dixon, and Clyde Harvard, local cowboys who worked for Upper Nowood ranchers; and George Saban, who had moved from Shell. Saban, together with his father-in-law, W. T. Whaley, had purchased the Bay State Ranch near Ten Sleep in 1908. Before April 2, 1909, though, Saban had rarely been seen in this part of the Upper Nowood.[12]

Felix Alston's investigation focused on these men, upon such things as their whereabouts on April 2, the horses they rode, and the guns they used. Alston rode about the Upper Nowood, from Ten Sleep to Big Trails (twenty miles south), and spoke to each one of the suspects about what each knew regarding the raid. Of special note was a certain rifle, a .35 automatic, owned by a man who worked for Bill Keyes, Farney Cole. It had been left in Keyes's living room on April 2, at a time when George Saban was visiting Keyes. That same day Cole went to Hyattville, but when he returned, his .35 automatic was missing. Alston was a friend of George Saban's, and Alston knew that Saban did not carry a gun. The sheriff might have been reluctant to draw the conclusion, but Farney Cole's rifle was certainly handy for George Saban, and he might have used it the night of April 2. The calibers of the guns used by the other suspects were also interesting. Alston learned that Keyes, Faris, and Alexander used .30–30s, and that Brink shot a .25–35, and Dixon, a .45 pistol, calibers that corresponded exactly to the fired cartridges found at the scene of the raid.[13]

Alston remained in the Upper Nowood for about a week, not returning to Basin until Sunday, April 11. When he did return, though, he brought Bounce Helmer, an important witness who had just become an even more important witness. While in the Upper Nowood, Alston had learned of threats to Helmer and decided to take him into protective custody. Then, at some time, whether in the Upper Nowood or while riding back to Basin, Helmer had admitted to Alston that he had recognized one of the raiders. Bounce told Felix that when he and Cafferal were being led back to the south wagon, he had noticed a man at a place near a blazing fire, trying to untie a buggy from a wagon. As the man leaned forward, his mask fell away from his face, and Bounce recognized Ed Eaton, a man he had known his entire life and a man with a distinctive build (Eaton was six feet tall and only 150 pounds). Helmer said that he had not told Percy Metz of this identification because he was afraid that if it got out, someone would try to kill him.[14]

Immediately upon his return to Basin, Sheriff Alston swore out a warrant for Ed Eaton's arrest, and Eaton was taken into custody on Thursday, April 15. The day after the Eaton warrant was issued, Alston again returned to the Upper Nowood but came back to Basin only two days later. Another warrant was then issued, for the arrest of Herb Brink, evidently based on some loose talk by Brink to some people in Big Trails, talk that indicated Brink had more than secondhand knowledge about the raid. Brink was also arrested and placed in the Big Horn County jail with Eaton.[15]

Around this time, the prosecution team, consisting of William and Percy Metz, E. E. Enterline, and Felix Alston, met and discussed strategy. Percy Metz was putting up a brave front to the public, declaring to the press that the cases against Brink and Eaton were very strong, but they were not.[16] The prosecution did not have any evidence putting Herb

Brink on the scene the night of April 2, 1909, and the evidence against Ed Eaton was shaky. Helmer had first denied having recognized anyone, and this denial was well known to cattlemen. More than that, Bounce Helmer was not an overly bright young man, and he seemed subject to confusion; in the statements he had made to Percy Metz, he put a lumber wagon at the scene of the raid, a wagon that had been at least two miles away the evening of April 2.[17]

The subject of a grand jury was addressed. Alston likely reported that some of the citizens in the Upper Nowood were hostile, opposing any prosecution, and many were intimidated, reluctant to talk because of fear of retribution by the raiders. A grand jury can be an excellent investigative device; in this case, it could provide a mechanism to inquire further, pulling witnesses into a closed and secret proceeding to grill them in depth, thereby overcoming their reluctance to tell all they knew. The local district judge, C. H. Parmelee, was in favor of convening a grand jury, at least in part because of the prompting of Governor Brooks, and members of the prosecution were surely aware of a dialogue among the governor, the judge, and the sheriff.

From the beginning, Governor Brooks had assisted the prosecution as actively as he could. Brooks did not just send his attorney general up to the Big Horn Basin to tell war stories; at some time, apparently only a few days after the raid, the governor had personally gone to the Big Horn Basin and had conferred "at length" with Alston and Parmelee. A special session of the Big Horn County commissioners was convened on April 23. At that meeting, it was the unanimous opinion that a grand jury should be convened, and the members of the prosecution were authorized and directed to do so.[18]

13

Another Grand Jury

The prosecution was not going to do this halfway. The attorneys issued more than a hundred subpoenas, so many that Percy Metz declared many years later that they intended to issue subpoenas to every man, woman, and child on the east side of Big Horn County. All those subpoenas commanded their recipients to appear in Basin City on April 29, 1909; consequently, for a day or so before that date, the road between Ten Sleep and Basin was congested with people making their way to the county seat.[1]

The grand jury was selected, and it consisted of men from Meeteetse, Lovell, Cowley, Byron, Greybull, Basin, and Burlington. The men from Cowley, Burlington, Byron, and Lovell were probably Mormon, which was significant for several reasons. Within Wyoming, especially southwestern Wyoming, sheepmen were frequently Mormon. Indeed, an element of the struggle between sheepmen and cattlemen was religious prejudice against Mormon sheep ranchers. Perhaps as significant, though, was the ugly history of mob violence against Mormons. Almost certainly, the Mormons sitting on the grand jury strongly disapproved of those who harassed sheepmen.[2]

District Judge Parmelee read a long charge to the grand jury, which embodied a great deal of his own philosophy of law and order. Parmelee first pointed out to the grand jury that there would be "certain offenses . . . requiring investigation," by which he meant the Spring Creek Raid. He cautioned the grand jury, though, that they should proceed "truly and impartially," in accordance with the evidence before them and make their resolutions in a deliberative way, proceeding "under all the authority and under the safe-guards of the law as well." Parmelee reminded the grand jury that their deliberations and votes must be secret. Some of the actions of the 1903 grand jury must have been leaked to the public, because Parmelee disapprovingly commented that in the past, "certain transactions and deliberations of the jury room gained circulation on the outside."[3]

Parmelee completed his charge by turning to "the particular matter which will be chiefly before you for investigation," and he delivered an eloquent condemnation of mob rule:

> To permit such things to be done in a civilized community is to sub-
> stitute for law and security tyranny and terror. It is to submit to the
> domination of the methods of the Ku Klux, the Black Hand and the
> "night riders." It is to cast aside the results of a thousand years of
> struggle for liberty and enlightenment. . . .
>
> No man or body of men, however wise or well-intentioned, may
> safely be entrusted to pronounce upon or to redress public wrongs or
> private grievances outside of the forms of the law. All acts of a mob
> give occasion for reprisal. The spirit of lawlessness grows by what it
> feeds on. And when one set of men or class of men on the one hand
> indulge in acts of lawlessness, it simply invites retaliation by like acts
> on the part of others. The example of a single mob is worse in a
> community than a pestilence. . . .
>
> Very much of the peace, security and happiness of this community
> depends upon your action. Do your duty fearlessly, pursue your
> investigations thoroughly and demonstrate that law and not violence
> is the ruling principle in Big Horn county.

And then the grand jury started hearing witnesses. A grand jury proceeding is like a criminal trial, in that witnesses are called by the prosecuting attorneys for the state (here being represented by E. E.

Enterline and Billy Simpson), are sworn, and are then asked questions by the prosecutors. An important difference between a grand jury proceeding and a trial, though, is that at a grand jury proceeding, there is no attorney present for people who might be charged with crimes; only the prosecution presents evidence.

The first two witnesses called before the grand jury were Al Morton and Felix Alston. Al Morton, the Ten Sleep deputy, the first lawman on the scene, was a good witness to well inform the grand jury about the grisly scenes on Spring Creek the early morning of April 3. Alston told the jury about the results of his tracking of horses, and about all the shell casings he found. The testimony of both men was helped by a map drawn by Clyde Atherly, the Big Horn County surveyor. On April 26, at the request of the prosecution, Atherly had gone to Spring Creek. He undertook a survey, starting by placing his survey instrument directly over the spot where Joe Emge's body was found inside the burned sheepwagon, and this was the basis for the map he drew.[4]

Bounce Helmer was the next witness. After being brought to Basin, Helmer had been quickly whisked away to the Sheridan area, evidently to protect him. He worked at a ranch near Sheridan until returning to Basin to testify before the grand jury. Bounce told what he knew about the events of the evening of April 2, including his identification of Ed Eaton. Pete Cafferal's testimony was then presented, followed by two men who had been at the Greet cabin on April 2, Porter Lamb and Fred Greet.[5]

Several witnesses were then called whose testimony demonstrated such things as the presence of Tommy Dixon, Milton Alexander, and Herb Brink near Spring Creek on April 2, other locations of Dixon and Brink on the 2nd and 3rd, and comments made by Herb Brink to the effect that he would take his rifle and drive back Emge and Allemand.[6]

Nothing really dramatic or surprising was presented to the grand jury until the testimony of William D. ("Billy") and Anna Goodrich. Billy Goodrich's testimony, however, at least in its second form, was probably the biggest break in the whole case. When Goodrich was first called, he stated that he knew very little about the case. There must have been something about his testimony that did not ring right, though, because it was not long after Billy Goodrich left the grand jury room that Joe LeFors, the Wyoming Woolgrowers' detective, took him aside and, in some manner, persuaded him to return and testify to what he actually knew.[7]

What Billy actually knew were startling admissions from three men, Herb Brink, Tommy Dixon, and Bill Garrison, who had been working at Billy's ranch at Big Trails. Two of these men, Brink and Dixon, had made the huge mistake of talking to Goodrich after the raid. Goodrich first related what Herb Brink told him just a couple of days after April 2, 1909. As Goodrich revealed this discussion, the grand jury must have been so quietly attentive that everyone in the room could have heard a pin drop.

Just after the raid, Brink and Goodrich had gone to the Greet house and had heard Felix Alston say there were eight raiders. Brink told Goodrich, though, that Felix was mistaken; there were only seven. When Goodrich then noted that Brink must have been at the raid, Brink responded, "I was." Brink told Goodrich that Saban, Dixon, and Alexander had also taken part, and he related many details of the raid. Tommy Dixon talked to Goodrich a little later and provided more information, that Charlie Faris, Bill Keyes and Ed Eaton were participants in the raid, and that it was either Saban or Brink who had shot and killed Allemand after he had emerged from the burning wagon.[8]

The testimony of Billy Goodrich must have elated the prosecuting attorneys. Lawyers look at a case from the standpoint of the proof of essential elements; prior to Goodrich's statements, the case against the raiders was slim. Goodrich's testimony as to what Brink and Dixon told him, however, was all admissible in evidence, and, together with other easily established information, sufficed to fully meet the elements of the crime of murder. Anna Goodrich corroborated many of the things to which her husband had testified. In addition, she also told of odd and suspicious behavior by Herb Brink and provided some other helpful details.[9]

Clyde Harvard was then called to testify; he had been a suspect, and the prosecuting attorneys questioned him extensively, but then they dismissed him. As the evidence evolved in the grand jury proceedings, it became apparent that Clyde Harvard was not a raider, and he was never formally accused of being one. It appears, however, that he was involved in the raid, just not in a way that anyone suspected in 1909. Years later, Clyde Harvard's story came out. During the evening of April 2, 1909, seven men gathered at the ranch house of Bill Keyes on Otter Creek for the purpose of planning a sheep raid. Clyde, who was a very young man, was booted out of the ranch area by the older men. His curiosity was aroused, however, and so when the seven men rode out from Keyes's place, Harvard followed them from a discreet distance. He is supposed to have gone all the way to Spring Creek and watched all the events before slipping off into the darkness.[10]

Farney Cole was next called as a witness. The prosecution wanted to present the admissions Cole had made to Alston regarding his .35 automatic rifle. When Farney got on the stand, though, he first denied what he had told Alston. Some stern persuasion was required, but then Cole came back to what he had said at first. He admitted that he had kept the rifle standing in a corner of the kitchen, where all the men present at Keyes's on April 2, including George Saban, could see it. Then Cole had left for Hyattville, and when he came back, the rifle was gone. Much later Bill Keyes had talked to Cole about the gun, and Keyes suggested that Farney should say he had lost it.[11]

Several of the raiders were called as witnesses, including Herbert Brink, who was not a good witness. His anxiety was so great that he could not wait to blurt out his alibi, and when asked the simple question of where he found Tommy Dixon on April 2, he took off and rattled on and on, relating in a nonstop manner everything he was asserting happened to him on April 2 and April 3. Brink was about the twentieth witness, and the grand jury already knew much of the truth about the evening of April 2; the jurors probably listened with incredulity and felt that Brink's performance established his guilt, not his innocence.[12]

Herb Brink and Tommy Dixon had a bunkmate, Bill Garrison, and he was called as a witness, apparently shortly after Brink was. After the raid, Brink and Dixon had freely spoken to Billy Goodrich (and others), and it was a reasonable inference that they both spoke freely to their friend Garrison. More than this, Garrison had done something else that involved him in the case. In the first few days after the raid, when Alston was still in the Upper Nowood, Garrison and Frank Helmer, Bounce Helmer's father, visited the home of Ade Goodrich, Bounce's mother. They were there to speak to Bounce, but only Goodrich was at the house when they arrived. Ade and Frank had been divorced, and it had not been an amicable parting, so Garrison went into the house alone and spoke to Ade, while Frank remained outside. Frank Helmer later testified that he wanted his son to be told to relate only what he knew, "and nothing else." The prosecution gave this visit a more sinister twist, asserting that the message, at least from Garrison, was that Bounce had better keep his mouth shut or someone might dry-gulch him. Regardless of exactly what was intended, this visit opened Garrison to many questions. He was called as a witness and was subjected to grueling examination. Garrison was finally dismissed but told to be available for recall.[13]

This experience was devastating to Bill Garrison, apparently creating terrible conflicts within him, and causing him to feel he was losing his mind. He left Basin on foot, though he had ridden his horse there, and wandered south through the night of Saturday, May 1. The next morning found him about ten miles south of Basin, at a ranch near Manderson, Wyoming. During that day, he acted in a strange manner; he ate two meals at the ranch house, but then returned to a haystack, near which he spent the day. About seven that evening, a search was undertaken for Garrison, and his body was found by the haystack; he had apparently shot himself.[14]

There was a sensation about his death, some people asserting Garrison had been murdered, but little evidence supported this supposition, and a coroner's inquest concluded that he had committed suicide. The grand jury adjourned for Garrison's funeral but then forged on, hearing the evidence of many more witnesses. These people did not provide any startling new information, but they did supply additional evidence corroborating the involvement of other raiders, including Milton Alexander, Bill Keyes, and Ed Eaton. The testimony also served to negate different theories about the raid. Statements had been made that Joe

Allemand was struck a shovel blow to the neck, but Dr. George Walker refused to accept this theory. There was also speculation that one or more of the raiders had been wounded, but no facts were ever developed to establish this supposition.[15]

The last witness was heard either late on May 5 or early May 6, and the grand jury then made its decisions regarding indictments. Arson charges were voted against seven men: Saban, Alexander, Keyes, Faris, Eaton, Brink, and Dixon. More significantly, three counts of first-degree murder were also charged against each of these seven men. The grand jury did not take long to make these decisions; the indictments were drawn up on May 6, and arrest warrants were served on every defendant that same day.[16] The *Big Horn County Rustler* described how the sheriff deputies fanned out around Basin City and arrested first Alexander, then Dixon, then Saban, then Keyes, and, finally, Faris. They were all taken to the Big Horn County jail, where they joined Eaton and Brink. Bail was shortly set, but at an unusually high level, $10,000 per charge; consequently, all the defendants had to remain in jail until their trials.[17]

The indictment and arrest of the seven defendants were, of course, greatly satisfying to Felix Alston, and on May 7 he wrote a letter to Governor Brooks, proudly announcing these developments. Alston had no way of knowing it on May 7, but only a day or two later, the state's case would become considerably stronger. Two of the raiders confessed and turned state's evidence in return for lenient treatment.[18]

Bill Keyes and Charlie Faris were stunned by the indictments, but, as Percy Metz later told it, they were also angry. Keyes and Faris had been induced to go along on the raid by the representation that there would be no killing, but there had been killings, and here they both were, facing charges that carried the death penalty. It is not clear how the two men were able to do it, when they were in a small jail with five of their co-defendants, but they managed to get a message to the sheriff that they wanted to speak to the county attorney. They were brought out of the county jail and soon agreed to tell everything.[19]

The confessions of Faris and Keyes substantiated the prosecution's entire case. The two men told that seven cattlemen had gathered the afternoon and evening of April 2, after sending two of the hired hands away. They confirmed that Saban had indeed obtained and used Farney Cole's automatic, that the men had ridden from Otter Creek to Spring Creek, and that then they had broken up into two groups, with Brink and Saban going to the north wagon and the remainder of the men to the south wagon; Saban was in overall command, but Alexander led the group of men who went to the south wagon. The plan called for each group to take prisoners. A short time later, however, when Saban was taking Faris from the south wagon to the north wagon, Faris asked Saban where his men were. Saban said that he did not know but thought they were all dead. They were not all dead, though, at least not yet, as Faris soon learned. Brink started a fire under the sheepwagon, and after it started to burn well, a man came out of the wagon; he was only twelve or fourteen feet in front of the wagon when Faris first saw him. The man was Joe Allemand, and he was stooped but was holding up his hands. Then Faris watched Herb Brink gun Allemand down and heard Brink proclaim, "It's a hell of a time of night to come out with your hands up." After Allemand was shot to death, Saban announced that the group would leave, and they all returned to Otter Creek. Faris understood that Eaton would be going west, to a camp in the badlands, that Saban and Alexander would return to Alexander's place, just north of Otter Creek, and that Brink and Dixon would go to their bunkhouse at Billy Goodrich's.[20]

As strong as the prosecution's case now appeared, all the attorneys knew that it could be undercut by the loss of just a few witnesses, as had happened in the Johnson County Invasion cases, when crucial witnesses had been kidnapped.[21] So the woolgrowers' help again was important. Faris and Keyes were quickly removed from Basin and taken to the Sheridan County jail by Joe LeFors. Of course, the attorneys for the other defendants wanted to know why Faris and Keyes, who were their clients just a short time ago, were suddenly being moved away and refused to talk to them. They would have known exactly had they credited newspaper stories that closely tracked these events. Although the defense attorneys were probably skeptical of the reporting in these stories, the reports proved to be remarkably accurate about the confessions and how they had been obtained.[22]

Bounce Helmer was also sent away from Basin to protect him. His location was secret, and it would not come out until the trial, but Sheriff Alston paid all the expenses to send Bounce Helmer to Dungeness, Washington, a small town on the Olympic Peninsula, near the Strait of Juan de Fuca.[23]

There was a last interesting footnote to all these events. A man named Virgil Chabot lived near Big Trails in 1909; he, like Joe Allemand, was French. The two men could speak to each other as Frenchmen; for each, the other was one of the few people with whom he could converse in his native tongue. (Allemand had been competent in both French and English.) Chabot reacted strongly to Allemand's death, writing a letter to the French ambassador to the United States. Chabot told the ambassador of a "heinous crime" that had just been committed in Big Horn County, Wyoming, and how he had heard of the crime at 10:00 A.M. on April 3, had immediately proceeded to the scene, and had found an awful sight. Chabot told in graphic detail what he had seen and concluded with a plea for international assistance: "It is absolutely necessary that the guilty be arrested so that there shall be no recurrence of such crimes and as it seems that the counties and the State of Wyoming have wholly neglected to arrest the offenders when such crimes have been committed heretofore it seems to me that it behooves the Government at Washington to take the matter up and bring the guilty to justice."[24]

This letter prompted the French ambassador to write the U.S. secretary of state, telling him, among other things, "It would seem that the case here reported is not an uncommon or solitary instance and impunity could not but cause further crimes; Americans and Frenchmen alike are, as shown by this occurrence, interested in having such cruelty brought to an end." Huntington Wilson, the acting secretary of state, then wrote Governor Brooks, sending him the chain of correspondence. Brooks, in turn, passed on all this information to Judge Parmelee, with a request that he keep it confidential. He also told Parmelee, "The whole state is deeply interested in the proceedings of the grand jury, and I have heard many expressions concerning your able and explicit instructions to the grand jury. I earnestly trust we may be able to secure some convictions in connection with these outrages."[25]

Given the developments in Big Horn County, Brooks was able to inform Acting Secretary Wilson that "the State and local authorities will use every possible effort to bring the perpetrators of this outrage to justice," and that "we confidently hope, despite the difficulties surrounding raids of this character, to secure a number of convictions and wipe out for all time this sort of thing in Wyoming." Indeed, at that time, the first part of May 1909, it appeared that the prosecution was in complete control, that the ugly lessons of the past truly were no longer applicable in 1909, and that it was just a matter of quietly waiting until the time of trial (set for the fall term, in October). Then the State of Wyoming would present its compelling case in a businesslike and efficient manner, and the whole business would be done. Alas, very little time would pass before any person who held such a notion would be sharply disabused. The powerful allies of the raiders would soon start flexing their muscles.[26]

14

♦

The Cattlemen Fight Back

Cattle interests moved early to support the raiders, and although it was not apparent at first, there was never a question that they would do so. Cattlemen throughout the Big Horn Basin quietly contributed to a defense fund and put together a huge war chest, which they initially used to retain virtually every attorney in the Basin except Billy Simpson. When Ed Eaton appeared at his bond hearing on April 22, having been arrested even before the indictments, H. S. Ridgely had already been hired and was there to represent Eaton, no doubt being paid through the defense fund.[1]

The support for the raiders, although muted at first, went far beyond money. Basin had two newspapers, and at first, both strongly supported prosecution of those who had killed Allemand, Emge, and Lazier. As noted earlier, at the time of the raid, the *Basin Republican* had unequivocally condemned the raid, using phrases such as "bloodthirsty and fiendish atrocities" and the "horrible outrage." Three weeks later, the *Republican* editor evidently still felt that the raid was a terrible thing, and he ran the entire charge of Judge Parmelee to the grand jury, even though Parmelee's remarks were so extensive they required several long columns in two different issues.[2]

In May 1909, however, the editorial policy of the *Republican* changed. Alston told Governor Brooks at one point that "the defense had purchased one of our leading newspapers," and shortly thereafter told the governor that Ridgely and W. S. Collins, the Basin mayor who had also been retained by the cattle interests, were controlling four newspapers. Alston did not reveal the source of this information, but given the articles that were published, Alston's statements are certainly plausible. Then again, perhaps both Basin newspapers were just coming back to original positions; their mastheads said quite a lot about their editorial stances. The *Big Horn County Rustler* began life in Bonanza in 1889, and from the beginning, its name was an announcement that it did not favor the interests of big cattlemen. Those interests were more closely represented by Wyoming Republicans, and had been since at least the early 1890s.[3]

The May 14 issue of the *Republican* commented negatively, but not overly harshly, on the attorney fees granted to William S. Metz. Then, on May 21, the *Republican* launched a vitriolic attack on William and Percy Metz, an assault that continued through three issues of the weekly newspaper, abating only when the *Republican* found another profound grievance against those prosecuting the raiders. In a span of less than a month, the *Republican* completely shifted its outrage from the raiders to the prosecutors.

The *Republican* began its May 14 editorial page by declaring that the people of Big Horn County had been "sadly buncoed" by "tinhorn politicians," referring to Percy and William Metz. Then the editorial referred to "greed for graft" on the part of unscrupulous politicians who caught "suckers" to serve their "schemes," all of which was "dirty politics" by a fellow unworthy to be trusted "in any public position to which he may have the 'gall' to aspire."[4]

Complaints were made about the size of the fees, but the primary thrust of the *Republican*'s position was that Metz had promised to help the new county attorney without charge but was now charging a substantial fee. The clamor was enough that Will Metz wrote a letter to the county commissioners on May 27, explaining why he felt he was entitled to a fee. What he stated, essentially, was that when he pledged to help his son, he was thinking of the ordinary run of criminal cases (and had, in fact, already helped Percy in a number of such cases), but no one could have anticipated that a case of the magnitude of the Spring Creek Raid would come along, requiring almost all his time; another factor Metz cited was that monies were being furnished to the county from sources such as the woolgrowers, and therefore the citizens of Big Horn County would not have to bear the cost of his fees.[5]

The *Rustler* was quite satisfied with this explanation, observing that what really counted here was bringing the Spring Creek miscreants to justice, "no matter what the cost." The *Republican,* on the other hand, found the "explanation" to be woefully inadequate, asking the rhetorical question: "Wasn't it a bummer?" The *Republican* asserted that "every right-thinking democrat" was "bitter in his denunciations of Metz, Sr." The paper further asserted, ambiguously, that it was wrong for any official to advance his political interests by "tooting his own horn" to the prejudice of those charged with murder on Spring Creek.[6]

In the same issue, the *Republican* printed a vicious allegory about "Percival, son of William." The theme was graft, an accusation directed against young Metz, who was "not versed in the wicked ways of the world." This piece, setting the Metz attorney fee controversy in a medieval setting, was written with apparent glee, the writer warming to his task and declaring, "this is graft such as we have never seen in the province and it must be that the younger a counselor may be the larger are his grafts and Lo! We will never have a grafter for governor or in Congress."[7]

Those behind the attacks on Will and Percy Metz did not stop at newspaper articles. Some of them made complaints to the Wyoming state examiner, one Harry B. Henderson. Henderson wrote a letter on May 20, 1909, to the Big Horn County commissioners; he announced that he was "astounded" to learn of the fees to be paid counsel to prosecute what he referred to as the "Ten Sleep murder cases." He made a declaration that must have frightened the county commissioners, noting they were personally liable on their official bonds for their "hasty action," and told them they had no right to so proceed "from either a legal or a moral point of view." He closed his letter by issuing an order: "You will please advise this office why the board permitted these conditions to obtain."[8]

The odd thing about this fearsome letter is that it seems to have disappeared as fast as it arose. There is no further reference in the historical record to Henderson or to a response by the county commissioners. Probably the answer to this enigma is revealed by the location of this letter today—in a file from Governor Brooks's office. In other words, the letter was apparently immediately referred to Governor Brooks. Brooks, in some manner, most probably squelched this whole challenge. Henderson was out of line to tell county commissioners how they should spend money they had available (whether from their own sources or outside contributors). The cattlemen were spending huge sums on lawyers, probably quite a bit more than the state was spending, and the state examiner had no right to take an official stand that preserved this unfair advantage to the cattlemen. People were intensely emotional about this event, however, and were frequently taking stands that were not the product of objective and fair analysis. The emotional upset was not confined to the cattlemen's side. After one of the articles was published, Percy Metz trekked to the newspaper's office and strongly complained about the unfairness of the stories. The only effect of this visit was to give the *Republican* the opportunity to paint the episode in its own words and make Metz look bad.[9]

The emotional nature of the event was well demonstrated by the next big blowup. Every one of the people associated with the prosecution had vivid and ugly memories of mob violence and influence, whether from the Johnson County War, the 1903 lynchings in Basin, or the struggle in Sundance on behalf of S. A. Guthrie. They feared the menacing control of the county seat's streets by cowboys, and worse, by direct mob action. Thus, very early, Alston started talking to Governor Brooks about ordering some members of the militia to Basin City. He wrote the governor on May 7, 1909, and told Brooks that he wanted "a dozen or so" militiamen; Alston was especially concerned because the grand jury had condemned the jail as unsafe. The feared intimidation related not just to a possible jailbreak, but to such things as threats against the prosecuting attorneys; all the attorneys for the state felt threatened and carried personal firearms. Brooks expressed his reluctance to call in the militia, saying that in some instances "it is liable to create an adverse public sentiment," but conceded that Alston was in a better position to judge "the urgency of these matters."[10]

Alston, or other members of the prosecution team, must have mentioned the militia in public settings, because it was not long before the *Republican* caught wind of the talk about militia being called in and objected to it. On May 21, the *Republican* published an article in which the writer declared that any fear of attempts by a mob to liberate the Spring Creek raiders was "absolutely groundless." The writer then declared, "The day of resorting to mob violence to liberate prisoners belongs to the lawless past, when small respect was felt for the laws and little effort made to support them." Apparently feeling that this whopper was not grand enough to carry his point, the writer announced that the people of Big Horn County "have a profound respect for the courts and are willing to abide by the decisions of the court, and stand ready to uphold the peace and dignity of the county at all times."[11]

It is hard to feature a perspective in which these are fair and accurate comments. They certainly made no sense to Felix Alston, who must have wondered where the writer of the editorial had been living for the last several years, and the sheriff continued to press the governor for militia. In late May, Sheriff Alston traveled to Cheyenne to make a personal request to the governor for soldiers. Shortly thereafter, on June 10, seven members of the militia from Cody arrived and pitched their tents around the courthouse. Predictably, the *Basin Republican* was irate.[12]

In a front page story with the headline "Why Has Militia Been Employed?" the *Republican* declared that the people of Basin were "dumfounded" when they watched a squad of militia set up to protect the courthouse. The newspaper viewed this action as "simply being a move to arouse prejudice against the men accused of the murder of Allemand, Emge and Lazier." The *Republican* declared that a petition would soon be circulated, and that 90 percent of the citizenry would sign it. In fact, attempts were made to circulate petitions, but they must not have met a favorable reception, because no petition was ever presented to Governor Brooks.[13]

The whole question of the stationing of the militia in Basin City became a lightning rod. Cattlemen and their supporters saw it as an affront, an insult to them. As the *Republican* put it, bringing the militia in left the impression "that we are a lawless class, beyond the control of the authorities." Those on the other side saw the militia as simply an important device to maintain control, to allow the processes of the justice system to work. E. E. Enterline felt especially strongly that the militia was necessary, not merely because of the ugly episodes he had just witnessed in Sundance, but upon the scarring memory of what happened in the flimsy Big Horn County jail to two of his clients just six years earlier. Enterline had the deepest kind of determination that the resolution of this case would be decided by what happened inside the courtroom and not by a mob outside the jail. Of course, George Saban had vivid memories, too, of the night of July 19, 1903, but his perspective was diametrically opposed to Enterline's. Saban remembered it as a time when the mob controlled, when the intentions of officials were thwarted, and that is exactly what he wanted again.[14]

By all appearances, Saban and the other raiders were not very distressed over their indictments and incarceration. They were reported to be "in the best of spirits," and "all goodnatured and full of fun." Their stay in the jail had been comfortable; friends of the raiders visited them virtually every day, "with their arms full of fruit cakes and cigars." All the raiders viewed the coming trial as a farce and firmly believed that the case would never come to trial; Saban talked about a big dance to be held when they all got out, as part of a "great celebration." Based on his experience, perhaps Saban's confidence was justified, but the man who reported these attitudes of the raiders was more skeptical, noting that there were "just as many good men trying to get him [Saban] hanged as he had working to get him turned loose."[15]

As time rolled on into the autumn of 1909, and the time for the trials grew ever nearer, the battle continued, and the strategy of the cattlemen became very clear. They would continue earnestly to importune the

governor to remove the troops. They would try to undercut the prosecution in every way they could; money, or the lack of it by the state, looked
like their best bet here. Finally, they had an ace in the hole, a challenge to
the whole jury panel. The cattlemen believed they could repeat the
Sundance experience by making it impossible to seat a jury; or at least, if
one were seated, it would have enough cattlemen on it to hang the jury,
or there would be enough intimidation that the jurors who were not
cattlemen would be afraid to bring in a conviction. Many times it appeared
that the cattlemen would surely succeed, that this whole ruinously
expensive and emotionally exhausting process would be a wasted exercise,
with the cattlemen triumphantly demonstrating at the end that the State
of Wyoming had no way of gaining a conviction. There was not enough
money or emotional strength to repeat the process. An acquittal was not
necessary for the cattle interests to prevail; a failure to obtain a conviction
for almost any reason would surely mean that all the charges against all the
raiders would have to be dismissed.

The whole matter of the militia continued to fester, but the prosecuting attorneys were certainly not willing to withdraw the soldiers.
Rather, they believed that the squad of soldiers at the courthouse needed
to be augmented, and in early October started to importune the governor
to do so. On October 16, Billy Simpson wrote the governor, stating his
belief that the defense intended to bring into Basin "a great many sympa-
thizers," for the purpose of "intimidating witnesses and influencing
jurors." Simpson stated that he was "looking for trouble during the trial,"
that it was "in the air" and sooner or later would break out.[16]

Governor Brooks took Simpson's letter seriously and dispatched the
Wyoming adjutant general, P. A. Gatchell, to Basin to do whatever was
necessary "to see that the laws are impartially enforced." At first it seemed
that quite a few extra troops would be forthcoming, but then there were
indications they might not. This situation prompted E. E. Enterline to
write a long letter to W. E. Mullen, the Wyoming attorney general.
Enterline wrote earnestly and cogently to Mullen about cowboys coming
into Basin, "several hundred men . . . whose interests and feelings will be
hostile to the state," and he pointed out that if the Big Horn County

sheriff could not control the county seat, then sheepmen would probably also come in, with the distinct possibility that the main street would turn into a battlefield.[17]

The governor finally decided to send more troops; on October 30, twelve more soldiers arrived, bringing the total number to about twenty. As the governor would have predicted, the cattlemen were hot about these new troops. Mayor Collins fired off a telegram to Governor Brooks requesting that the governor "remove the detachment of state militia." He declared that the situation did not warrant their presence, that the militia was "a menace to the peace and quiet of the town," and that if the sheriff "will not do his duty I as Mayor will guarantee to see that peace and good order shall be maintained." The *Republican*, in its November 4 issue, proclaimed by headline that the governor should "Recall the Militia," demanded to know who had asked for the troops to be sent in "at a time of profound peace," and insisted that the governor inform the citizens of Basin who made statements to him that resulted in the national guard being brought in. At that time, P. A. Gatchell, the Wyoming adjutant general, was in Basin, and he contacted Governor Brooks and gave his emphatic opinion that the troops were necessary and Mayor Collins was misusing his position (Collins was representing one of the Spring Creek defendants). Brooks treated Collins's telegram as the bombast it was. The Governor did not respond until November 8, when the first trial was almost completed, and then he simply informed the mayor by telegram that "troops there at request of sheriff and Prosecuting Attorney and will remain as long as they seem necessary to preserve order."[18]

Turning aside the challenge to the militia did not solve all the prosecuting attorneys' problems, however. A potentially greater problem still plagued them, and in his October 16 letter to the governor, Billy Simpson referred to it: "One of the most serious matters we are up against is the lack of funds in this County, the limit of indebtedness having now exceeded all appropriations for the year 1909[,] and the banks here have given out that under no conditions will they buy at any price any certificates of indebtedness issued in payment of Juror or witness fees. The defense are making as much as possible out of this fact and I believe we have got to do something along this line."[19]

In other words, the county was in debt and had no money to pay such things as jurors' and witnesses' fees, essential if there is to be a jury trial. The primary response by the county was to issue scrip, a promise to pay from the following year's revenues, but the local Basin banks were pro-cattlemen and refused to honor the county's scrip. As Simpson noted, the forces supporting the raiders quickly picked up on the situation. When the *Republican* demanded that the militia be recalled, it also complained about the "enormous bills" to pay the troops and asked: "Is the county not heavily enough in debt now?"[20]

This matter worried the prosecution very much and was not finally resolved until the eve of the first trial against the raiders. The first case to be tried was *State v. Herbert Brink,* and only a short time before that trial was convened on November 4, a number of sheepmen finally stepped up and purchased much of Big Horn County's scrip; on November 3, the First National Bank of Meeteetse agreed to purchase any remaining scrip.[21]

Of course, the ultimate targets of all this effort were the jurors who would decide Herb Brink's fate. Every tactic was aimed at something relating to the jurors, whether their fears, their fees, or what they would hear if they were ever presented a case. The forces supporting Brink and his compatriots were acutely aware of the central role of the jury. Indeed, their strongest challenge was mounted against the whole process of selecting a grand jury and a trial jury.

A panel of prospective jurors would normally have been selected on October 18, 1909, the first day of the fall term, but this process was delayed after the defense filed a plea in abatement. This pleading was sworn to by George Saban, and Saban asserted a whole litany of things. He stated that the jury list in Big Horn County was not properly prepared, that it had been "clandestinely, unlawfully, illegally, improperly and fraudulently" made up by Felix Alston and the chairman of the county commissioners, not by the county treasurer and the county clerk, as it should have been. Saban went on and asserted that as a result of this improper behavior, the jury list comprised only 731 names, whereas there were at least 1,746 qualified jurors, and that the jury list was "void and invalid," and all indictments should be thrown out.[22]

Hearings were necessary to address the plea in abatement. Over several days, Judge Parmelee heard the testimony of people involved in selecting the jury, including the Big Horn County clerk, treasurer, clerk of court, Sheriff Alston, and Alex Linton. On Monday, October 25, 1909, Judge Parmelee entertained arguments from the attorneys and rendered his decision. To the surprise and consternation of the prosecution and the joy of the defense, he granted the plea. The judge did not give much weight to a number of the contentions of the defense, such as an allegation that the grand jury was prejudiced against cattlemen, but he ruled that the fact that a large number of qualified men were not on the jury list was a serious matter that had to be remedied. The judge declared, "A list must be obtained which is above suspicion."[23]

The indictments against all five men in jail were thrown out, and the prosecution had to proceed by information. That is, the prosecution would have to refile all the charges by means of a signed declaration by the county attorney. It would also have to compile a new list of prospective Big Horn County jurors. Of course, both were done very quickly (the raiders never left the jail), but it must have been a real scramble for a few days.

The newspapers supporting the raiders covered all these events closely and, when the decision came down, exuberantly. The *Republican* devoted three long, excited articles in its October 29 issue to the decision. The *Worland Grit* also carried several ecstatic articles. All this coverage repeated the same themes, that Judge Parmelee's "most righteous decision" was like "a zephyr of refreshing and cooling ozone," that had saved the jury box from "pollution" and undercut a "cunningly devised scheme."[24] It had been noted that the jury was selected long before the Spring Creek Raid, which was seemingly a complete rejoinder to the contentions of the *Worland Grit* that some kind of conspiracy existed to commit a wrong against the raiders. The *Grit,* though, turned this argument on its head with a neat bit of sophistry, asking the question: "For whom was the wrong intended?" The correct but embarrassing response of the prosecution would have been that county officials had been careless by not keeping the jury lists current, but that they certainly never intended to compromise anyone's rights.

The cattlemen believed they had won a major victory, one that was crippling to the prosecution, and that somehow heralded the complete vindication of the raiders. It is certainly true that the prosecution had been embarrassed, but the harsh reality for the raiders was that nothing in this proceeding affected the underlying case. All the evidence was intact, and there was no restriction on the prosecution presenting every last bit of it. Furthermore, a crucial question remained that the cattlemen, in their euphoria, never paused to think through: What kind of jury would be produced under the new list? After the county officials prepared a new jury list and came up with even more names than the defense had said existed, some 2,600, the *Worland Grit* crowed. It issued a sarcastic headline, blaring: "The Rapid Growth of Big Horn County—The Jury List Has Increased the Past Ten Days from 755 To 2600." The assumption of the *Grit* was that all this was a very bad thing for the prosecution and a very good thing for the raiders. The accuracy of these assumptions would soon be tested; the trial of Herbert Brink began just ten days after Judge Parmelee's decision on the plea in abatement.[25]

15

The Brink Trial Begins

On November 4, 1909, the attention of almost every person in Big Horn County was turned to the big trial in Basin City. Indeed, almost every person in Big Horn County seemed to be in Basin on that day. Simpson and Enterline had been right, large numbers of cowboys and sheepmen had appeared, but so did a sizeable number of people who were not aligned with either camp and were simply curious. Oddly, though, those on opposing sides were apparently not belligerent toward one another. This probably had a lot to do with the fact that downtown Basin was full of soldiers and lawmen, and that guns were collected. Even so, the reports of contemporaneous newspaper articles give the distinct impression that the mood in Basin was almost festive. The trial was covered by reporters from several newspapers, not simply the local newspapers, such as the *Big Horn County Rustler* and the *Basin Republican,* but those from around the region, including the *Cheyenne Daily Leader* and the *Denver Post.* Many people were directly involved in the trial, and these people alone greatly added to the crowds in Basin. They included witnesses, court personnel, lawyers (for the prosecution, E. E. Enterline, Will Metz, Billy Simpson, and Percy Metz; for the defense, R. B. West, W. S. Collins, Thomas W. Hyde, and C. A. Zaring of Basin; C. F. Robertson,

W. L. "Billy" Simpson.
Courtesy the Colorado
Historical Society and the
Denver Post.

and J. T. Jones of Worland; H. S. Ridgely and W. L. Walls of Cody; and
J. L. Stotts of Sheridan), and, the largest group, prospective jurors.[1]

Using the new, much larger jury list, a hundred men had been
summoned to Basin; about ninety appeared on November 4. Now the
great test would begin, to see whether a jury could even be selected, and
if so, whether it could or would render a verdict of guilty. Even among
those supporting the prosecution, there was pessimism that a guilty
verdict could ever be achieved; the *Big Horn County Rustler* openly
admitted that "disinterested persons predict that the outcome will be a
mistrial resulting from a hung jury." The makeup of that initial group of
ninety men must have worried the defense, however; only twelve were

from the deadline area, that oddly shaped territory that took in most of the Nowood River, and of those twelve, two were no friends of the raiders: J. M. Becker, a sheepman from Nowood, and F. M. Sheldon of Big Trails, who was Joe Allemand's brother-in-law.[2]

If the defense had its way, every man on the jury would have lived along the Nowood River, or on a tributary of the Nowood, where large numbers of men did not believe the raiders had even committed a crime.[3] The defense knew that was not probable, but it at least wanted three or four men from this area. Just ten men from the Nowood area, however, worked out to only one in nine of the panel members.

The first step in selecting a jury in a criminal case is to choose twelve names. This was done in *State v. Brink,* and the results were even more foreboding to the defense. Unlike the jurors in the Gorman trials, this was not a group of ranchmen. Instead, those first twelve included a carpenter from Worland, an undertaker from Cody, and several farmers. There was one sheepman and one cattleman.

The first challenges to a jury are those for cause; that is, a challenge based upon a juror's inability to render a fair decision. The attorneys question the prospective jurors, and if they are able to elicit some grounds showing a juror would not or could not be fair, that juror can be excused for cause. In *Brink,* there were only two successful challenges for cause from the initial twelve panel members, and both were made by the prosecution. One of them was to Mark Warner, the lone cattleman, and a strong one at that, and he was probably excused because of comments he had made against sheep. These two men were replaced by two others, a barber and another farmer, both of whom were passed for cause.[4]

The situation quickly became this: Twelve neutral jurors were ready to try Herbert Brink, and the only way he could prevent his immediate trial by this jury was to use his limited number of statutory peremptory challenges; that is, challenges to jurors without having to establish cause. Such challenges may delay the final seating of a jury for a short while, but they will soon be exhausted. For every lawyer in the courtroom, it must have been a time of momentous realization. This trial would be no Sundance case, in which virtually every potential juror was dismissed for

THE BRINK TRIAL BEGINS

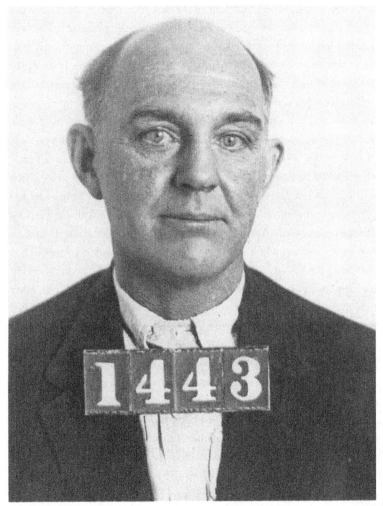

Herbert Brink. Courtesy Washakie Museum.

cause; there were too many men on this jury panel who had no personal
knowledge of any of the people or issues involved in the case.

Peremptory challenges were made. Of course, the defense challenged
the one sheepman, and the prosecution also made a challenge in the first
round (each set of challenges is referred to as a "round"). These jurors

were replaced by others, but none of the new men selected were offensive to the prosecution, and so by the fourth round, the prosecution waived any challenge. In other words, the State of Wyoming was perfectly content with the existing jury members. Not so the defense. Indeed, the defense had to make every last challenge it could in the hope of somehow pulling someone onto the jury who was so biased (and so willing to conceal his bias) that he would hang the jury. Not until the very last round, however, was a man selected who was unacceptable to the prosecution. "Denver Jake" Winslow was chosen, a man from Worland with a seamy reputation who had come into the country as a cowboy. The prosecution felt it could not leave Winslow on the jury and therefore used its last peremptory challenge.[5] The defense had also used its last challenges, and thus new jurors had to be selected. Herb Brink finally had a little luck, as two men came up whom the defense liked. One was John Rutrough, a sheepman from Cody, who should have been good for the prosecution but had apparently made some comments indicating otherwise. The other man was even more pleasing to the defense, John Donahue, a rancher from Hyattville. Over fifty years later, Percy Metz said, "Ridgely was thrilled beyond words. He figured, 'Well, here's a fellow to hang the jury.'" Yet Donahue had never been identified as a strongly committed cattleman, as Mark Warner was. Donahue was an older man, nearly sixty years old in 1909, and members of the prosecution who knew him believed he was honest and independent. The prosecution finally decided not even to try to disqualify Donahue, because it probably could not develop an adequate basis for challenge and would only irritate him.[6]

The entire jury was selected before 3:30 P.M., to the "genuine surprise" of all sides. The members of the jury were from Penrose, Cody, Greybull, Burlington, Meeteetse, Clark, Lovell, Cowley, and Hyattville, and they were primarily farmers and farm laborers, with one undertaker, one beekeeper and farmer, one barber, one sheep raiser, and, of course, Donahue, a farmer and rancher.[7]

When Judge Parmelee had charged the members of the grand jury, he had told them that "very much of the peace, security and happiness of this community depends upon your action." Now the indictments of that

The Spring Creek Five, beginning with Herbert Brink, top row left, and proceeding clockwise: Ed Eaton, George Saban, Thomas Dixon, and Milton A. Alexander. Courtesy Washakie Museum.

grand jury had been thrown out (although replaced by informations), and this new jury was either the last hurdle before freedom for the raiders, or, on the other hand, the last hope for peace, security, and happiness in the community. This jury was similar to juries in the recent past, being all male and prosperous, but it was different in important ways.

A photograph of the Spring Creek Raid jurors has surfaced, more than ninety years after the event; they are sitting and standing next to a building, almost surely in Basin, and are accompanied by Sheriff Alston. Twelve lean men face the camera, men inured to a lifetime of hard, physical work. By and large they look young, but several are older men, such as W. H. Packard, the short and full-bearded man seen in the back row, who was fifty-eight; Joseph Vogel, a man of German descent, forty-seven; Frank Young, the barber, forty-four; and Jack Donahue, about sixty. This was a jury of farmers, not ranchers, and in this way it was different from previous juries; however, in one highly important way this jury was like earlier juries, or, at least, like the second Gorman jury. A solid number of the jurors were members of the Church of Jesus Christ of Latter Day Saints. Packard's parents came to Utah in 1850, and he was born there on August 12, 1851.[8] Charles Duncan was born in Utah about 1877, and then came to Lovell; and C. E. Nielson also came from Utah, was temporarily working near Cody, but soon moved to Cowley, and then Lovell. Charles Walter was probably also Mormon, being from Cowley, and he had probably also come to Wyoming from Utah. Neither the prosecution nor the defense particularly noted that fully one-third of the jurors were Mormons, men from a culture that traced its deepest common memories to ugly incidents in which men ran amok in mobs, remembrances that were the foundation for the strongest kind of common bond among adherents of the faith.[9] Packard's parents probably came to Utah by wagon, and they made this pioneer trek in 1850, when incidents of persecution by those who lynched and burned were fresh and raw; it had been only six years since Joseph Smith was murdered and only three since the saints had arrived in Utah. The defense, so desperately focused on getting a solid number of cattlemen on the jury, apparently never worried about such things as the religious culture and history of

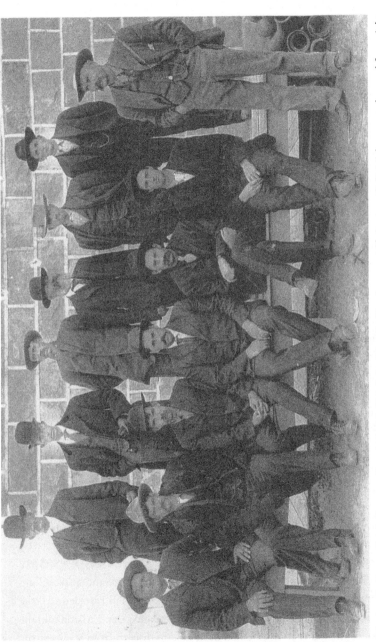

The jury in *State v. Brink*. Courtesy Karma Smith (Salt Lake City, Utah), whose grandfather was C. E. Nielson, seated second from right in the bottom row.

the jurors, and never realized that there *was* a solid cadre on that jury, but one that certainly did not consist of cattlemen. Of course, a trial is exactly that, a test in which seemingly numberless crucial considerations are thrown at lawyers, and in *State v. Brink,* the defense had many other things to be concerned about, as the opening statement for the prosecution soon made clear. The jury having been selected, that opening statement would be delivered early the next day, Friday, November 5, 1909.

The trial had been moved from the regular courtroom to a larger facility, Fraternal Hall, but that Friday morning this building could not hold all the spectators. Not even standing room was available, and the people spilled back into the front doors. E. E. Enterline opened for the prosecution; he had a lot of ammunition, and, seemingly, he used it all. Enterline had that wonderful quality of a good trial lawyer, the ability to command and forcefully present a complex set of facts. Enterline told the jury about everything Herb Brink did on April 2, 1909, the places he went, the men he saw, the plans made for the raid, and everything the raiders did to carry out those plans. Enterline cited detailed, persuasive information, such as the calibers and types of every gun used by every raider, and all the physical details of the setting of the raid, using the map drawn by the county surveyor and photographs taken of the scene. He was able to quote one crucial conversation after another, ending in the chilling pronouncement by Herbert Brink right after he shot down Joe Allemand: "This is a hell of a time of night to come out with your hands up." The defense made no opening statement, apparently reserving it for the beginning of their case.[10]

The first witness for the state was Felix Alston. The general plan of the prosecution was to show gradually how all the facts had come to light, beginning with the initial investigation, and then to present each succeeding witness so that the jury was brought closer and closer to exactly how three men were murdered the evening of April 2. W. S. Metz questioned Sheriff Alston, and Alston set the basic groundwork, telling what he found on April 3 and what his investigation revealed. All the spent cartridges found at the scene were introduced, and Alston told the jury of the many things he had been able to discern from tracks at the

Fraternal Hall in Basin. The first Gorman trial and the Brink trial were held in this building, which was at a different location. Courtesy Jack Gage, Jr.

scene, even after an intervening snowfall. H. S. Ridgely was the lead
attorney for the defense, and in his cross-examination, he immediately hit
Alston on a weakness of the prosecution's case; Alston had to acknowledge that there was nothing unusual about the shells he had picked up
and that he had not marked them in any way. Ridgely did not take immediate advantage of these admissions but went on to pick at other points of
weakness. He brought out that Alston was not presenting all the spent
cartridges he had collected because, oddly, he had given some of them
away. He also demonstrated Alston's uncertainty when the sheriff said
he knew there were seven horses, but there might have been more than
seven, and he "would not say there was not ten." In the examination,
Ridgely implied that the entire crime scene had been tracked up and that
the intervening snow had spoiled the ability to find clues. He also probed
for areas in which Alston's knowledge of facts was incomplete and firmly
established that Alston did not know who had killed Joe Allemand or
when he had been killed. On redirect examination, Metz brought out
that on the evening of April 3, the defendant, Herb Brink, had shown up
at the Greet house, accompanied by Billy Goodrich, and had spent a fair
amount of time there.[11]

Alston was followed by Clyde Atherly, the county surveyor, who had
prepared a plat from the survey he had undertaken. Atherly did not take
long, but immediately after his testimony was finished, Ridgely made a
motion to "strike out the evidence of the shells" because they had not been
properly identified, and Judge Parmelee granted the motion. At least for
the time being, the shell casings were no longer evidence the jury could
consider.[12]

Deputy Al Morton was then called to the stand. His testimony was
similar to Sheriff Alston's, although he did add some things; for instance,
that he had found gold teeth lying under one of the burned bodies in the
sheepwagon, and that he knew Joe Emge had several gold crowned teeth.
These may seem like mundane observations, but one of the tactics of the
defense was to insist that the prosecution could not prove the identities of
those hideously burned bodies in the sheepwagon. Morton was able to
solidify certain facts that the cross-examination of Alston might have

shaken, such as that most of the area around the wagons was not "tracked up" before Alston arrived, and that there were exactly seven raiders.[13]

Morton was followed by an unexpected witness, Percy Metz. It turned out that the county attorney had directly received the shells gathered at the scene and had marked a few of them, and this was sufficient to re-admit the shells. This brief appearance as a witness was Percy Metz's only direct involvement in the trial.[14]

Dr. George Walker was the next witness called. Dr. Walker was a well-qualified physician, being a graduate of the Barnes Medical College in St. Louis, and having practiced medicine in Nowood and Hyattville for seven years. The doctor testified about his medical findings upon the examination of the body of Joe Allemand. Dr. Walker established that there had been two bullet wounds, one of which passed through several vital organs, the necessary result of which was death. The other, along the collarbone, was from a bullet that mushroomed after hitting another object and was not a fatal wound. The cross-examination of Dr. Walker was a contentious battle of wills between the witness and the examining attorney, to no apparent good purpose. A great deal of time was spent bickering over whether the entry wound was the size of a certain pencil.[15]

Fred Greet was next called to the stand. He was the first witness who had been near the raid, but he could disclose very little about who committed the crime. Still, his testimony was invaluable to show myriad circumstances surrounding the crime and facts that were consistent with the defendant having committed it. Fred Greet testified that he had left Allemand, Emge, and Lazier in good health the night of April 2, and that the only other person near them was Pete Cafferal (who was alive and well, as would soon be demonstrated when he testified). He stated that he heard rapid shooting at first, near what he termed the "northeast" wagons, shooting that in his opinion came from an automatic; within about a half hour, he heard two shots at that wagon and watched two men (he could not identify them) walk over to the location of Allemand's body, bend over, and then move along. Fred Greet told the jury that gunfire went on some two hours after it first started; that there was quite a bit of light at the scene, with the moon and the fires at the wagon (they were still burning the next morning); and that it was a comparatively warm night. He said that when he and his companions (his brother, Porter Lamb, and John Meredith) investigated the next morning, they found the various bodies, four dead dogs, and a cut telephone wire. Finally, Greet said that he had seen Herb Brink the afternoon of April 2, about 9.5 miles south of the crime scene, and that he was then riding south.[16]

The defense ignored most of these fine details, probably because it intended to employ Fred Greet to another purpose. One of the theories of Herb Brink's attorneys was that the real aggressors here were Emge and Allemand, that they had armed themselves to the teeth and forced their way through the deadline, and those who represented cattle interests had justly repelled them. On cross-examination, Ridgely vigorously forwarded this position, demanding that Fred Greet tell him if it was not true "that there was a line drawn and agreed upon between the sheepmen and the cattlemen in that country which excluded the sheep from coming into the country where the sheep were that night?" The prosecution objected strenuously to this question, and Judge Parmelee refused to allow it, but Ridgely kept hammering away. He declared (using the device of an improper offer of proof, apparently before the jury) that "there was an agreement between the sheep and the cattle interests as to the range that each should occupy, . . . and that no sheep under the agreement had a right to range or feed in that vicinity or travel through that country." The prosecution again strenuously objected to the offer being made, correctly proclaiming that it was not proper and that "it would in no sense be a justification for the crime of murder." The objection was sustained, but all those words by Ridgely had been bellowed forth, and all the objections in the world would not erase what the jury had just heard.[17]

Poor Fred Greet was irrelevant to this blowup, merely a pawn in a bid by Ridgely to try to prejudice the jury, and he must have watched in bewilderment as lawyers bitterly clashed; however, this scene also meant that true cross-examination would probably not be pressed strongly. It was not, and Fred Greet's time on the witness stand was soon over.

Fred Greet's examination had begun on a Friday afternoon and was completed on a Saturday morning, a day in which the crowd watching the trial reached peak numbers; the *Rocky Mountain News* estimated that seven hundred people were crammed in the courtroom.[18] That crowd knew that this Saturday would be the day the prosecution would present its most important witnesses: Bounce Helmer, Bill Keyes and Charles Faris. Bounce Helmer was the first of these, called to the stand after the comparatively brief testimony of Porter Lamb and Pete Cafferal. Lamb and Cafferal were witnesses like Fred Greet; they were at the scene and were very helpful but were unable to identify anyone as a perpetrator. Bounce Helmer could, though, and the defense correctly viewed him as a grave threat, the first witness who could tell the jury the name of a raider.

Bounce's age at the time of the trial was somewhere around seventeen or eighteen; a picture of him taken at that time seems to show a reasonably mature young man, but he was not. He had offered impossible versions about his experience in the raid, saying in his grand jury testimony, for example, that there was another wagon on the scene the night of the raid, a lumber wagon driven by employees of George McClellan, and that he had heard Jake Frison's voice during the raid. These statements were just plain wrong, which had been firmly established before the grand jury's work was completed. Bounce's identification of Ed Eaton was so important, though, that the prosecution was certainly going to put Helmer on the stand; still, there must have been great nervousness when the name of "Charles David Helmer" was announced as the next witness.[19]

Bounce testified that on the evening of April 2, 1909, he went to bed about 8:00 P.M. and that he slept "out west of the wagon right behind the buggy." He said nothing had occurred until his dog began to bark; Bounce told the dog to "shut up" and went back to sleep, but then he was awakened by gunfire. He sprang up, started running, and was then captured by two men and told to put his hands up. He remembered that the men asked him, "Where is Joe Emge?"[20] Bounce and Cafferal were taken to a place just under the hill on which the north wagon set, and while making this walk, Bounce noticed that there were about seven raiders. When Helmer was lying at the bottom of the hill, the raiders

Charles David "Bounce" Helmer. Courtesy Washakie Museum.

were shooting into the sheep, and then Bounce heard someone issue a command to "light that wagon." Bounce heard rapid shooting thereafter, apparently into the wagon, and not long after he heard someone holler to "get them hands up," followed by some shots.[21]

Bounce and Pete were then taken back to the south wagons. The light was plain, and as they came up to these wagons, Bounce noticed a man stooped over, untying the buggy from the supply wagon, and "the mask flew away from his face." This was the time Helmer made that important identification of Ed Eaton. Bounce told the jury that after recognizing Ed Eaton's face, he also identified him by his build, and that he had known Eaton "ever since I was a little bit of a kid."[22]

Bounce Helmer's testimony was the most damaging yet to Herb Brink, and the defense responded with rigorous cross-examination. Ridgely went to some lengths to point out that after the raid, Bounce was moved to several places, in every instance with the sponsorship of Felix Alston and usually to a ranch owned by some prominent sheepman. The defense attorney emphasized the great amount of reward money available to witnesses and tried to get Bounce to say that much of the firing he heard had come *from* the north sheepwagon and not necessarily *toward* it. The real thrust of the cross-examination, however, centered on the belated identification of Ed Eaton. Ridgely hammered on this young, frightened witness about those initial days when Bounce had denied to so many people that he had recognized anyone in the raid. He referred to Percy Metz's first interview, when Bounce was taken aside and still did not reveal his identification of Ed Eaton; and to the times Bounce had spent with Felix Alston and still supposedly did not tell of the identification; and to an April 4 dinner with I. B. Latham, Bob Goodrich, and their wives, when Bounce declared that he had not recognized any of the raiders because he had been too scared. At least Bounce did not deny to Ridgely that he had told these things to the Lathams and Goodriches, and it was a good thing, because I. B. Latham, his wife, and Bob Goodrich were all listed as witnesses by the defense, and would no doubt have been called to contradict his testimony if Bounce had not admitted what he had told them.[23]

In the redirect examination, Billy Simpson worked to rehabilitate his witness. The defense fought it, but Simpson was able to pull out of Helmer that the reason he had not told Latham that he recognized Eaton was that, "I didn't want to tell them for fear it might leak out, and I was afraid they would kill me if I told, and I didn't want to let it out." In re-cross-examination, Ridgely again came strongly at Helmer, so strongly that Bounce made the mistake of saying that he had thought he should wait to say that he had recognized Eaton until testifying before the grand jury. His statements that he had not recognized anyone had come long before anyone knew there was going to be a grand jury.[24]

Simply based on the trial transcript, it would seem that the cross-examination of Bounce Helmer should have seriously impaired his credibility. The journalists covering the trial did not think so, though, and actually reported that he was a good witness. No one would know the jury's response until the final verdict. The problem for the defense was that witnesses following Bounce Helmer would be even more deadly to Herb Brink. Bill Keyes immediately followed Bounce to the stand. On that Saturday, it took a while just to bring witnesses to the stand, to work them through all the people, because the crowd was so large. Some of the gallery had stood on chairs throughout that long day, and they must have craned their necks to get the first look at one of the two raiders turning state's evidence.[25]

Bill Keyes was a single man who was forty-three in 1909; he and Charles Shaw ran about 400 cattle from a ranch on Otter Creek, one just downstream from the ranch of Keyes's friend Charlie Faris. Keyes told the jurors that the raiders—George Saban, Herb Brink, Milton Alexander, Faris, Tommy Dixon, and Ed Eaton—had come together at his ranch, and then they had all ridden toward Spring Creek at about 8 P.M., under the general command of Saban. Keyes testified that Saban had, in fact, taken Farney Cole's .35 automatic (and that he, Keyes, had later hidden it in accordance with Saban's directions). Near Spring Creek, the seven men had split into two groups, five men under Alexander going to the south wagon, and Saban and Brink to the north wagon.[26]

Remarkably, Bill Keyes did not learn that evening that men had been killed at the north wagon, and perhaps this explains why Ridgely's cross-examination of Keyes was not ferocious. Ridgely picked at Keyes, implying that the only reason he was testifying was so "you won't be hung," and noting that Keyes had carried a .30–30 rifle on what Ridgely sarcastically referred to as that "peaceful mission" (following Keyes's testimony that he only went on the raid because he was assured there would be no killing).[27]

Charlie Faris followed Keyes and, as Keyes had done, first told the jury about his general background.[28] Enterline took Faris down what was by then a familiar path to the jury, and Faris confirmed everything Keyes had said, but then he went on and told the jury much more about the murderous things done that night at the north wagon. He had first been at the south wagon, and then Saban had taken him to the north wagon. Faris knew that each of the two groups of raiders was to take charge of prisoners, and he asked Saban where his men were. Saban told him he did not know where the sheepmen were, "but thought they were dead." Saban then told Faris to go back to the south wagon and start a fire. Faris refused, and Ed Eaton was told to start the fire instead. There was no fire at the north wagon when Faris arrived there, but one was soon started when Brink pulled some sagebrush and placed it "at the hind end of the wagon."[29]

After the fire was burning well, a man emerged from the wagon whom Faris shortly learned was Allemand. Faris described how this man was stooped as he came out of the wagon, and he was holding up his hands in response to a command someone hollered to "Halt there. Halt, throw up your hands." When Allemand was only about twelve or fourteen feet from the front of the wagon, however, a shot was fired by Herb Brink, and Allemand fell. Brink followed his rifle shot with the comment that Faris quoted to the jury, that it was "a hell of a time of night to come out with your hands up." Then Milton Alexander went up to where Allemand had fallen, came back, and said, "It is Allemand." George Saban declared, "That is enough, we will leave," and that is what the raiders did.[30]

Denver Post story about the Spring Creek Raid. Photographs depict the Big Horn County Courthouse, W. S. Metz, H. S. Ridgely, and W. S. Collins. Photograph of article courtesy the Colorado Historical Society and the *Denver Post*.

Ridgely's cross-examination of Faris was much more aggressive than that of Keyes. Ridgely strongly implied that it was Faris, not Brink, who shot Allemand. The attorney made Faris admit that he was carrying a .30–30 along with some thirty shells, and that he was at a place so that Allemand's left side (where he had been shot) was to Faris. Enterline conducted the redirect examination of Faris, and he asked the witness to explain to the jury exactly where Brink was in relation to him (Faris), apparently to counter Ridgely's implications that Faris shot Allemand.[31]

Then the day was over. That grueling, fascinating day was completed just before 6 P.M. The large crowd finally left the makeshift courtroom and filtered out into the dark, no doubt buzzing about all they had seen and heard. The *Denver Post* filed a report about this day that said, "The prosecution in the Ten Sleep murder cases today played its trump cards against Herbert Brink, . . . and when court adjourned, it was admitted on all sides the state had scored in an unmistakable manner."[32]

16

The Brink Trial Concludes

The prosecution still had several witnesses it could present. The prosecuting attorneys might have been tempted to cut their presentation short, because the trial had gone remarkably well for them, and subsequent witnesses might mar what had already been presented. The testimony of Bill Keyes and Charlie Faris, standing alone, seemed powerfully persuasive. The problem for the prosecution, though, was a rule of law requiring that the testimony of an accomplice could only be considered if it was corroborated.[1] This rule was one of the reasons Bounce Helmer's testimony was so important. Although Helmer could identify only one of the raiders, that information, as well as his general knowledge about the circumstances of the raid, strongly supported Keyes and Faris. The witnesses not yet called could support Keyes and Faris on other points. Then, too, given the almost hysterical emotional climate in which the trial was being held, it would have been folly to assume that the case had been made. So on the following Monday, November 8, the prosecution continued with its parade of potent witnesses.

William Gibson, a deputy sheriff, was called to the stand. He was shown a .35 automatic rifle, and he testified that he had gone to a chicken coop on Bill Keyes's ranch (apparently right after Keyes's confession, in which he revealed the location of the rifle) and found the rifle rolled up in a gunny sack, "all covered with sand," underneath a box and with "some chickens there and some eggs there." The defense sputtered a futile objection; the rifle was admitted into evidence. Farney Cole was then called, and although he did not want to help the prosecution, he had to acknowledge to the jury all the details regarding his .35 automatic rifle that had been left in Bill Keyes's living room the afternoon of April 2.[2]

Four witnesses were called, each of whom had seen Brink near Otter Creek the afternoon of April 2 (along with Tommy Dixon and four or five other riders). Ridgely countered the testimony of these witnesses by showing that they all saw Brink riding south, away from Spring Creek, but then the prosecution presented John Callahan, a local trapper, who had seen Brink head back north after riding a few miles south of Otter Creek. Ridgely's cross-examination of Callahan was a direct assault, demanding that Callahan admit his testimony was false, but Callahan refused to retreat at all from what he had told the jury.[3]

The state then called four witnesses who had overheard Brink either make threats against Emge and Allemand or, after the raid, tell what only a raider would have known. These were Fred Widmeyer (saying that Brink had proclaimed that if Emge and Allemand came into cattle country, something was going to happen), W. G. Colethorpe (Brink said that he "was ready with his rifle to go out and mob the sons of bitches and drive them back"), and Eliza and Frank P. Brown (after the raid, Brink told the Browns that the "supposition" was that Allemand had come out of the wagon and had "looked around as though he was listening to something, or had heard something, and was shot and fell down, . . . and got up and staggered over to where he was laying when they found him"). None of this testimony was earth shaking, but none of it helped Brink's cause.[4]

The most important witness that day, however, was Billy Goodrich. Goodrich's testimony followed that of his wife, Anna, who acted as a lead-in to her husband. The Goodriches lived at Big Trails, about thirteen miles south of Spring Creek, and Herb Brink, Tommy Dixon, and Bill Garrison bunked at the Goodrich's place. Anna Goodrich remembered that during April 2, Dixon and Brink were at the ranch only in the morning; she did not see them again until the next morning. She further recalled that when she first learned about the raid, on April 4, she told Brink about it, who then acted nervous and excited, going to the telephone three or four times, calling Mrs. Brown and asking her if she knew "who they supposed did it." She later had a discussion with Herb Brink, and Brink asked her if she knew anything about the killing. She replied that she did not and did not want to know anything about it, and Brink responded, "I guess you are better off not to know anything about it." On cross-examination, Anna stated she had suspected Brink early and that her husband had told her what Brink had said to him.[5]

The diminutive Billy Goodrich then took the stand. Billy was a talkative man and was not well regarded in the Upper Nowood. Prosecuting authorities, however, do not have the luxury of choosing their witnesses. The State of Wyoming had to use the people who had knowledge of the relevant facts, and Billy Goodrich was at the very center of this most contentious case.[6]

E. E. Enterline carefully established background information, showing that Goodrich had lived in Big Horn County since 1890, that he knew all the defendants, and that on the day of the raid, he had been surveying at Mahogany Buttes. He first learned of the Spring Creek Raid on Sunday, April 4, when his wife told him about it while he was in the bunkhouse with Bill Garrison, Herb Brink, and Jack Rebidaux. He decided to go to Spring Creek because Mrs. Lamb was concerned about her husband, Porter, and Goodrich asked Herbert Brink to go with him. Goodrich stated that he and Brink set out on the sixteen-mile ride and arrived at the old Greet house about sundown; they went into the house, where there were two bodies, one of which was Allemand. While they were there, Felix Alston made several statements, that eight persons carried out the raid, that it appeared the wagon had been completely surrounded, and that it looked as though "they had made a fight from the wagon."[7]

After leaving Spring Creek, the two men stayed overnight at "the William's ranch," and then went back to the Goodrich place. At some point during this long horseback ride, Herb Brink apparently felt the need to demonstrate his importance to Goodrich, and he started talking about the raid. He told Billy that "Felix was mistaken about the tracks, that there was only seven." He said that the wagon was not completely surrounded, that it was taken by only two men, and that contrary to the conclusion of Alston, "there was not a shot fired from the wagon." Brink told Goodrich that he told those in the wagon to strike a light, that he was going to count three, and said, "and if there ain't a light lit in the wagon, we will riddle the snap with bullets." The first shot Brink fired was right into the door of the wagon, and Brink said, "there was a hell of a racket in the stove and pots and pans."[8]

Goodrich's testimony showed that Herb Brink was proud of his role in the raid and was eager to expound at length about it. Brink had identified Saban and Alexander as participants in the raid and proclaimed that he (Brink) had begun the fire at the north sheepwagon with sagebrush. Goodrich completed his direct testimony by telling how Brink had declared that "Callahan was the only man who had seen him go down there, and if necessary, he would take care of him."[9]

Surprisingly, Enterline did not ask Goodrich about the incriminating statements Tommy Dixon made to him, statements Goodrich had told to the grand jury. Perhaps they were being saved for the trial against Dixon.[10] Not that this diminished the ferocity of Ridgely's attack; the defense attorney conducted his strongest cross-examination of the trial against Goodrich. Billy had been talking to his neighbors, people who very much disapproved of the fact that he would be testifying against Herb Brink. Several of these neighbors had contacted the defense attorneys and provided ammunition to use against Goodrich in the form of inconsistent statements Billy had made.

According to Porter Lamb, Billy Goodrich had declared that Felix Alston told him "he [Goodrich] would get the fattest pocket book you ever had" for giving his testimony. Frank Helmer was ready to testify that Goodrich had said Felix Alston told him that he was to have his share of the reward. And Oscar McClellan was available to tell the jury that on one occasion, Goodrich had declared that Dixon, Brink, and Garrison were not "in it, as they were at home that night." Ridgely hurled every one of these statements at Goodrich and challenged him to deny them.

From the trial transcript, it appears that Goodrich had trouble handling the accusations, and that was certainly the opinion of some of the newspaper reporters covering the trial.[11]

The last witness for the prosecution was Adeline Allemand, Joe Allemand's widow. The prosecution carried out this sad exercise, bringing her to the stand "dressed in deep mourning." The state's transparent purpose was to underline the tragedy of Joe Allemand's death by having the jury watch this pretty young woman, the mother of Joe's two fatherless sons, give her somber but brief testimony. The defense was not foolish enough to cross-examine her, and after Ada's testimony, the prosecution rested.[12]

The next morning, Tuesday, November 9, the attorneys representing Herb Brink presented his defense. Only five witnesses were presented, and they were all done testifying by noon. George Pickett, a local rancher, wanted to testify that the bullet hole he had seen in Joe Allemand's body (as a juror in the coroner's inquest), came from a .30-30. Of course, the point was to try to pin the crime on Charlie Faris, who shot a .30-30, rather than on Herb Brink, who shot a .25-35, but Pickett's testimony was a poor effort by the defense. Even on direct examination, Pickett had great difficulty establishing his credentials for making such a conclusion, and on cross-examination, his testimony was further weakened. Pickett did not know the size of a .30-30 bullet, nor even how to tell the exact measurement, and he had no idea of the effect on a soft-nosed bullet of passing through several layers of clothing.[13]

Three of the defense witnesses testified that Billy Goodrich's reputation for truth and veracity was not good, but all three were clearly diehard cattlemen, and Enterline even managed to pull some facts from them that helped the prosecution. For instance, one of these witnesses was Frank Helmer, Bounce Helmer's father, and Enterline got him to admit that he did not doubt the veracity of his son's testimony. Another defense witness was Porter Lamb, who testified that Goodrich had, in fact, said that he (Goodrich) was to get the "fattest pocket book for giving his evidence that he had ever had." Enterline again used a defense witness to establish favorable evidence for the state; Lamb had to admit that

Goodrich had been reluctant to testify against the raiders, and that Goodrich's testimony was completely consistent with what he had told Lamb immediately after the raid.[14]

After the presentation of these five weak witnesses, whom the *Cheyenne Daily Leader* termed "seemingly immaterial," the defense rested its case. It was apparent to everyone in the courtroom, and to those following the case around the state of Wyoming, that Herbert Brink had no defense, and that the chief reliance of his lawyers was the hope for a hung jury.[15]

That afternoon, the attorneys for the prosecution and for the defense haggled over instructions to be given to the jury. The defense was forced to argue for instructions that would have twisted the law in favor of Brink, and Judge Parmelee ruled against all the defense's contentions. The judge presented conservative instructions to the jury, but even these statements, safely within the letter of the law, sounded a death knell to Brink. They included one whereby the jury was told that if a murder was committed during the commission of a felony (such as arson), then Brink was guilty of felony murder, the same as first-degree murder. Another instruction said that if Herb Brink had assembled together with other people to commit a wrongful act associated with the raid, then he was guilty of first-degree murder even if the murder was not intended but was merely "probable in the nature of things." Still another stated that the testimony of an accomplice (such as Keyes and Faris) did not have to be corroborated in detail, but if the corroborative evidence "tended to connect the defendant" with the charged crime, that was enough, and such evidence did not have to be sufficient to establish the defendant's guilt. The defense wanted an instruction saying that the testimony of Faris and Keyes could not be accepted unless the case was fully and completely proved without reference to anything they said, but Judge Parmelee would not agree to that.[16]

The attorneys who practiced in front of juries in the first few years of the twentieth century were good orators. Indeed, jurors probably expected to be treated to a skillful oration. It is impossible to know how much difference the final arguments made—most experienced trial attorneys do not think that final argument makes much difference—but the attorneys in *State v. Brink* gave the jury what they expected. Will Metz made the opening final argument for the state. He had a mountain of favorable evidence to work with, and, from his own writings (he wrote his wife that he "made *the* speech" of his life) and newspaper reports, it sounds as if he did justice to the material he had.[17]

On every important point, Metz had two or three solid sources of evidence. He could demonstrate without question that in the evening of April 2, 1902, seven men under the leadership of George Saban and Milton Alexander rode out from the ranch of Bill Keyes on Otter Creek to raid the camp of Emge and Allemand. These seven men—Saban, Alexander, Keyes, Eaton, Dixon, Brink, and Faris—went to Spring Creek, where they split into two groups. One consisted of Saban and Brink, who walked to the north wagon, and the other consisted of the remaining five men, who went to the south wagon. At the south wagon, men were only kidnapped, property burned, and sheep and dogs killed; but at the north wagon, Brink and Saban shot a sheepwagon full of holes, a wagon with three men in it—Emge, Allemand, and Lazier. Then Brink set fire to the sheepwagon, forcing Joe Allemand, apparently the only one of the three who was still alive and able to walk, to come stumbling out into the night. Herb Brink then shot him down without mercy. The sheepwagon continued to burn through the night, hideously deforming the bodies of Emge and Lazier.

In an unforgettable moment of drama, Ada Allemand entered the courtroom during Metz's final argument. She was clothed in her widow's black clothing and carried Joe Allemand's nine-month-old baby boy; the baby cooed and waved at the jurors. Toward the end of the argument, Metz had Billy Simpson put on Joe Allemand's coat and made a demonstration to the jury, showing, Metz asserted, that a bullet from the known location of Brink would make a straight line to the bullet holes in the coat, and that it was impossible for Faris, from his position that night, to have caused the wound Allemand suffered. This demonstration should have been persuasive, because Faris's position the night of April 2 was farther to the south than Brink's; therefore, a bullet from Faris's rifle would have exited Allemand's body toward his back, not his side, as the actual bullet did. The *Basin Republican* reported that during this demonstration, Ada Allemand "averted her head and her frail, black-garbed figure shook with emotion."[18]

It was powerful, emotional theater, but the defense was ready to put on its own show. The opening argument for the defense would be given by Joseph Stotts, the man who had sat as the district judge in the first Gorman trial, and who had not participated in the trial to this point. (One of the unusual aspects of this trial was that former district judges for both the prosecution and defense, that is, W. S. Metz and Stotts, made presentations to a third district judge, their successor, C. H. Parmelee.)[19] Joseph Stotts had been hired for his oratorical ability. "Judge" Stotts railed at Keyes and Faris, the two witnesses the defense obviously saw as most damaging. He referred to Faris as a "low-browed rascal," who was "not satisfied with three murders on his blood-stained hands," but would now "swear away the lives of five others." He declared that Faris and Keyes, in order to "escape the hangman's noose," were purchasing "their own miserable existences" by their testimony, and asserted that this testimony "was not corroborated in a single point." Finally, he gave what the *Basin Republican* referred to as a "thrilling picture of an open grave and a gallows," asking each juror by name whether he would "pull the rope" and "fill the grave?"[20]

When H. S. Ridgely followed Stotts, he addressed what had to be the weakest point of Stotts's oration, that the testimony of Faris and Keyes "was not corroborated in a single point." Ridgely had no difficulty doing this. He simply asserted that nothing Billy Goodrich said was believable, because his neighbors had testified his reputation for truth and veracity was bad. Then Ridgely stated Anna Goodrich had not told the truth, and neither had Bounce Helmer, nor Mrs. Brown, nor John Callahan. Taken from the view of a debating point, it was probably true that if the jury discarded the testimony of all these witnesses, there was inadequate corroboration. This kind of logic was not relevant here, though, because the jurors had seen and heard each of these witnesses and no doubt had their own firm opinions about each witness's veracity and significance. This is exactly what Enterline talked about when he gave the final argument of the day. Enterline carefully went through all of the testimony, showing how the testimony of each witness provided corroboration. He condemned what he termed the only defense offered by Brink's attorneys, the "vituperation and vilification of the state's witnesses." Enterline closed by declaring, "Justice demands a verdict of guilty be returned against the defendant."[21]

The case went to the jury shortly before 6 P.M. George Mead took charge of the jurors and led them to a small log cabin to deliberate. One wonders what Mead's thoughts were that night as the jury decided the fate of Herbert Brink, charged with committing murder when taking the law into his own hands. Mead had searing memories of a similar event just six years earlier, memories he would surely take to his grave, of a mob attacking the jail, killing Earl Price and two of the men Mead was trying to protect, and led by one of the Spring Creek defendants. We have nothing to reveal what his feelings were, however; the contemporaneous reports merely indicate that Mead discharged his duty when small groups of people paused too long by the jurors' cabin, having them move along by gruffly saying such things as "I guess you have seen enough."[22]

The newspaper reports supplied great detail about the session of this jury, and from these reports, as well as other information from court files, the deliberations can be reliably reconstructed. The first act of the jury was to select a foreman, which turned out to be very bad news for Herb Brink; the jury selected W. H. Packard, the Burlington beekeeper and Mormon bishop. The initial vote of the jury showed that most of the jurors were already convinced of Herb Brink's guilt of first-degree murder; the vote was eight for first-degree murder, two for second-degree murder, and two for acquittal. The two men who voted for acquittal were probably William Lewis and John Rutrough. Both were viewed as problem jurors by the prosecution, but more tellingly, several years later, both had signed petitions urging clemency for the Spring Creek defendants. There were sharp differences among jurors—one newspaper reported that "shadows of men passing to and fro could be seen within. Sometimes two figures, like shadowgraphs, would face each other and an index finger or a hand would aggressively point toward the face of one of the ghostly figures outlined on the window curtain." The commitment of those supporting leniency, however, was obviously not firm, because in rapid succession, the vote went to eight for first-degree murder and four for second-degree murder (on the second ballot); then to ten for first-degree murder and two for second; then eleven for first-degree, one for second; and, finally, on the fifth and last ballot, all for first-degree murder. The jury completed its work shortly before midnight.[23]

The unavoidable inference is that the eight men in favor of the most severe finding could muster such powerful arguments to support their position that the remaining four jurors had to concede. Despite all the turmoil surrounding the trial, in the end, all twelve men obeyed their oaths as jurors (to "well and faithfully try the matter in issue . . . and render a true verdict according to the evidence"), and did their duty as citizens.[24]

The next morning, the jurors arose early and announced they had reached a verdict. Court was convened at 8:45, when Judge Parmelee mounted the bench. All participants were present: Brink (with a jailer immediately behind him for the first time in the trial), Brink's lawyers, the lawyers for the state, and all the court personnel, not to mention hundreds in the gallery.[25]

Judge Parmelee began the ritual, asking the jury, "Gentlemen of the jury, have you reached a verdict?" Packard replied, "We have, your honor," and stepped forward, handing the verdict to the judge. Parmelee read over the verdict slowly and handed it to Clerk of Court Russell. Russell finally ended the suspense by announcing that the jury found Herbert Brink "guilty of murder in the first degree."[26]

The response in the courtroom was muted, but the verdict produced banner headlines throughout Wyoming and even on the front page of the *Denver Post*. The newspapers made sure all their readers were aware that the verdict meant that the first raider tried was to be sentenced to death.[27]

In retrospect, the decision to challenge the jury panel by the plea in abatement was a blunder by the defense. The attorneys correctly perceived that the existing jury list was flawed and could not resist using this fact to strike at their hated adversaries, but the defense team and their cattlemen supporters did not think through the consequences of this pyrrhic victory. Because the plea in abatement was granted, the jury rolls were completely re-done, changing the number from 755 men to 2,600. The smaller number no doubt reflected the population of Big Horn County at an earlier time, when cattlemen were an outsized percentage of the population. But the new jury list, more than three times larger, had to include all those settlers, mostly farmers, who had come into the Big Horn Basin after 1900. The presence of several members of the Mormon faith was no doubt very important to the final decision of the jury, but it would have mattered little had there been three or four zealous cattlemen on the jury, men dedicated to frustrating the prosecution. Because of the actions of the defense, however, the presence of such cattlemen on the jury panel, and there were certainly a number of them, was greatly diluted. When cattlemen were selected as trial jurors, the prosecution could easily handle the problem by peremptory challenge. All this is as it should be; the members of a jury should fairly reflect the entire society from which they are drawn, but it is ironic that in *State v. Brink,* it was the defense that brought this situation about, not the prosecution.

Despite what must have been euphoria over a verdict the prosecuting attorneys feared would never come, these lawyers still had four more cases to try. Within two hours of the *Brink* verdict, they began the case of *State v. Thomas Dixon.* Jury selection was undertaken, and by 3 P.M., a new jury was in place, a jury that looked very much like the old and was the product of similar processes; the defense used all twelve of its peremptory challenges and the prosecution only two. The men selected were from Greybull, Byron, Basin, Cody, Kane, Sunlight (or Sunshine), and Cowley, and they were all farmers except for one teamster, one banker, one barber, and a cattleman.[28]

One man, W. H. Lewis, had served on the *Brink* jury. The defense did not challenge him, having apparently heard that he was favorable to them. The prosecution did not challenge him, because, after all, he had voted for a conviction of first-degree murder against Brink. It is surprising that the state did not challenge another of the jurors, J. J. Davis, as it had done in the *Brink* trial. Then again, the prosecution had learned that the fact that a man was a cattleman did not automatically mean he would violate his oath as a juror and refuse to vote for conviction. Nor, for that matter, did the fact that a man was *not* a cattleman mean that he would automatically vote for the prosecution. Another consideration surely was that Davis lived in the far western part of the Big Horn Basin (whether in Sunshine or Sunlight), completely on the other side of the basin from the Nowood Valley. The *Dixon* jury looked even worse for the defense than the *Brink* jury had. Five of the jurors were probably Mormon, and this group was from areas a long way from Nowood; the residence of the jurors closest to Upper Nowood, W. H. Smith and W. J. Jones, was Basin.

The defense had to do something to keep all five of the raiders from being convicted of crimes carrying the death penalty. Brink had broken down completely, going "plumb wild," apparently thinking he would be hanged immediately, and this added greater urgency to the situation. The leaders of the cattlemen supporting the raiders, including George McClellan and Milo Burke, demanded that negotiations with the prosecution be opened.[29]

The problem for the defense attorneys was that they were not dealing from a strong position. The negotiations went back and forth, at one point breaking down entirely when the state's attorneys refused to agree to a lenient deal proposed by the defense. The settlement negotiations were resurrected, though, and, finally, after some grueling sessions, a deal was reached. Saban and Alexander agreed to plead guilty to second-degree murder; the governor would be petitioned for clemency by the defense and prosecution (in order to spare Brink from execution); and Eaton and Dixon would plead guilty to arson. Judge Parmelee would decide the sentences to be imposed.[30]

Early the next morning, Saturday, November 13, the five defendants were brought into the courtroom. Apparently, until it happened, none of them believed they would ever be convicted, and all five men were devastated. The three who would receive the harshest penalties were especially affected. Saban was described as "a broken hearted and broken spirited man," and as having aged twenty years over night. Brink appeared to have been crying for hours, and during the sentencing, Alexander's eyes also filled with tears. Judge Parmelee sentenced both Alexander and Saban to terms not less than twenty years, nor more than twenty-six, in the Wyoming State Penitentiary. Brink was sentenced to be executed, but, of course, it was expected his sentence would soon be commuted, and it was. Eaton and Dixon were both sentenced to not less than three nor more than five years.[31]

Suddenly, it was all over; all the cases were resolved. The Spring Creek Raid cases were finished so abruptly that some on the prosecution team must have needed a while to absorb the full significance of what they had done. Still, all knew they had accomplished something very important, and some had already formulated strong opinions. The very day of the *Brink* verdict, Will Metz was interviewed by the *Cheyenne State Leader,* and he had quite a bit to say. He first declared that Brink's conviction "marks the end of the assassination and warfare on the open range," and that the conviction would prevent "for all time" the "disgrace" that "has stained the fair name of Wyoming in the eyes of the rest of the world." Metz then noted that the conviction was the first ever obtained in a sheep raid, and went on to make some very broad and bold statements:

> It is significant of the beginning of a new era, of a period where lawlessness in any form will be no more tolerated by citizens than in the more densely settled communities of the east.
>
> The 'gunman' has had his day in Wyoming. From this time on settlers may come in assured that the law will give them its fullest protection, that the open range will be as safe as the peaceful prairies of Iowa or Illinois. It is a triumph of law and order, the culmination of a struggle waged for two score years, by those with the best interests of the state at heart, against the domination of its broad acres usurpers of the open range who have opposed the passing of the old order of things and have desperately fought it.[32]

Metz's declaration could have been dismissed as a pompous bit of crowing, but he turned out to be exactly right: The convictions in the case of *State v. Brink* did mark the end of the toleration of violence in the Big

Horn Basin, and, indeed, throughout Wyoming. There was only one
later sheep raid within the basin and only one other in the whole state of
Wyoming; in neither was anyone hurt or killed. In all of Wyoming, there
was only one other lynching. It occurred in the Wyoming State Penitentiary in 1912, and Herbert Brink, then an inmate, was one of the
perpetrators. A black man, Frank Wigfall, who had been convicted of
raping a white woman, was lynched by fellow prisoners. It would not be
fair to say that the convictions of Brink, Dixon, Saban, Alexander, and
Eaton were directly responsible for the virtual cessation of lynching in
Wyoming. A number of factors contributed to that result, not least a
growing disapproval of lynching in the society at large, coupled with
increased efficiency of law enforcement authorities. Putting George
Saban and his cohorts in prison, however, certainly underlined the
severity of the penalty for flouting that disapproval and how much more
powerful the legal authorities had become, and it is surely correct that
these were developments most people of the Big Horn Basin welcomed.[33]

The *Worland Grit,* which had done its part harassing the prosecutors
of the Spring Creek raiders, still grudgingly got in step with the attitude
of the majority of its readers. In a December 18, 1909, editorial, the *Grit*
first noted that newspapers around the state were disposed to stop writing
so much about the raid and the convictions. It then stated, though, that
"one pleasing feature connected with the regretful affair is that it has
completely vindicated the good name of Big Horn County and Wyoming
as the home of law and order." The truth is that the good folks of
Wyoming, for all their contrary independence, very much cared about
how they appeared in the eyes of people in the rest of the country. Just
before Herbert Brink's trial began, the *Rocky Mountain News,* a Denver
newspaper, ran a piece written by Arlan W. Coons, the editor of one of
Basin's papers, the *Big Horn County Rustler.* The article had a defensive
tone, in which Coons argued that "change is taking place, that the march
of progress has made its mark upon the country that once belonged
wholly to the cattleman and to the sheepman." Almost plaintively, the
Rustler editor insisted that Basin was "the home of intelligent, patriotic,
home-loving, home-building progressive people. Its streets are as peaceful

on this sunny Sabbath day as those of any village of Puritanical New England." Before the conviction of Herbert Brink, though, editor Coons was really talking about what he wanted Basin to be, not what he could confidently say that it was. After that conviction, it could justly be said that the words of one of the prosecuting attorneys were finally true: "Wyoming has passed the border stage of her history. It has been a hard, bitter growth, but we have arrived and the world will know that the law is held in regard by the big majority of our people."[34]

♦

Epilogue

On November 15, 1909, there were train departures from Basin City to Billings, Montana, departures reminiscent of Maggie Gorman's exile six years earlier. Bill Keyes, Charlie Faris and his wife and baby, and Billy and Anna Goodrich and their child all boarded the train in Basin for a trip north. All knew they could not stay in the Big Horn Basin. When they came into the depot, they were "treated like lepers," and people pointedly avoided them.[1]

During the night of Wednesday, November 9, the very time when the jurors were deciding the fate of Herbert Brink, the sawmill at the Goodrich ranch had been burned to the ground, probably to send a message to Billy. The anger toward Faris and Keyes was stronger yet. An editorial in the *Cheyenne State Leader* demonstrated the deep contempt in which Faris and Keyes were held among cattlemen. The editorial referred to Benedict Arnold and spoke of how Faris and Keyes were "guilty but by the law made guiltless." None of these people being banished felt that simply going to Billings would suffice; all of them intended to relocate farther west.[2]

On the other hand, the cattle community treated the convicted raiders as heroes. Just before the five men left Basin on November 20, they were treated to a "splendid dinner," while being visited by as many as a hundred people, many of whom brought fruits and flowers. When the raiders were taken to the train depot, a bigger crowd yet followed them there, showering them with parting handshakes and words of sympathy. More than fifty years later, Percy Metz still found this spectacle "unbelievable," and was disgusted by the "killing" that was made by "outfits in Denver" from the sale of all the flowers bestowed upon the raiders.[3]

Still, the irrevocable reality remained. These five men might have been treated as heroes by some in the Big Horn Basin, but they were vanquished and fallen heroes, and they would not be allowed to rise again until they had paid their debt to society. When they got on the train that day, the end of their long train trip was to be the state penitentiary in Rawlins, and all five were delivered there on November 23.[4]

Loose ends had to be wrapped up, of course. One was the disposition of the reward money. Both Felix Alston and Billy Simpson declined to accept any of it. Joe LeFors probably got the lion's share of the money, but since most of it was from private people who refused to divulge how they disbursed the reward monies, we will never know its disposition. There was a final skirmish with regard to Will Metz's attorney fees; he chose to accept the initial $2,500 forwarded by the county commissioners, but not to request further payment. The men in the militia who had stood guard at the Big Horn County Courthouse were never properly paid. Governor Brooks was written and told this in May 1910, but he had to respond that there was no money for payment unless the legislature approved it, and, apparently, the legislature never did.[5]

Elections were held every two years for county officials in the early twentieth century, and in 1910, both Percy Metz and Felix Alston were up for re-election. Metz was defeated, but Alston was retained. Metz was defeated probably because he had strongly enforced the gambling and liquor laws, making him unpopular in some of the larger towns, such as Greybull, Basin, and Worland. The most interesting results were from the areas within the 1897 deadline. As might be expected, both Metz and Alston lost badly in Shell, but in the Red Bank Precinct (just south of Big Trails, the home of "Bear George" McClellan), Alston evenly split the vote with his opponent, and Metz beat his, 19–14; and in the Spring Creek

Joe LeFors. Courtesy Washakie Museum.

Precinct, Alston won handily, by about the same margin that Metz lost. At the state level, Joseph M. Carey, running as the Democratic candidate, won the governorship. The consequence of this was that in April 1911, Carey appointed Felix Alston as warden of the Wyoming State Penitentiary, and when a new judgeship was created for the Big Horn Basin in 1913, Carey appointed Percy Metz as the district judge, supposedly the youngest person in the United States (at twenty-nine) to hold such a position.[6]

The five raiders quietly served their time for about a year and a half, but then Saban and Alexander retained lawyers to challenge their convictions. About the same time that Felix Alston took over the penitentiary, in April 1911, Samuel King, a Salt Lake City attorney, and W. E. Mullen, who had just been the attorney general of Wyoming, filed a verified petition for writ of *coram nobis*. Saban and Alexander sought a new trial, swearing that in Big Horn County, sheepmen had brought about "a practical reign of terror," with "threats of mob violence," and that as a result, they had been intimidated and compelled to enter an "extorted" plea of guilty. The courts gave short shrift to these cynical distortions, although the opinion of the Wyoming Supreme Court in *State v. Alexander* remains fascinating reading.[7]

Herbert Brink was punished after the lynching of Frank Wigfall, but his penalty did not amount to much. He was put in solitary confinement briefly but then was released because he was needed in the blacksmith shop. In the same year of these events, 1912, both Eaton and Dixon left the penitentiary, although under quite different circumstances. Eaton was bitten by a tick while with a road gang in the Big Horn Basin. He died on June 1, 1912, in Meeteetse, and was then buried in the Ten Sleep Cemetery. Dixon was in Rawlins in July 1912, when a fire broke out at the prison broom factory. He and Alexander, along with others, fought the fire all through the night. Dixon had been an exemplary prisoner, a trustee who drove the wagon carrying supplies to the prison, and in consideration of this record and his help with the fire, the board of pardons commuted Dixon's sentence, and he was released on November 1, 1912. Dixon apparently did not return to the Big Horn Basin, although

Wyoming State Penitentiary baseball team, ca. 1911. The little boy in the photograph is Felix Alston, Jr. George Saban is in the back row, third from the right. Courtesy Jack Seaman.

it appears he remained in the West. There are differing reports of his final fate; one states that he became insane in Montana and another that he died in Oklahoma in an oil field accident in the 1930s.[8]

In late 1912, agitation began for the release of the remaining three prisoners. Petitions and letters were sent to Governor Carey on behalf of Saban, Alexander, and Brink (Brink's complicity in the prison lynching was ignored). Carey sought advice from prominent sheepmen about what he should do. He was a cautious politician, and when he received mixed recommendations, he declined to take any action. Throughout 1913, letters and petitions seeking pardons kept coming in, but before acting, Carey wanted a resolution of support for probation or parole by the Big Horn County Woolgrowers. No such resolution was approved, and Carey expressed reluctance to take action, a position that was becoming increasingly frustrating to George Saban.[9]

For the previous two years, George had been on a road camp crew in the Big Horn Basin and had been allowed to live with his wife. In December 1913, though, orders were sent out to return Saban to Rawlins, and Saban must have thought that he would not be released from his sentence soon. He was being given such unusual freedoms that his guard had no objection to delaying the trip to Rawlins so that Saban could do some banking he said he had to do. Saban went to a Basin bank on his own, but all he did at the bank was get money for an escape. From the newspaper reports of the day, it sounds as if Saban did his banking business and then just went out the back door of the bank. He found a man who was willing to drive him to Laurel, Montana, for one hundred dollars; they drove through the night and arrived at six o'clock the next morning. Saban's guard did not even know he was gone until two o'clock that afternoon. By that time, Saban had surely caught a train (Laurel sits on the Northern Pacific rail line) and was long gone.[10]

Saban made good his escape, but by doing so, he made himself a perpetual wanderer. No one knew for sure where Saban had gone, but he was reported in many faraway places, ranging from Alaska to Argentina. His absence was devastating to his wife and children. Felix Alston put out a flier proclaiming a $250 reward for Saban's capture.[11]

George Saban never was found, though, and the worst of this family's tragedy was that Saban would almost certainly have been paroled within a year. That is what happened to both Alexander and Brink, as cattlemen and their supporters mounted more petition drives and wrote hundreds more letters to Governor Carey. Milton Alexander and Herbert Brink were paroled on December 14, 1914.[12]

Alexander was told not to return to the Big Horn Basin, and he did not, at least not until 1917, when Governor John Kendrick pardoned him. He and his wife then came back to the Upper Nowood but sold the ranch in 1920. The Alexanders moved to Ten Sleep, where Milton acted as the town marshal in the 1920s; he died on January 20, 1931, and as with many people associated with the raid, was buried in the Ten Sleep Cemetery. Herbert Brink spent the rest of his life in and out of prison, mostly in, because he could not stay out of trouble. Still, he was the last of the defendants to die, not doing so until the late 1950s.[13]

Not much information is available about the subsequent history of the jurymen, but we do know what became of the foreman, W. H. Packard. In the year following the trial, 1910, he and most of his family left Burlington and went north to Canada. He did not have the same kind of success in Canada as he had had in the United States, knocking around from one job to another, and on October 29, 1917, in Glenwoodville, Alberta, he died.[14]

Another one of the Spring Creek players who went to Canada was Bill Keyes; at least, he was there in 1911, but his whereabouts thereafter are not known. Charlie Faris returned to Montana, probably to a place near where he grew up. He is mentioned in two places in Montana: Bozeman, where he is supposed to have become a preacher, and Manhattan, which is a small town about thirty miles northwest of Bozeman. Billy and Anna Goodrich remained away from the Upper Nowood for nine years, but then, apparently believing that old animosities had faded, they returned to Big Trails in 1918. Both of the Goodriches lived long lives; Billy died in 1960, and Anna not until 1974.[15]

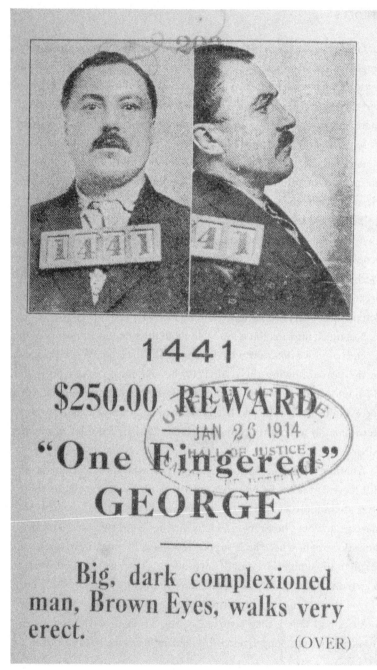

George Saban, wanted flier (front), issued by Felix Alston. Photograph of flyer courtesy Gary Pfeiffer, Worland, Wyoming.

This man is wanted for murder, escaped from prison, is described as follows: 5 feet, 10¼ inches high, hair chestnut age 40, weighs about 185 to 200, dim vac scar above left elbow, all fingers off right hand but the index finger, pit of back and legs hairy; has a loud, hearty, peculiar, attractive laugh, is a good c⟨o⟩ puncher, ropes and shoots left han⟨d⟩ does not drink or use tobacco, nor ⟨ab⟩le, very attentive to the ladies, w very poor hand, has very little ⟨educati⟩on; want this man very much, he ⟨ha⟩s deserted a good wife and 6 children.

Wire all communications to

FELIX ALSTON,
Warden,

(over)   **Rawlins, Wyoming.**

George Saban, wanted flier (back), issued by Felix Alston. Photograph of flier courtesy Gary Pfeiffer, Worland, Wyoming.

The historical
marker erected on
Wyoming State
Highway 434 on
the site of the
Spring Creek
Raid. Photograph
by author.

After the trial, a romance developed between Ada Allemand and John Callahan, the trapper who had given such damaging testimony against Herbert Brink. They married and moved to Washington State, near Ellensberg. Bounce Helmer worked as a sheepherder all his life, although he did marry and have children. He retired in Cody in 1953 and died in 1956.[16]

Ken McClellan and his family moved to Fremont County, just south of the Big Horn Basin; they appear in Fremont County in the 1910 census. In Natrona County, the Wyoming county directly east of Fremont County, 1920s land records show an intriguing name: "Margaret Gorman, a widow." The Natrona County seat is Casper, and in 1924, residential property in what was then the southwestern part of Casper was conveyed from people named Jordan to Margaret Gorman. Only a few months later, "Margaret Gorman, a widow," gave a $2,800 mortgage to the Casper Mutual Building and Loan Association. This was probably the means by which Gorman paid for the house and land she had just purchased. The person listed in these conveyances was most likely *the* Maggie Gorman, formerly of the Dry Fork of Brokenback Creek. She would have been forty-four in 1924, an age when she might have purchased a home. Given Wyoming's tiny population (194,402 people in 1920), two Margaret Gormans, both widows, probably did not live within the state. The home that was conveyed still stands; it is a modest home, and one that she might have seen as affordable while working as a waitress, which was evidently Maggie Gorman's chosen occupation. Unfortunately, the last recorded entry relating to Margaret Gorman appears to be a deed in lieu of foreclosure. On April 25, 1928, Margaret Gorman conveyed her property to her mortgagee, the Casper Mutual Building and Loan Association. Such a conveyance usually means that a person cannot pay the mortgage and is setting the mortgaged property over to the lender as part of an agreement to avoid formal foreclosure and a deficiency.[17]

If this person in Natrona County in the 1920s is, in fact, Maggie Gorman, it is remarkable that this woman, known for her beauty, never remarried, and that she continued to present herself as a widow. Why people act as they do is a complicated question, but her actions are consistent with a woman who perceived herself as the victim of a great tragedy that she never again wanted to risk repeating, not with a scarlet woman who casually took lovers and shed husbands.

Percy Metz would never have to worry about a foreclosure against his home. Beyond the support of his prosperous father, Percy became well-to-do very early because of his investment in one of the pioneer oil fields in the Big Horn Basin. Metz lived a long life, a good part of it—almost forty years—as the district judge for the Big Horn Basin. After he retired, he considered writing a book about the Spring Creek Raid, something he never got around to doing, but he did travel to several places in the state and tell local historical societies about the last great sheep raid in Wyoming. Percy's colleague, Felix Alston, served for many years as warden of the Wyoming State Penitentiary, then moved to California, where he died in the 1950s. Joe LeFors retired in Buffalo and died there in 1940.[18]

One early spring day in 1936, the editor of the *Basin Republican-Rustler* (the two formerly antagonistic Basin papers had merged in 1928) looked out his office window and observed "the peaceful quiet of Big Horn County's beautiful court house square," and recalled the time when a mob attacked the Big Horn County jail.[19] The editor wrote an article that was unusually interesting, not simply because it recounted "the most tragic page in the history of Big Horn county," but because it showed the attitude of some 1936 Basin residents toward the 1903 lynching. The disturbing thing is that even thirty-three years after the event, the editor made excuses for the actions of the mob, indicating that the incident was particularly unfortunate because of the killing "of an innocent man," but asserting that the actions of the lynch mob were at least understandable because of "the law's delays" and comparing the Gorman case to more recent examples of "America's slow method of dealing with criminals" (such as the kidnapping and murder of the Lindbergh baby). Perhaps the editor was following the lead of Justice Charles Potter, who visited Basin only a few years after the lynching (while running for re-election) and apparently forwarded an apology when he delivered an address about "the law's delays."[20]

During the twentieth century, the Big Horn Basin grew to about 50,000 people; it has been a reasonably prosperous, though still remote, corner of the United States. The residents enjoy its wildness, taking advantage of the excellent hunting and fishing. The Basin has an unusually low crime rate; indeed, after the Brink trial, the area settled into a domestic tranquility (at least from the standpoint of criminal activity) that it still maintains.

In 1957, the United States Supreme Court addressed the case of *Green v. United States*. Everett Green had been tried in a federal court, the United States District Court for the District of Columbia, for the crime of arson and first-degree murder. He was found guilty of second-degree murder, and he appealed that conviction; the conviction was reversed, but upon retrial, Green was convicted of first-degree murder and sentenced to death. He again appealed, this time on the grounds of double jeopardy, but the court of appeals denied his appeal, saying that he had waived his protection against double jeopardy by taking the appeal. The United States Supreme Court granted a writ of certiorari and reviewed the case.[21]

It was a close decision, and the five-member majority framed the question before the Court by paraphrasing the basic contention of the government, saying it came down to saying that, "in order to secure a reversal, a defendant must be willing to barter his constitutional protection against a second prosecution for an offense punishable by death as the price of a successful appeal." The Court ruled unambiguously: "The rule should not, and in our judgment does not, place the defendant in such an incredible dilemma. Conditioning an appeal of one offense on a coerced surrender of a valid plea of former jeopardy on another offense exacts a forfeiture in plain conflict with the constitutional bar against double jeopardy." The majority opinion was unusually strong, firmly rejecting the notion of waiver as "indefensible," and closing with a stirring pronouncement: "The right not to be placed in jeopardy more than once for the same offense is a vital safeguard in our society, one that was dearly won and one that should continue to be highly valued. If such great constitutional protections are given a narrow, grudging application they are deprived of much of their significance."[22]

The *Green* case arose out of the federal system and therefore was not expressly applicable to the state criminal systems. Nor, for that matter did it directly address the more common situation, such as that faced by Jim Gorman, wherein a defendant seeks a new trial after being convicted of a lesser included offense (such as manslaughter after being charged with first-degree murder). The *Green* opinion, however, was so strong and so broadly worded that there could be little doubt how the United States Supreme Court would rule if it were to consider a case such as *State v. Gorman*. In fact, after *Green*, the issue has never again arisen in a state jurisdiction, apparently because state trial courts have uniformly determined that *Green* resolved the issue against the prosecuting authorities.

All of this means that as of December 16, 1957, it was the law of the land, throughout the United States, that no defendant could be retried as Jim Gorman had been. This ruling came fifty-four years too late for Jim, but even fifty-four years earlier, it would have been a close issue requiring a careful weighing of a number of considerations. It was an issue that should have been resolved by the quiet deliberation of appellate judges, not by the frenzied bloodlust of a mob.[23]

Under modern laws, Jim Gorman would have been convicted only of manslaughter (and a new trial would not likely have been granted), a crime carrying a maximum penalty of twenty years in the penitentiary. Joseph Walters's conviction would almost certainly have been reversed because of the refusal to give defense counsel a reasonable time to prepare, and it is problematic what would then have happened. Perhaps Walters still would have been convicted of first-degree murder and sentenced to death after a trial, but it appears that the man was mentally ill. Jurors, however, still rarely enter an acquittal in a murder case on the basis of insanity; however, even if a modern jury found Walters guilty of murder, it might have been second-degree murder. A jury could well have believed that Walters's mental condition precluded premeditation and might have acquitted him of first-degree murder.

One should always be careful not to judge the fairness of an event in one time by the standards of another time, but even by the standards of 1903, the first-degree murder convictions of Walters and Gorman were suspect. In other words, when these two men were slaughtered by the lynch mob, their guilt of capital crimes was not at all clear in law. Jim Gorman's case, especially, involved fine legal considerations; his appeal would have addressed some of the most important issues in the history of American jurisprudence. As Hamlet observed, the law's delays are sometimes so frustrating that they might cause a person to consider suicide. But there are exercises in this world that require time to do correctly, and that should only be completed after calm and considered reflection.

When Judge Parmelee told the grand jury in 1909 that no "body of men, however wise or well-intentioned, may safely be entrusted to pronounce upon or to redress public wrongs or private grievances outside of the forms of the law," he was right, and his admonition was equally valid to any kind of mob action, whether a lynching or a sheep raid. It meant that the killing of Gorman and Walters was no more justifiable than that of Earl Price. Of course, it is hard to avoid the feeling that there are varying degrees of justification for nonofficial actions. A moral difference seems to exist between, say, the actions of the Montana Vigilantes, taken virtually in self-defense against men clearly guilty of murder, and the lynching of a jailed person awaiting trial, unpopular because of his race. Such distinctions are dangerously made, but it is also hard to shake the feeling that the lynchings of Gorman and Walters were particularly unfortunate because the fairness of their convictions of capital crimes was so questionable.

Judge Lynch should never have rendered a decision.

♦

Notes

CHAPTER ONE

1. Marriage license and certificate of marriage between Thomas C. Gorman and Margaret M. McClellan, Sept. 3, 1898 (license), and Sept. 19, 1898 (filing of certificate), Book A of Marriage, p. 418, Johnson County Clerk. The 1900 census, Big Horn County, Wyoming, shows Maggie to have been born in August 1880.

2. Homestead Proof—Testimony of Claimant by Henry E. Miller, homestead file #1288 for Henry E. Miller, Land Office at Buffalo, Wyoming, July 6, 1905, RG 40, Bureau of Land Management, National Archives and Records Administration; McPhee, *Rising from the Plains*, 63. Gloria Cutt, interview by author, Feb. 5, 2000. Fred and Gloria Cutt are present owners of the land.

3. "Big Horn County's Terrible Tragedy," *Cheyenne Daily Leader,* Nov. 10, 1902. Much of the available information about the Gormans is found in contemporary newspaper stories. Most of the articles in local newspapers (e.g., those in Basin and Meeteetse) are unfortunately not available, but articles from outside the Big Horn basin are, such as those from the *Laramie Boomerang*, the *Sheridan Post*, and the above excellent *Cheyenne Daily Leader* report. See also the 1900 census; Bob Swander, interview by author, June 10, 2003. Swander now lives in Cody, Wyoming, and is pushing seventy. He grew up and ranched near Ten Sleep, and recalled a discussion, which probably took place in the 1970s, with Jim and Topsy Bull, then an elderly couple who had known the Gormans. The subject of the Gorman murder came up. Topsy, a lively lady, said to her husband, "Everybody thought that Maggie Gorman was good looking; you didn't think so, did you?" Bob thought the scene was cute, as Jim Bull

recognized this husband's predicament, and just stopped saying anything. Bob thought that Jim probably did think Maggie Gorman was quite good looking, but certainly was not going to declare this to his wife.

4. "A Foul Murder Unearthed," *Wyoming Dispatch*, June 13, 1902; "Murder near Hyattville," *Sheridan Enterprise*, June 21, 1902; "Big Horn County's Terrible Tragedy."

5. Frison, *Under the Ten Sleep Rim*, 45; interview notes taken by Frison, which are in the author's possession (hereafter cited as Frison notes); Bowes, "Vigilante Vengeance," 28. This last reference is in large part a fictionalized, sensationalized version of the event, but at least the article started life honestly, beginning with interviews of some of the participants, including Fred Bader. The "photograph" of Maggie Gorman in that article is clearly a construction.

Many contemporaneous newspaper reports and later writings address the inquiries about Tom, not always in the same manner, but consistently enough to show that nosy neighbors thought something was not right at the Gorman house and that they were not satisfied with what they were told. See Frison, *Under the Ten Sleep Rim*, 38; "Murder near Basin," *Wyoming Derrick*, June 19, 1902; "Murder near Hyattville"; and "Jim Gorman Convicted," *Big Horn County News and Courier*, Nov. 1, 1902. The problem with the discussion here is that there is much general recollection but not nearly enough contemporaneous documents; therefore, I had to draw conclusions from a review of all materials available, determining what is the most plausible, considering internal consistency and known facts.

6. 1900 census; Fred Bader, interview by Paul Frison (no date or location available for Frison interviews), Frison notes; Paris Bader, interview by author, Feb. 2000. On June 10, 1900, when the 1900 census interviews were undertaken, Tom and Maggie Gorman reported no children, but by May 1902, a child is being described as "a little girl," not as a baby, and the girl is speaking.

7. "Murder near Hyattville." The chronology here is a puzzle. Contemporary reports are unclear, but apparently, Jim and Maggie Gorman were arrested several days later. The warrant for their arrest was sworn out on June 7 and returned on June 13. The natural expectation is that they would have gone directly to Montana, and it did not normally take several days to reach Montana from the location of the Gorman house. One possible reason for delay is that Maggie Gorman might have talked Jim into leaving Rose at Maggie's parents, the McClellans, who lived a few miles south of Brokenback Creek.

8. "Big Horn County's Terrible Tragedy"; "Murder near Hyattville"; "Murder near Basin"; Carter, "C. Dana Carter, Pioneer Doctor"; Skovgard, *Basin City*, 52; "Black Page in Basin History," *Basin Republican-Rustler*, Mar. 19, 1936; "A Foul Murder Unearthed." The attempt to burn the body was reported consistently enough

that it must be credited, but the evidence at the trial indicated that the fire was confined to an attempt to conceal the burial spot.

In *State v. James Gorman*, criminal case 109, all the witnesses were endorsed on the information (a charging document). Oddly, Dr. Carter is not listed, but the statements in his autobiography leave no doubt that he was at the Gorman place and helped in the search. Apparently, though, Dr. Walker conducted later examinations of Tom Gorman's body. In Skovgard, *Basin City*, 51–52, the author incorrectly states that C. A. Zaring was the county attorney. Though Zaring was later involved with the case, the Big Horn County attorney in 1902 was W. S. Collins, who swore out the complaint against the defendants. See the Big Horn County District Court Journal, vol. 1, 440, Big Horn County Clerk of the District Court.

9. Skovgard, *Basin City*, 53.

10. During the fur-trading era, in the 1820s and 1830s, several white men and even one black man, Edward Rose, visited the basin, but to my knowledge, Woodruff was the first man to build a cabin, which he did so on Owl Creek before 1878. See Woods, *Wyoming's Big Horn Basin*, 30, 80–82.

11. Murray, "Short Grass and Heather," 99, 103; Woods, *Wyoming's Big Horn Basin*, 73, 76, 78, 82, 83, 86; Edgar and Turnell, *Brand of a Legend*, 38; Lindsay, *The Big Horn Basin*, 100.

12. DeVoto, *The Year of Decision*, 82.

13. Interestingly, the crime problems were confined to certain offenses, primarily livestock theft and violent crimes against the person. See Robertson *A History of the Worland Valley*, 19, wherein Robertson describes the undisturbed use of an open cigar box as a cash register in Dad Worland's hole in the wall. McGrath, in *Gunfighters, Highwaymen and Vigilantes*, 199, reports a similar situation with respect to Bodie, California, in the 1870s and 1880s. This frontier mining town was subjected to myriad shootings and shootouts, but "The old, the weak, the female and the innocent were generally left untouched." In an excellent appendix about the extent of violence in the west, McGrath cites Holden's article "Law and Lawlessness on the Texas Frontier," wherein Holden makes a similar observation with regard to west Texas.

14. *The Compiled Laws of Wyoming, 1876*, chap. XIV, sec. 1–212 (criminal procedure); chap. XXXV, sec. 1–154 (crimes); and chap. XXVII (counties and county boundaries); chap. LXXI (justices' code), sec. 395–435. P. K. Simpson, "History of the First Wyoming Legislature."

15. 1900 census (even this late, more than 70 percent of the population was male, and the average age was only 24.6 years); Edgar and Turnell, *Brand of a Legend*, 49, quoting Arland's December 5, 1884, letter to Camille Dadant. The originals of Arland's letters are found in manuscript collection no. 2, Victor Arland Collection.

They are cited at length, including many of the quotations herein, in Wasden, *From Beaver to Oil*, and in Edgar and Turnell, *Brand of a Legend*.

16. 1999 Wyoming Official Highway Map. I am not aware of any criminal prosecutions in Green River or Rawlins for crimes committed in the Big Horn Basin around 1879.

17. Hanson, ed., *The Papers of J. Elmer Brock*, 188; Wasden, *From Beaver to Oil*, 124; Wister, *The Virginian*, 35. Skovgard states that Wister visited Basin City in August 1917 and at that time said he had first come to the Big Horn Basin in 1883. *Basin City*, 117.

18. See the minutes of the Johnson County Board of Commissioners, Mar. 29, 1881, Johnson County Clerk, vol. 1, p. 1, the first set of minutes of the county commissioners of the new county. See also *Compiled Laws of Wyoming, 1876*, chap. XXVI, 198; "Johnson County," *Buffalo Echo*, Aug. 2, 1883.

19. Edgar and Turnell, *Brand of a Legend*, 37; See *Territory v. Angus*, Johnson County criminal case 1, *et seq.*, Johnson County Clerk of District Court.

20. Records of the Johnson County Board of Commissioners (hereafter cited as Johnson County Commissioners), vol. 1, 95; Sweetwater County Commissioners' Record, Wyoming Territory, vol. B, 197, Sept. 24, 1882, Sweetwater County Clerk; Black, *Black's Law Dictionary*, 383, 1003.

21. See Sweetwater County Commissioners' Record, vol. B, especially the minutes for Apr. 21, 1881; June 24, 1881; May 10, 1881; Dec. 26, 1881; and Sept. 24, 1883. Minutes of the Johnson County Commissioners, July 16, 1883, 138. The latter minutes note an appearance by W. P. Noble regarding mistaken payment of taxes to Sweetwater County.

22. Edgar and Turnell, *Brand of a Legend*, 39.

23. 1999 Official Wyoming Highway Map.

CHAPTER TWO

1. Wasden, *From Beaver to Oil*, 107, 124. See also Woods, *Wyoming's Big Horn Basin*, 77.

2. Edgar and Turnell, *Brand of a Legend*, 46–47, 49, citing Arland to Dadant, Mar. 16, 1884.

3. Edgar and Turnell, 49, citing Arland to Dadant, June 17, 1884.

4. Letter from Tom Osborne to unknown recipient, in Edgar and Turnell, *Brand of a Legend*, 50–51. In this account, Osborne never provides McWallace's first name. Osborne also incorrectly identifies George Smith as Jim Smith. On Labor Day 2003, Smith's remains were reburied at Old Trail Town in Cody, Wyoming, and the ceremony was attended by descendants of Smith and of Ira Hamilton. Bob Edgar, interview by author, Nov. 17, 2003.

5. Woods describes this event well in *Wyoming's Big Horn Basin*, 135. See *Territory v. Anable*, Johnson County criminal cases 57, 63, and 64. Frank Canton was a notorious figure in Johnson County in the late 1880s and early 1890s. He served as sheriff until 1886, and then became a range detective. When he again sought the office of sheriff in 1890, though, the Democrats of Johnson County preferred Red Angus, and Angus became the new county sheriff. Canton was charged with two murders in 1891 but managed to beat the charges, and in April 1892, he was one of the leaders of the fifty men who invaded Johnson County to assassinate, among others, Red Angus. See Smith, *The War on Powder River*, 98, 119, 165, 175, 188, 197, and 201.

From 1882 to 1887, the primary prison facilities used were those in Joliet, Illinois. For an excellent discussion of Wyoming territorial penitentiary arrangements, see Larson, *History of Wyoming*, n. 6, p. 146.

6. Minutes of the Fremont County Board of Commissioners, Mar. 23, 1884, Commission's Record of Proceedings, vol. A, p. 1 *et seq.*; Records of the Johnson County Clerk, Sept. 6, 1884, meeting, p. 211. Old Meeteetse was located on Meeteetse Creek below Arland, and when its post office was moved to a location on the Greybull River, the name "Meeteetse" was transplanted to the new town. Larry Edgar, interview by author, Feb. 1, 2002. Edgar now lives on Meeteetse Creek between what were the towns of Arland and Old Meeteetse.

7. Fremont County Commission's Record of Proceedings, vol. A, pp. 25, 148–49; Johnson County Commissioners, vol. 1, 387.

8. Fremont County Commission's Record, vol. A, p. 7, 100; Johnson County Commissioners, vol. 1, 307; Woods, *Wyoming's Big Horn Basin*, 169–71; *Lander Clipper*, June 28, 1888.

9. Woods, *Wyoming's Big Horn Basin*, 135; *Territory v. Gross*, Johnson County criminal case 148.

10. Lindsay, *The Big Horn Basin*, 139–40; quotation from Edgar and Turnell, *Brand of a Legend*, 55.

11. Edgar and Turnell, *Brand of a Legend*, 56.

12. Sentence, *Territory v. Booth*, Johnson County criminal case 77; *Booth v. Territory*, 3 Wyo. 159 (1886). The minutes of the Johnson County commissioners are filled with references to items such as the purchase of lumber for a scaffold and payment for such things as participating in a death watch. See vol. 1, 345–46, in the minutes. For a complete exposition of this case, see Brown, *You Are Respectfully Invited to Attend My Execution*, 111–33.

13. Edgar and Turnell, *Brand of a Legend,* 59, citing Arland to Dadant, Mar. 26, 1887; Woods, *Wyoming's Big Horn Basin*, 119. For patents granted between 1890 and 1892, see Johnson County transcripts 1, 2, and 4, pages 53, 58, 59, 60, 62, 63, 68, 69, 70, 71, 72, 75, 87, 89, 94, 98, 99, 102, and 103, Records of the Washakie County Clerk.

Because of the requirements of the applicable land laws, patents were not granted until three to five years after the initial settlements.

14. Wasden, *From Beaver to Oil*, 309.

15. Ibid., 221 (Arland quotation); Woods, *Wyoming's Big Horn Basin*, 139.

16. Wasden, *From Beaver to Oil*, 221.

17. Ibid., 222.

18. Lindsay, *The Big Horn Basin*, 144. Gormand was shot in the spring of 1888, and Inglas in September 1888. See also Woods, *Wyoming's Big Horn Basin*, 135.

19. See Johnson County criminal case 155, Fremont County Commission's Record, vol. A, 740. An affidavit by Jack Hollywood, case 155, states that Jack Hill was stationed in the Big Horn Basin as a Johnson County deputy sheriff. Wasden indicates that in 1893, John Price of Embar was the first deputy sheriff of "northern Fremont County," but that is probably incorrect, unless Robinson did not accept the position. *From Beaver to Oil*, 56.

20. Wasden concluded that McComb shot and killed her and took her money, but other historians feel otherwise; Bob Edgar feels that most likely McComb was involved in Edna Wilson's accidental death but not in her murder. Wasden, *From Beaver to Oil*, 309; Bob Edgar and Larry Edgar, interview by author, Mar. 12, 2002.

21. See Wyo. Stat. § 6–117 (1957). This statute does not appear after 1970.

22. Indictment, Fremont County criminal case 74.

23. Woods, *Wyoming's Big Horn Basin*, 153; *McCray v. Baker*, 18 Pac. 749, 3 Wyo. 192 (Terr. of Wyoming 1888).

24. Edgar and Turnell, *Brand of a Legend*, 66–67. The LU Ranch, which is still an operating cattle ranch, is located primarily on Grass Creek, but its headquarters are on Gooseberry Creek. The exact location of this fight is unknown.

25. Edgar and Turnell, *Brand of a Legend*, 67; Woods, *Wyoming's Big Horn Basin*, 139

CHAPTER THREE

1. Map from Wyoming Department of State Parks and Cultural Resources (The towns shown are "Meteetse [sic]", Arland, Franc, and Corbett. The 1990 population of Meeteetse was 368.) In 1890, the Big Horn Basin was part of Fremont and Johnson Counties, and there are, therefore, no separate population figures. This estimate is based primarily on the number of people voting in the Big Horn Basin 1888 election precincts, which was 1,250, but also from general discussions, such as in Wasden, *From Beaver to Oil*, 59, and Lindsay, *The Big Horn Basin*, 160, 168. See also Larson, *History of Wyoming*, 262; 1890 census.

2. See Woods, *Wyoming's Big Horn Basin*, chap. 14. See also Wasden, *From Beaver to Oil*, chap. 4.

3. Woods, *Wyoming's Big Horn Basin,* 188; thirteen county map in Larson, *History of Wyoming,* 264.

4. Woods, *Wyoming's Big Horn Basin,* 136–38; "A Tragedy: The Awful Result of a Basin Fight," *Buffalo Bulletin,* Apr. 16, 1891.

5. "Discharged," *Buffalo Bulletin,* June 18, 1891.

6. "A Tragedy"; "Discharged"; "Robbed the Mails," *Buffalo Bulletin,* May 7, 1891.

7. "Robbed the Mails."

8. "Discharged." See also Indictment, *State v. Madden, Kearney, and McDermott,* Fremont County criminal case 138, July 13, 1891.

9. Woods, *Wyoming's Big Horn Basin,* 137; "James McDermott Fears His Reputation Is Being Injured by the State Press," *Buffalo Bulletin,* Aug. 20, 1891.

10. Woods, *Wyoming's Big Horn Basin,* 138.

11. "The Killing of Pete Madden," *Buffalo Bulletin,* Nov. 25, 1893; Woods, *Wyoming's Big Horn Basin,* 138; Information, *State v. Madden,* Johnson County criminal case 260, Apr. 26, 1893.

12. *State v. Galigar,* Fremont County criminal case 132; *Board of Commissioners of the County of Fremont v. Perkins,* 5 Wyo. 166, 38 Pac. 915 (1895); *State v. Galigar,* Fremont County criminal case 136. Will Simpson, known as Billy, was to have a long and storied career in the Big Horn Basin, and his progeny would secure renown for the family. Billy Simpson was the father of U.S. senator and Wyoming governor Milward Simpson and the grandfather of U.S. senator and minority whip Al Simpson.

13. *Board of Commissioners of the County of Fremont v. Perkins,* 5 Wyo. 166.

14. Clover, *On Special Assignment,* 232.

15. Of the many accounts of this incident, two of the best are Smith, *The War on Powder River,* and David, *Malcolm Campbell, Sheriff.* David tells the story from the standpoint of the big cattlemen. See pages 344–51. See also Journal Proceedings of Commissioners, vol. 5-B, 16, 72, Johnson County Clerk.

16. Woods, *Wyoming's Big Horn Basin,* 124–29; Information, *State v. Rodgers, et al.,* Johnson County criminal case 245.

17. Minutes of the Fremont County Commissioners, Oct. 1, 1894, Commission's Record of Proceedings, vol. A, pp. 405–406, and minutes of the Johnson County Commissioners, vol. 2, 138.

18. *State v. Hollywood,* Johnson County criminal case 248; *State v. Hollywood,* Johnson County criminal case 288.

19. See *State v. Hollywood,* Johnson County criminal case 303; *State v. Dillingham,* Johnson County criminal case 309.

20. Woods, *Wyoming's Big Horn Basin,* 143; *Hollywood v. State,* 19 Wyo. 493, 120 Pac. 471 (1912).

21. Woods, *Wyoming's Big Horn Basin,* 139; Edgar and Turnell, *Brand of a Legend,* 77; Bob Edgar, interview by author, Mar. 25, 2002.

22. *State v. Wheaton,* Fremont County criminal cases 182 and 187. Wheaton's case apparently turned on a letter Houlihan wrote after he had been shot and knew that he was dying. Bob Edgar reports that when he excavated the grave of Houlihan, it was obvious from the skeleton that Houlihan had been shot in the back. Interview by author, Apr. 14, 2001.

23. Edgar and Turnell, *Brand of a Legend,* 77; Bob Edgar, interview by author, Apr. 14, 2001. Edgar points out that strychnine was readily available at this time; Rose Williams had expressed unhappiness about Belle Drewry's conduct in the Gallagher affair; and there had been nothing to indicate ill health on the part of Williams, a relatively young woman. The inscription on Drewry's grave at Old Trail Town in Cody states that "a few days later, an unknown assassin came into the house and killed Belle, apparently in revenge for their comrades death."

24. *State v. Chapman,* Johnson County criminal case 270; *State v. Murray,* Johnson County criminal case 284.

25. *State v. Conway,* Johnson County criminal case 275 and 298. In other areas of Wyoming during the 1870s and 1880s, convictions seemed hard to obtain. Judge Jeffrey A. Donnell, district judge for Wyoming's Second Judicial District, reports that during this time, numerous charges for serious crimes were brought in Laramie, but very few convictions were obtained.

26. Johnson County criminal case 286.

27. See Woods, *Wyoming's Big Horn Basin,* 140–42; Johnson County criminal cases 299 and 300. Nard's former wife was Jack Hollywood's sister.

28. Slick Creek is hardly a reliable source of water, but one farm was established there, in 1920, when water was diverted from the Upper Hanover Canal to fields along the creek. The farm was owned by William and Bertha Beadle, my maternal grandparents. Mr. Beadle had to grub small fields out of the sagebrush bottomland along Slick Creek.

29. *Board of Commissioners of the County of Fremont v. Perkins;* Wasden, *From Beaver to Oil,* 59.

30. See Davis, *Worland Before Worland,* 1–2, for a discussion of how the German Voss, Bihr, Wostenberg, Loudan, and Bosch families first settled in the Big Horn Basin; Saxton, *The Packard Legacy,* 148–74; Loveland, *Sagebrush and Roses,* 399; Arrington and Bitton, *The Mormon Experience,* 120. Apparently, Packard's selection was informal, but he was later confirmed as bishop by church authorities in 1899.

31. Basin had 474 votes, Otto, 430, and Cody, 238. Skovgard, *Basin City,* 11; Woods, *Wyoming's Big Horn Basin,* 191. The November 19, 1887, *Fremont Clipper*

(page 2, no article title) notes that Collins and three men were homesteading in the Basin and spoke highly of the place. Quotations from Skovgard, *Basin City,* 8.

32. "Double Killing in Wyoming," *Wind River Mountaineer,* Sept. 13, 1897.

33. 1900 census.

34. See 1900 census, Ten Sleep Precinct. One of these sixty-seven men states that he is a "partner," but the apparent partner, his father, lists "farmer" as his occupation. All of Otto Franc's hired men, who certainly would be called cowboys today, refer to themselves as farm laborers. See 1900 census, Meeteetse Precinct.

35. 1900 census, Ten Sleep Precinct.

36. Frison, *When Grass was Gold,* 49.

37. 1900 census, Ten Sleep Precinct.

CHAPTER FOUR

1. "Kills Brother," *Cheyenne Daily Leader,* June 13, 1902.

2. "Murder Near Hyattville."

3. "Lynched at Basin," *Wyoming Dispatch,* July 4, 1902. The article consists of two paragraphs. In the first, the *Wyoming Dispatch* quotes an item from the *Natrona County Tribune,* and in the second, it takes the Casper paper to task for its many erroneous statements.

4. "State Happenings," *Sheridan Enterprise,* Nov. 15, 1902.

5. Skovgard, *Basin City,* 56; Frison, *Under the Ten Sleep Rim,* 45; T. Walker, *Big Horn Basin,* 230–33; Fred Bader, interview by Paul Frison, Frison notes. Records from the Wyoming attorney general indicate that Jim Gorman weighed 150 pounds and was slender, five foot eight, with red hair. Big Horn County sheriff prison register, 6, Wyoming Department of Commerce Archives and Records Division. Bowes, "Vigilante Vengeance," contains a photograph of subjects identified as Jim and Tom Gorman, but this identification is probably wrong. The same photograph is found in the Washakie Museum, with a statement that the two men were brothers from Lost Cabin. The two men shown look similar; certainly, one could not be described as "homely" while the other is described as "good looking."

6. Big Horn County Commissioner's Journal, vol. 1, 346.

7. Big Horn County Dist. Ct. Journal, vol. 1, 423. The justice docket described in Skovgard, *Basin City,* 52, which covers events between June 7, 1902, and June 16, 1902, lists John P. Arnott as employed by the defendant; see also the March 14 article in the Rhodes series "All the World's a Stage: Basin County History," *Basin Republican-Rustler,* Mar. 7, Mar. 14, Mar. 21, Mar. 28, and Apr. 4, 1940.

8. In criminal prosecutions, one of the most common—and effective—defenses is to paint one's client as "the good guy" and one or more of the co-defendants as "the

bad guy," and to offer to provide evidence supporting these positions, in return for lenient treatment by the prosecution.

9. This account directly follows the detailed description of Maggie Gorman's testimony in "Big Horn County's Terrible Tragedy" and incorporates the recollection of Zinny McCreery from Pendergraft, *Washakie,* 41–42.

10. Big Horn County Dist. Ct. Journal, vol. 1, 415.

11. At this time, Big Horn County was part of the Fourth Judicial District, which also included Sheridan County. See Wyo. Rev. Stat. § 3299 (1899). Joseph L. Stotts served as a district court judge until January 1905. Between 1898 and 1906, more than sixty cases from Judge Stotts's court were appealed to the Wyoming Supreme Court. See *State ex rel. Burdick v. Schnitger,* 17 Wyo. 65, 96 Pac. 238 (1908).

12. Woods, *Wyoming's Big Horn Basin,* 204; Davis, *Sadie and Charlie,* 14. The modern statute setting out terms of court is Wyo. Stat. Ann. § 5–3-101 (2001). The applicable statute in 1902 was Wyo. Rev. Stat. § 3299 (1899). See also *Younger v. Hehn,* 12 Wyo. 289, 75 Pac. 443 (1904), an interesting case in which E. E. Enterline challenged the validity of the term statute.

13. Big Horn County Dist. Ct. Journal, vol. 1, 423; "This Morning the Jury Returned with a Verdict of Murder in First Degree," *Worland Grit,* Nov. 11, 1909; *Bryant v. Cadle,* 18 Wyo. 64, 104 Pac. 23 (1909); Wyoming State Bar 2002 Directory, 8. Any Wyoming lawyer will immediately recognize the name Fred Blume. He had a storied career as a justice of the Wyoming Supreme Court and is generally considered the finest jurist the state of Wyoming has ever produced. For an excellent biography of Blume, see Golden, "Journey for the Pole."

14. Big Horn County Dist. Ct. Journal, vol. 1, 424; Wyo. Rev. Stat. §§ 3345, 3346 (1899). See also *Gunnell and Elder v. State,* 21 Wyo. 125, 128 Pac. 512 (1912), p. 129, with a reference to chapter 80, *Compiled Statutes* 1910 (Section 1010). "Incompetent" here refers to legal incompetence, meaning that a person is a minor or is mentally impaired, but, as noted later, it might have been applied more liberally.

15. Wyo. Stat. Ann. § 1–11–106 (2001); SuZann Whitlock, clerk of the district court for Washakie County, interview by author, June 10, 2002.

16. See Wyo. Rev. Stat., § 1779 (1899); Big Horn County 1903 assessment tax roll, Office of the Big Horn County Treasurer; Larson, *History of Wyoming,* 84–85.

17. Big Horn County Dist. Ct. Journal, vol. 1, 414; 1900 census; Davis, *Worland Before Worland,* 4. For specific juror names and residences, see 432–37. About 1,100 of the approximately 3,100 men in the Big Horn Basin were married (about 35 percent).

18. *State v. Bolln,* 10 Wyo. 439, 70 Pac. 1 (1902), p. 470.

19. Big Horn County Dist. Ct. Journal, vol. 1, 440–41. One of these men was apparently related to one of the listed witnesses on behalf of the state against Jim

Gorman, Arthur Ilg. See Information Verified by Witnesses, Big Horn County criminal case 109.

20. Ibid., 441–43.

21. Ibid.; 21 Wyo. 125, 129, 128 P. 512 (1912); 594 P.2d 978 (Wyo. 1979).

22. Big Horn County Dist. Ct. Journal, vol. 1, 440, 443; "Jim Gorman Convicted"; Skovgard, *Basin City,* 39. Quotation from p. 440 of the journal.

23. The other well-known Basin paper, the *Basin Republican,* did not begin publication until 1905. The *Cheyenne Daily Leader* typically printed thorough accounts, often indicating that they were a "special to the *Daily Leader,*" which is consistent with the Cheyenne paper engaging the services of a local reporter. See, for example, the July 20, 1903, issue. It is also possible that "Big Horn County's Terrible Tragedy" is a reprint of a now-unavailable *Big Horn County Rustler* story. All discussion of the trial that follows comes from that November 10, 1902, *Cheyenne Daily Leader* article, unless otherwise indicated.

24. Although the November 10, 1902, *Cheyenne Daily Leader* article is the most reliable source of information about Maggie Gorman's testimony, other recitals are found in the historical record, such as in T. Walker, *Big Horn Basin,* 230–33; Rhodes, "The Road of Yesteryear," 89; and Frison, *Under the Ten Sleep Rim,* 45–48. These sources, however, contain obvious reconstructions from secondhand information and distant memory, are replete with inaccuracies, and are simply not trustworthy, at least in their specifics. Another of these recitals, found in Gustafson, "History of Vigilante and Mob Activity in Wyoming," 149, has much detail, some of which may be accurate. So much of it is clearly wrong, however, that it is hard to know what part is reliable. For instance, Jim and Maggie did not pull out for Montana shortly after the killing, as in Gustafson's account, but waited until June, and Maggie Gorman did not have "little girls," but only one daughter. See Pendergraft, *Washakie,* 42. As before, all subsequent discussion of the trial, including testimony, comes from "Big Horn County's Terrible Tragedy" unless otherwise indicated.

25. See Wyoming's Criminal Pattern Jury Instructions, revised Apr. 1996, 4.03A. The instruction including lesser offenses is referred to as a "lesser included offense instruction." See also Davis, Comment, "The Lesser Included Offense Instruction, Problems With Its Use." The Gorman file cannot be found, and the instructions given to the jury are, therefore, not available, but subsequent events (that is, the legal battle over the consequences of such an instruction) show that it must have been given. Such instructions were given to juries even in territorial times. See, for example, *Territory v. William Booth,* Johnson County criminal case 77, and *Territory v. Elias R. Smith,* Johnson County criminal case 114.

26. "Big Horn County's Terrible Tragedy" does not recite Collins's name but simply refers to "the prosecuting attorney," who was Winfield Scott Collins.

27. Wyo. Rev. Stat. § 4950 (1899). The probable defense argument directly follows *Ross v. State*, 8 Wyo. 351, 383, 57 Pac. 924 (1899), in which the Wyoming Supreme Court laid out clear rules for when deadly force is permitted in self-defense.

28. Big Horn County Dist. Ct. Journal, vol. 1, 450.

CHAPTER FIVE

1. "Jim Gorman Convicted." As now, manslaughter carried a penalty of not more than twenty years. Wyo. Rev. Stat. § 4954 (1899); Wyo. Stat. Ann., § 6–2-105 (2003). "Black Page in Basin History" states that the result "astonished" the prosecution.

2. *Thermopolis Record,* Nov. 7, 1902, front page; Rhodes, "All the World's a Stage," Mar. 7, 1940.

3. Preston Workman, interview by author, June 4, 2002. Preston Workman was Cornelius's grandson and was raised by him. Thomas W. Harrington, interview by author, Mar. 3, 2003; Harrington was the Washakie County prosecuting attorney from January 1995 until January 2003.

4. Big Horn County Dist. Ct. Journal, vol. 1, 452; "State Happenings," *Sheridan Enterprise,* Nov. 15, 1902.

5. Apr. 20, 1903, was the first day of the 1903 spring term; see Big Horn County Dist. Ct. Journal, vol. 1, 469.

6. See Annotation, "Conviction of Lesser Offense as Bar to Prosecution for Greater on New Trial," 61 A.L.R.2d 1141 (1957), particularly §§ 6 and 7. The phrase "lesser included offense" is used in the context of the kind of criminal offense, such as assault and murder, that admits of degree. Manslaughter and second-degree murder are lesser included offenses of first-degree murder. See Davis, Comment, "The Lesser Included Offense Instruction."

Sections 13 and 14 of the Annotation appear to present the cases most closely in point to the situation in *State v. Gorman,* but as pointed out in the Annotation, other decisions generally address the question, such as those in Texas and California. These are not particularly helpful, though, because of the special circumstances in these jurisdictions.

7. Big Horn County Dist. Ct. Journal, vol. 1, 467; Rhodes, "All the World's a Stage," Mar. 14, 1940. Ridgely represented parties before the Wyoming Supreme Court in some twenty-four cases, including wins in significant cases such as *Samuelson v. Tribune Publishing Co.,* 42 Wyo. 419, 296 P. 220 (1931); *State ex rel. Walls v. District Court,* 38 Wyo. 427, 267 P. 1060 (1928); and *Chicago, Burlington and Quincy Railroad v. Lampman,* 18 Wyo. 106, 104 P. 533 (1909). Ridgely was also politically active. He ran for governor as the Republican candidate in 1914 but was defeated by John B. Kendrick. Larson, *History of Wyoming,* 387.

8. Big Horn County Dist. Ct. Journal, vol. 1, 485; "Judge Charles E. Carpenter," *Thermopolis Record,* Oct. 24, 1902. The Second Judicial District included Fremont County, which, in turn, included Thermopolis.

9. "Judge Charles E. Carpenter"; "Republican State Ticket," *Thermopolis Record,* Oct. 24, 1902.

10. Big Horn County Dist. Ct. Journal, vol. 1, 488; "Guilty of Foul Murder," *Cheyenne Daily Leader,* May 4, 1903.

11. "Guilty of Foul Murder"; Big Horn County Dist. Ct. Journal, vol. 1, 488.

12. Big Horn County Dist. Ct. Journal, vol. 1, 488–89.

13. Big Horn County Dist. Ct. Journal, vol. 1, 487–88, 490–92.

14. Ibid., 493.

15. 10 Wyo. 439, 70 Pac. 1 (1902); Big Horn County Dist. Ct. Journal, vol. 1, 494.

16. 1900 census; Big Horn County 1903 tax assessment roll, Big Horn County Treasurer; Big Horn County Dist. Ct. Journal, vol. 1, 495. Four jurors were born in Utah and, being residents of Cowley, Burlington, and Otto, were almost certainly Mormon. Three others not born in Utah came from the heavily Mormon community of Otto, and therefore were probably Mormon. 1903 tax assessment roll, 74, 76, 81, 96, 97, 104, and 119. See also Davis, *A Vast Amount of Trouble,* 154, 228, and 247.

17. Big Horn County Dist. Ct. Journal, vol. 1, 495; "Guilty of Foul Murder." "Quondam," a word seldom seen in modern writing, means former, or sometime.

18. Big Horn County Dist. Ct. Journal, vol. 1, 496–98.

19. Ibid., 500.

20. Ibid., 501–502; "Guilty of Foul Murder."

21. Big Horn County Dist. Ct. Journal, vol. 1, 502.

22. "Guilty of Foul Murder."

23. Ibid.; Biennial Report of the Attorney General to the Governor of Wyoming, 1903–1904, Archives Division, Wyoming Department of State Parks and Cultural Resources. Of these cases, only two resulted in an opinion by the Wyoming Supreme Court, *State v. Keffer,* 12 Wyo. 49, 73 P.1 556 (1903), and *State v. Horn,* 12 Wyo. 80, 73 P. 705 (1903). In both cases, the decision of the district court was sustained, and the death penalty carried out. The Horn case, in particular, is fascinating reading, because the supreme court, in an exhaustive sixty-four-page opinion, addressed every relevant point raised in the case, essential reading for those interested in the real story of the Tom Horn case.

24. Big Horn County Dist. Ct. Journal, vol. 1, 508.

CHAPTER SIX

1. Brief of Plaintiff in Error, *Walters v. State* (doc. 2, no. 391), 1; Skovgard, *Basin City,* 41. The state, in its Brief of Defendant in Error, conceded the accuracy of the recitation of the facts in the Brief of Plaintiff in Error.

2. Skovgard, *Basin City*, 41–42; Big Horn County Sheriff prison register, 6, records of the Wyoming Attorney General, Archives Division, Wyoming Department of State Parks and Cultural Resources. See also the Reply Brief of Plaintiff in Error, *Walters v. State*; Saban, "20th Century Vigilante Justice."

3. Skovgard, *Basin City,* 41–42. See also Brief of Plaintiff in Error, *Walters v. State,* 12–13; "Gorman and Walters Shot," *Laramie Boomerang,* July 21, 1903.

4. Big Horn County Dist. Ct. Journal, vol. 1, 252, 258; Brief of Plaintiff in Error, *Walters v. State,* 1, 5, 9.

5. Brief of Plaintiff in Error, *Walters v. State,* 5, 7; Big Horn County Dist. Ct. Journal, vol. 1, 277.

6. Brief of Plaintiff in Error, *Walters v. State,* 12–13.

7. Ibid., 7, 8; Big Horn County Dist. Ct. Journal, vol. 1, 287.

8. Petition for Stay of Execution of Sentence before the Wyoming Supreme Court, *Walters v. State.*

9. Brief of Plaintiff in Error, *Walters v. State,* 15; *Ross v. State,* 8 Wyo. 351, 387, 57 P. 924 (1899). This is a close call, because there is no Wyoming precedent, but shortly after these briefs were forwarded, the Wyoming Supreme Court did address error asserted on the grounds of failure to grant a continuance to allow defense counsel to prepare, and the court showed very little sympathy for the defense position. See *Keffer v. State,* 12 Wyo. 49, 73 Pac. 586 (1903), decided on August 20, 1903.

10. Brief of Plaintiff in Error, *Walters v. State,* 13.

11. Enterline to Van Orsdel, July 16, 1902, *Walters v. State,* records of the Wyoming Attorney General, Archives Division, Wyoming Department of State Parks and Cultural Resources.

12. Enterline to Van Orsdel, Aug. 13, 1902, *Walters v. State,* records of the Wyoming Attorney General.

13. Enterline to Van Orsdel, Aug. 25, 1902, *Walters v. State,* records of the Wyoming Attorney General.

14. Metz to Van Orsdel, Dec. 26, 1902, *Walters v. State,* records of the Wyoming Attorney General.

15. See Brief of the Defendant in Error, *Walters v. State*; Wyo. Rev. Stat. § 4953 (1899).

16. Brief of the Defendant in Error, *Walters v. State,* 2.

17. Van Orsdel to Enterline, Mar. 30, 1903, *Walters v. State,* and Enterline to Van Orsdel, telegram, Mar. 31, 1903, *Walters v. State,* records of the Wyoming Attorney

General. Van Orsdel was not appointed to the federal bench; the last time he appears in a Wyoming case is in 1904, when there is one case showing him as private counsel (prior to that time, he is listed as the attorney general).

18. Reply Brief of Plaintiff in Error, *Walters v. State*, 2, 3.

19. "Three Men Shot," *Sheridan Post*, July 23, 1903.

CHAPTER SEVEN

1. "Lynching Feared," *Wyoming Tribune*, July 19, 1903; Big Horn County Dist. Ct. Journal, vol. 1, 508; "Black Page in Basin History."

2. "Lynching Feared"; "Gorman and Walters Shot," *Laramie Boomerang*, July 21, 1903. Law officers stepping aside was perceived as enough of a problem that in a few states, special statutes were passed providing for the removal of lawmen (for "official misconduct") who permitted a mob to take a prisoner. See Cutler, *Lynch Law*, 6. There were 103 lynchings in the United States in 1901, 92 in 1902, and 99 in 1903. Table 2, Lynchings, by Year and Race, 1882–1968, in Zangrando, *The NAACP Crusade Against Lynching*, 6.

3. "Murderer Gorman Escaped," *Laramie Boomerang*, July 19, 1903; "A Triple Killing," *Cheyenne Daily Leader*, July 20, 1903; "Shot Down by Lynchers," *Wyoming Tribune*, July 21, 1903; Rhodes, "All the World's a Stage," Mar. 21, 1940. The only "narrow defile" north of Basin that I am aware of is Sheep Mountain Canyon, but this is about fifteen miles north of Basin.

4. "Shot Down by Lynchers." See also "Lynching Feared"; "Murderer Gorman Escaped"; "A Triple Killing"; Big Horn County prisoner register, 6.

5. "Murderer Gorman Escaped."

6. "Shot Down by Lynchers."

7. Ibid. See, for example, "Lynching Feared"; "A Triple Killing"; "Black Page in Basin History"; and Rhodes, "All the World's a Stage," Mar. 21, 1940.

8. "A Triple Killing"; "Black Page in Basin History"; Smith was incorrectly identified as "Chot" Smith, but Chot Smith was born about this time. See Stephens and Erlich, eds., *The Shell Valley*, 87.

9. "Lynching Feared."

10. "A Triple Killing"; "Shot Down by Lynchers"; "Gorman and Walters Shot."

11. "Sheriff Wires for Militia," *Laramie Boomerang*, July 21, 1903; Davis, *A Vast of Amount of Trouble*, 13–14; Saban, "20th Century Vigilante Justice"; Rhodes, "All the World's a Stage," Mar. 28, 1940.

12. "Sheriff Wires for Militia" asserts that mob members were cattlemen (and, therefore, friendly to McCloud); two other articles assert they were both cattlemen and sheepmen. "Quiet in Northern Wyoming," *Laramie Boomerang*, July 22, 1903;

"Three Men Shot." Still another, "Shot to Death," *Thermopolis Record,* July 25, 1903, indicates that very little occurred.

13. "Sheriff Wires for Militia."

14. Rhodes, "All the World's a Stage," Mar. 21, 1940; Saban, "20th Century Vigilante Justice"; Rhodes, "The Road of Yesteryear."

15. Skovgard, *Basin City,* 57, 59; Saban, "20th Century Vigilante Justice," 42; "Black Page in Basin History."

16. In "20th Century Vigilante Justice," Saban cites 120 residents. The 1900 census figure is 146 people for the Basin Precinct (many of these people would have lived outside Basin). The most accurate source, though, is probably the May 1902 census of the town of Basin, reported by Skovgard in *Basin City,* 46–47, which shows 189 people at that time.

The description in this paragraph is taken primarily from Saban, "20th Century Vigilante Justice," 12, but also from other reports of men meeting at the Temple Lodge in Basin and staying at the Mountain View Hotel and the Antlers Hotel. See Skovgard, *Basin City,* 57; "Black Page in Basin History." Houses of prostitution were reported in operation in 1909. See Davis, *A Vast Amount of Trouble,* 92.

17. "Shot Down by Lynchers"; "Gorman and Walters Shot." Tillard is inaccurately referred to as "Filliard" in the former article, but the 1900 census and later articles, such as Saban's, show his correct name.

18. "Shot Down by Lynchers"; "Gorman and Walters Shot."

19. Rhodes, "All the World's a Stage," Mar. 21, 1940, provides an excellent description of the floor plan of the courthouse, and the following discussion follows this description closely. "Black Page in Basin History" is also helpful to show where the old courthouse was located.

20. "A Triple Killing"; "Shot Down by Lynchers." Unfortunately, the report of the local paper, the *Big Horn County Rustler,* is not available, although its stories might have been used by other newspapers. Contemporary information about the lynching comes almost entirely from newspaper reports, although there is a bit of information stemming from the subsequent grand jury indictments. The analysis here is a result of weighing the accuracy of the different reports.

21. "Gorman and Walters Shot." See also "Three Men Shot." "Shot to Death" reported that after Price had been shot, "Mead then ran into the clerk's office, shut the door and remained quiet."

22. "Black Page in Basin History." T. Walker reported that after the raid, Dr. Carter asked George Mead why he was crouched in a corner. Dr. Carter apparently stated that Mead "knew if he started for his gun, he would be killed just as Price had been so he had decided to keep out of the rain of bullets." *Big Horn Basin,* 233.

23. "Black Page in Basin History"; T. Walker, *Big Horn Basin,* 233.

24. "A Triple Killing"; "Shot Down by Lynchers."

25. "Shot to Death"; "A Triple Killing."

26. See "Black Page in Basin History" and the version given by Skovgard, *Basin City*, 58, wherein a witness stated, "It was an awful noise to hear in the night when the steel cells was ringing from the sledgehammer blows."

27. "Black Page in Basin History"; Rhodes, "All the World's a Stage," Mar. 23 and Apr. 4, 1940; Skovgard, *Basin City*, 57–58. The Antlers Hotel sat just east of the northeast corner of Fourth and C street, east of what is now a car wash.

28. Rhodes, "All the World's a Stage," Mar. 23, 1940; Skovgard, *Basin City*, 61.

29. "Shot to Death." Other reports, written many years after the event, describe different versions, such as "Black Page in Basin History," which states that Walters said, "There's no need to destroy county property, here I am." One of the more genteel descriptions of the killing states that Walters "was shot through the temple with death almost instantaneous." Saban, "20th Century Vigilante Justice," 42. Dr. Carter states that Walters was shot in both the right and the left temples. Carter, "C. Dana Carter, Pioneer Doctor," 17.

30. "Shot to Death" indicates that Walters came to the front of the cell before Gorman was shot, but Rhodes, in his writings, indicates that Gorman was first shot and then Walters. There being no strong basis to choose one version over the other, I assume that the contemporaneous report, "Shot to Death," is more reliable. See "A Triple Killing"; "Shot Down by Lynchers"; "Gorman and Walters Shot"; "Three Men Shot"; "Shot to Death."

31. "Three Men Shot" and "Gorman and Walters Shot" stated there were five volleys; "Shot Down by Lynchers" and "Murderers Shot," *Casper Derrick,* July 23, 1903, reported five bullets; and "Shot to Death" reported one bullet in the head and three in the body. Dr. C. Dana Carter states that Jim Gorman was shot five times; as a treating physician, Carter's statement should be accorded considerable weight. Carter, "C. Dana Carter, Pioneer Doctor," 17.

32. For instance, Skovgard, *Basin City*, 58, related a version of the raid apparently told about ten years after the event by Neil J. Anderson, the owner of the Antlers Hotel. In this report, Gorman tried to hide under the cell cot but was still shot.

33. T. Walker asserts that Guffy was innocent of horse stealing but was arrested because of mistaken identity. The district court journal does not indicate any charges filed against Guffy. T. Walker, *Big Horn Basin,* 242; Big Horn County Dist. Ct. Journal, vol. 1; Saban, "20th Century Vigilante Justice"; Carter, "C. Dana Carter, Pioneer Doctor," 17.

34. "Shot Down by Lynchers"; Rhodes, "All the World's a Stage," Mar. 28, 1940.

35. Skovgard, *Basin City,* 59.

36. Rhodes, "The Road of Yesteryear."

37. Skovgard, *Basin City,* 59. I am aware of no other report of this. If one or more of the lynchers were shot, it probably would have been reported in connection with the grand jury proceedings and subsequent trial, and it was not.

38. "Shot Down by Lynchers."

39. Ibid.; "Black Page in Basin History," This description comes primarily from "Shot Down by Lynchers," but also from Skovgard, *Basin City,* 61, and "Shot to Death," which further reported that Gorman was taken to Dr. Gillam's office, but all other references state that it was Dr. Carter's office, including *Basin City* and Carter, "C. Dana Carter, Pioneer Doctor." Dr. Carter is the only physician listed as a witness in the criminal charges against one of the mob for the murder of Walters, Gorman, and Price. See Big Horn County criminal cases 146, 147, and 148.

40. Zangrando, *The NAACP Crusade against Lynching*; "Shot Down by Lynchers."

41. Carter, "C. Dana Carter, Pioneer Doctor," 17.

42. The primary reference here is T. Walker, *Big Horn Basin,* 233, but also to articles that seem to follow Walker, such as that of Saban and Rhodes, "All the World's a Stage," Mar. 21, 1940. Some of this statement comes from "Shot to Death."

43. T. Walker, *Big Horn Basin*; Rhodes, "All the World's a Stage," all issues, and "The Road of Yesteryear"; and Saban, "20th Century Vigilante Justice."

44. Skovgard, *Basin City,* 59. Skovgard points out that the statement, apparently from Anderson, is dated 191_, meaning that it was provided sometime between 1910 and 1919.

45. Saban, "20th Century Vigilante Justice," 41.

46. Loveland, *Sagebrush and Roses,* 64.

47. Skovgard, *Basin City*, 62–63. The contemporaneous newspaper stories do not report this incident, but they are not inconsistent with it either. (Welling was located on the west side of the Big Horn River, about fifteen miles north of the present site of Worland.)

48. "Shot Down by Lynchers." See also Skovgard, *Basin City*, 62; "Quiet in Northern Wyoming."

49. "McCloud Case," *Thermopolis Record,* July 25, 1903.

50. "Quiet in Northern Wyoming."

51. "McCloud Case."

52. Wasden, *From Beaver to Oil,* 312.

53. "Quiet in Northern Wyoming."

54. "Sheriff Gets Warm Welcome," *Laramie Boomerang,* July 24, 1903.

55. "Quiet in Northern Wyoming."

56. Wasden reports that McCloud was claimed by federal authorities for robbing the post office in Buffalo. *From Beaver to Oil,* 313.

57. "Three Men Shot."

CHAPTER EIGHT

1. Cutler, *Lynch Law,* 1–6; Zangrando, *The NAACP Crusade Against Lynching,* 1. Cutler points out that the nearest thing to the practice of lynching found in Europe were the "summary measures" used against horse thieves in rural Russia, supposedly adopted because the crime was of great seriousness in that society and Russian law provided only a light penalty.

For an excellent discussion of the experience of members of the Church of Jesus Christ of Latter Day Saints (Mormons) before coming to the Great Salt Lake, see DeVoto, *The Year of Decision,* 76–98, and Arrington and Bitton, *The Mormon Experience,* chapters 3–5.

2. Zangrando, *The NAACP Crusade Against Lynching,* 5–8, shows that 3,446 of the total number of lynching victims were black, and that the total number of people killed in the named states was 3,443. Figures such as this are necessarily estimates, because of the difficulties in definition and, in some cases, the lack of clear information. When there are riots, with just general fighting, resultant deaths are not usually considered lynchings.

3. See Cutler, *Lynch Law,* 5–6, for an interesting discussion of the frontier example.

4. Hofstader and Wallace, *American Violence*; Dimsdale, *The Vigilantes of Montana.*

5. Dimsdale, *The Vigilantes of Montana.* Dimsdale clearly ignores the subsequent statement in the Declaration, that change should not be undertaken for "light and transient causes." Quotation from pp. 16–17.

6. Hofstader and Wallace, *American Violence,* 22; Dimsdale, *The Vigilantes of Montana,* 269; Gustafson, "History of Vigilante and Mob Activity in Wyoming," 53. See also Doob, *Social Psychology,* 288–89.

7. Larson, *History of Wyoming,* 44; Gustafson, "History of Vigilante and Mob Activity in Wyoming," 38, citing the *Wyoming Eagle,* Feb. 7, 1930.

8. Gustafson, "History of Vigilante and Mob Activity in Wyoming," 36–69, contains a thorough discussion of the activity of the Cheyenne vigilantes. See also 70–82.

9. Ibid., 85, 87. See also Larson, *History of Wyoming,* 60.

10. Gustafson, "History of Vigilante and Mob Activity in Wyoming," 88–90, which was taken in large part from chapter 5 of Pence and Homsher, *Ghost Towns of Wyoming.*

11. Gustafson, "History of Vigilante and Mob Activity in Wyoming," 104–109; Moulton, *Roadside History of Wyoming,* 247.

12. See Gustafson, "History of Vigilante and Mob Activity in Wyoming," 113–19.

13. Larson, *History of Wyoming,* 141–42.

14. See Larson, *History of Wyoming*, 269–70; Hufsmith, *The Wyoming Lynching of Cattle Kate*.

15. Gustafson, "History of Vigilante and Mob Activity in Wyoming," 134; Smith, *The War on Powder River*, 148–49; David, *Malcolm Campbell, Sheriff*, 143. This last book is a one-sided presentation of the Johnson County War, presenting the position of the big cattlemen.

16. Gustafson, "History of Vigilante and Mob Activity in Wyoming," 142–48. Probably the most reliable figure for the number lynched is thirty-four, which is the number stated by Brown in *You Are Respectfully Invited to Attend My Execution*, xiv, and by Zangrando, *The NAACP Crusade against Lynching*, 5. This number is generally supported by Gustafson in "History of Vigilante and Mob Activity in Wyoming." During territorial days, however, only seven were legally executed (see Brown), and it seems unlikely that in the following thirteen years, twenty-seven more people were legally executed. In the course of producing this volume, including a review of most criminal cases decided by the Wyoming Supreme Court between 1890 and 1903, I came across only three cases in which the penalty of death was carried out: those of Charles Miller in 1892 and Tom Horn and James Keffer in 1903.

CHAPTER NINE

1. Biennial Report of the Attorney General to the Governor of Wyoming, 1903–1904, 4, records of the Wyoming Attorney General.

2. *Sheridan Post*, editorial, July 23, 1903.

3. "Cattlemen Are to Blame," *Laramie Boomerang*, July 25, 1903.

4. "Murderers Shot"; "Shot Down by Lynchers."

5. "A Triple Killing"; Chatterton to Big Horn County commissioners, telegram, July 21, 1902, Governor Fenimore Chatterton Records.

6. "Demands Action," *Wyoming Tribune*, July 22, 1903. For instance, in the recent well-known prosecution in Laramie of the killers of Matthew Shepard, a notorious and expensive case, Albany County bore virtually all the cost. Jeffrey A. Donnell, district judge, Second Judicial District, interview by author, Sept. 5, 2003; "Governor Chatterton Is Opposed to Lynching and Is Not Afraid to Say So," *Wyoming Tribune*, July 22, 2003.

7. "Quiet in Northern Wyoming." Another factor in Chatterton's public tough-guy posturing might have been the governor's refusal to show leniency to Tom Horn. Despite strong pressure to commute Horn's death sentence, Chatterton did not, and Horn was hanged in November 1903. See Larson, *History of Wyoming*, 271–74.

8. "A Lynching," *Cheyenne Daily Leader*, Oct. 25, 1903.

9. Ibid. This was the first grand jury ever convened in Big Horn County. As will be seen, it was 1909 before another grand jury was called.

10. Big Horn County Dist. Ct. Journal, vol. 1, 543–44; 1900 census, Basin Precinct.

11. "Return Indictments," *Cheyenne Daily Leader,* Oct. 27, 1903; Cutler, Lynch Law, 255.

12. "Prosecute Mob," *Cheyenne Daily Leader,* Oct. 27, 1903.

13. "Return Indictments."

14. "Eight Indictments," *Cheyenne Daily Leader,* Oct. 30, 1903; "Nearing the End," *Cheyenne Daily Leader,* Nov. 1, 1903.

15. See *State v. James G. Tatlock,* Big Horn County criminal case 133; *State v. George Saban,* Big Horn County criminal case 134; *State v. Tyancum T. Taylor,* Big Horn County criminal case 137; *State v. Ralph Mercer,* Big Horn County criminal case 140; *State v. Colin F. Mackenzie* [McKenzie], Big Horn County criminal case 143; *State v. Daniel Lee Morse,* Big Horn County criminal case 146; *State v. Walter Feuder,* Big Horn County criminal case 149; *State v. Orville Hardee,* Big Horn County criminal case 152. Each man is charged in separate counts with the murder of Gorman, Walters, and Price.

16. "Saban in Toils," *Cheyenne Daily Leader,* Oct. 29, 1903; "Leaders of Mob," *Cheyenne Daily Leader,* Oct. 25, 1903; "Basin Court," *Wyoming Tribune,* Apr. 19, 1904; Rhodes, "The Rest That Came," 11. It was later remarked that if Saban had been convicted of the lynching of Jim Gorman, the Spring Creek Raid would never have occurred. Skovgard, *Basin City,* 64.

17. 1900 census, Horse Creek Precinct; Stephens and Erlich, eds., *The Shell Valley,* citing Vera Saban, 103, 105. Vera Saban, who was George Saban's daughter-in-law, states that he was only sixteen when he left home, but that he came to Shell in 1888. These are inconsistent; George Saban would have turned only fifteen in October 1888.

18. Friends of the Old Pen, *Sweet Smell of Sagebrush*; wanted poster for George Saban (see the figure later in this chapter); and Davis, *A Vast Amount of Trouble,* chap. 3, n. 9. Rhodes, "The Rest That Came," 9, n. 3.

19. Stephens and Ehrlich, eds., *The Shell Valley*, citing Vera Saban, 106; Davis, *A Vast Amount of Trouble,* 23.

20. See "Eight Indictments" and "Trial of Basin Mob Leaders On," *Cheyenne Daily Leader*, Apr. 20, 1904; Big Horn County Dist. Ct. Journal, vol. 1, 562. Apparently, all the men arrested were released on bail. The bail amounts per charge are found at *State v. Saban,* Big Horn County criminal cases 134, 135, and 136.

21. See 38 A.C.J.S., *Grand Juries,* §§ 176–179; Big Horn County Dist. Ct. Journal, vol. 1, 562–63.

22. "Eight Indictments"; "Nearing the End."

23. "Nearing the End."

24. Big Horn County Dist. Ct. Journal, vol. 1, 577; Challenge to Array and Motion to Quash Panel of Petit Jury, *State v. Tatlock*; affidavit of J. J. Fenton, *State v.*

Tatlock; "Peculiar Outcome of Jury Drawing," *Cheyenne Daily Leader*, Apr. 23, 1904. Of the jury panel members subsequently selected on Apr. 22, only one was from Burlington.

25. "Basin Court"; Big Horn County Dist. Ct. Journal, vol. 1, 618; "Alleged Leader," *Cheyenne Daily Leader*, Apr. 27, 1904.

26. "Alleged Leader"; "Fear of Rescue," *Cheyenne Daily Leader,* Apr. 28, 1904.

27. Big Horn County Dist. Ct. Journal, vol. 1, 629; Rhodes was also chosen for this jury, but he was excused by the defense. "Dan Lee Morse Goes Scott Free, *Cheyenne Daily Leader,* Apr. 29, 1904; "Lynching Case Dismissed," *Sheridan Post,* Apr. 29, 1904.

28. Session Laws of Wyoming, ch. 11 (1905).

CHAPTER TEN

1. Gustafson, "History of Vigilante and Mob Activity in Wyoming," 97.

2. For example, the Bay State near Ten Sleep and the LU on Grass Creek. The LU owned more lands, but most of them were not patented until the twentieth century, and the pattern that emerged was of forty-acre parcels running all the way up Grass Creek to the national forest. Virtually all of the vastly greater acreage around this property was owned by the federal government or the State of Wyoming. See Davis, *A Vast Amount of Trouble,* 2, 3.

3. Frison, *First White Woman in the Big Horn Basin,* 55.

4. Rollins, *The Struggle of the Cattlemen,* 286. Throughout the nineteenth century, the Congress forwarded a number of land-distribution arrangements. By the 1880s, a homesteader had the right to proceed under several different acts, including the 1862 Homestead Act, the Desert Land Entry Act, and the Pre-emption Act.

5. See Wentworth, *America's Sheep Trails,* 524.

6. Davis, *A Vast Amount of Trouble,* 12, map on 39.

7. Wentworth, *America's Sheep Trails,* 524.

8. O'Neal, *Cattlemen v. Sheepherders,* 97.

9. Davis, *A Vast Amount of Trouble,* 13.

10. Ibid., 14; Edgar and Turnell, *Lady of a Legend,* 36–37.

11. Wentworth, *America's Sheep Trails,* 525; Wasden, *Beaver to Oil,* 142; and "Law Abiding Be Damned!" *Garland Guard,* Aug. 25, 1905. See also Davis, *A Vast Amount of Trouble,* 14, 23, n. 15.

12. Davis, *A Vast Amount of Trouble,* 15.

13. Stephens and Erlich, eds., *The Shell Valley,* citing Richard Whaley and Stan Flitner, 89.

14. Wasden, *From Beaver to Oil,* 141.

15. Davis, *A Vast Amount of Trouble,* 9–10, 16, 62–63. LeFors was a renowned detective, a controversial figure held responsible for, among other things, the

conviction and execution of Tom Horn. There is a great deal of writing about LeFors, including his own autobiography, *Wyoming Peace Officer,* and Carlson, *Tom Horn.*

16. Legislation that assisted these developments included the important Carey Act, named for Wyoming senator Joseph M. Carey. See Larson, *History of Wyoming,* 303. Carey Act projects had already been undertaken by Solon Lysander Wiley on the Greybull River and William F. Cody on the Stinking Water. The large irrigation canals around Worland are all Carey Act projects.

17. Woods, *Wyoming's Big Horn Basin,* 230–31. The best description of Robertson's efforts is found in his own book, *A History of the Worland Valley.*

18. Pendergraft, *Washakie,* 72–74.

19. Woods, *Wyoming's Big Horn Basin,* 233–35; Skovgard, *Basin City,* 73–74.

20. The 1910 census. In 1910, Park County was separately enumerated, even though it would not officially be a county until January 1911. The figure in the text is Park County (4,909) in addition to the population of those still in Big Horn County (8,886).

21. The town of Worland in 1906 grew immediately to about 300, virtually none of whom was a rancher. See Davis, *Sadie and Charlie,* 17.

22. Woods, *Wyoming's Big Horn Basin,* 227–28.

23. Ibid., 193; Davis, *Sadie and Charlie,* 20.

24. Skovgard, *Basin City,* 31, 72; Davis, *A Vast Amount of Trouble,* 16.

25. Saban, *He Wore a Stetson,* 2, 44; Davis, *A Vast Amount of Trouble,* 16.

CHAPTER ELEVEN

1. 1903 tax assessment roll, 48. See Davis, *A Vast Amount of Trouble,* 25, and chap. 3, note 34; Rhodes, "The Rest That Came," 15.

2. See Davis, *A Vast Amount of Trouble,* 27; quotation from Rhodes, "The Rest That Came," 16. Spring Creek empties into the Nowood about seven miles south of Ten Sleep, and Otter Creek, about twelve miles south of Ten Sleep. As with virtually every tributary of the Nowood, they flow east to west, coming down off the Big Horn Mountains.

3. See 11 Mortgages 173 of the records of the Big Horn County Clerk. This mortgage recites $5,800 as the debt secured but also notes two other mortgages against the property, one for $4,500 and one for $1,700. Charles E. Shaw, grand jury testimony, 2, 3, Lola Homsher Collection, American Heritage Center, Laramie; Rhodes, "The Rest That Came," 17; Davis, *A Vast Amount of Trouble,* 49.

4. Davis, *A Vast Amount of Trouble,* 49. See C. D. Helmer, grand jury testimony, 190, 196, 203, Lola Homsher Collection; testimony in State v. Brink, trial transcript, 24, Archives Division, Wyoming Department of Parks and Cultural Resources. Regarding the guns, see trial transcript, 5, 55, 66. These guns were formidable

weapons in 1909 and are found today in the collection of the Washakie Museum, Worland, Wyoming.

5. Rhodes, "The Rest That Came," 18–19.

6. Frank Greet to Edna Greet, "Recollections of the Spring Creek Raid," 4, American Heritage Center, Laramie; *State v. Brink* trial transcript, 107.

7. Davis, *A Vast Amount of Trouble,* 47–49 and chap. 4, n. 15; trial transcript, 11; Lamb, grand jury testimony, 3, 9–10; Fred Greet, grand jury testimony, 4–6; Fred Greet, "Recollections," 3.

8. Fred Greet, grand jury testimony, 6, 14, 19; Lamb, grand jury testimony, 3, 6, 9; Frank Greet, "Recollections," 3; trial transcript, 3, 4, 34–35, 118–19.

9. Frank Greet, "Recollections," 3; Lamb, grand jury testimony, 3, 6, 9; Fred Greet, grand jury testimony, 3, 6, 19; Alston, grand jury testimony, 1–3; trial transcript, 52, 89.

10. Trial transcript, 5, 35, 39, 45, 53–55; Frank Greet, "Recollections."

11. G. W. Walker, grand jury testimony, 3, 4; trial transcript, 95, 101.

12. Trial transcript, 5, 32, 36, 37, 55, 66, 199. It is not completely clear that Cafferal was with Helmer then, but he probably was.

13. Trial transcript, 182.

14. C. D. Helmer, grand jury testimony, 10; trial transcript, 187; Davis, *A Vast Amount of Trouble,* 28.

15. C. D. Helmer, grand jury testimony, 12–13; trial transcript, 197.

16. Alston, grand jury testimony, 3–4, 5; trial transcript, 9, 12, 15, 19, 31, 33, 59, 65, 81, 85.

17. See Davis, *A Vast Amount of Trouble,* 59.

CHAPTER TWELVE

1. Enders to Brooks, Apr. 5, 1909, Sheep Raid File.

2. "Raiders Assassinate and Burn," *Cheyenne Daily Leader,* Apr. 7, 1909.

3. "Two Bodies Furnish Food for Flames," *Worland Grit,* Apr. 8, 1909; "Two Sheep Men and Herder are Killed," *Big Horn County Rustler,* Apr. 9, 1909.

4. "Three Sheepmen Murdered," *Basin Republican,* Apr. 9, 1909.

5. "Eaton Charged with Complicity in Murder," *Big Horn County Rustler,* Apr. 16, 1909. It is hard to establish exactly, but I estimate that the value of this money was somewhere between twenty and thirty times the present value of money. See Davis, Sadie and Charlie, 62 and 74, for a discussion of comparable values of money between the years 1915 and 1989. Delfelder to Brooks, Apr. 12, 1909, Sheep Raid File.

6. I am not aware of anyone from the State of Wyoming ever accepting this argument, however. At a much later time, 1980, the State of Wyoming, through the Wyoming Supreme Court, did declare that education was a fundamental right and

that the State of Wyoming could not avoid its responsibility to educate the state's children by simply turning over education to local authorities while providing taxing mechanisms that resulted in hugely disparate monies available to students within the state. See *Washakie County School District 1 v. Herschler,* 606 P.2d 310 (Wyo. 1980).

7. Larson reports that in 1899, the Wyoming legislature appropriated $18,000 for the costs of the cases. Larson, *History of Wyoming,* 279.

8. Delfelder to Wyoming Woolgrowers executive committee, Apr. 12, 1909, Sheep Raid File.

9. "Eaton Charged with Complicity in Murder." See Davis, *Sadie and Charlie,* 62, for an idea of prices of homes in Worland in 1918, a time when absolute prices had risen because of the inflationary effect of World War I.

10. Percy W. Metz, speech to the Park County Historical Society, June 9, 1961, Archives Division, Wyoming Department of State Parks and Cultural Resources; "Special Counsel Is Employed," *Big Horn County Rustler,* Apr. 30, 1909; "Four Indictments for Each Man," *Basin Republican,* May 14, 1909.

11. Davis, *A Vast Amount of Trouble,* 32.

12. Trial testimony of John Callahan, Sam Brant, George Walters, Walt Richie, John Buckmaster, and Mary Buckmaster, trial transcript, 281–99; Davis, *A Vast Amount of Trouble,* chap. 3, n. 17; Trial transcript, 323–24.

13. Cole, grand jury testimony, 3, 12; Davis, *A Vast Amount of Trouble,* 69, 101, 215.

14. "Eaton Charged with Complicity in Murder"; Davis, *A Vast Amount of Trouble,* 72; trial transcript, 186, 201–202; Davis, *A Vast Amount of Trouble,* 189.

15. "Eaton Charged with Complicity in Murder"; Davis, *A Vast Amount of Trouble,* 73; "Second Arrest for Spring Creek Raid," *Basin Republican,* Apr. 23, 1909.

16. See "Cowboy Said to Know about a Murder Is Jailed," *Denver Post,* Apr. 21, 1909, which states that Percy Metz had "'conclusive evidence' in the case."

17. Trial transcript, 199–201; Walter Nelson, grand jury testimony, 3; Rufus Barrington, grand jury testimony, 2; Davis, *A Vast Amount of Trouble,* 103.

18. Brooks to Huntington Wilson, acting secretary of state, May 7, 1909, Sheep Raid File. See also Parmelee to Brooks, Apr. 7, 1909, and Brooks to Parmelee, Apr. 10, 1909, Sheep Raid File; "Special Counsel Is Employed."

CHAPTER THIRTEEN

1. Percy W. Metz, speech to the Park County Historical Society, June 9, 1961.

2. "Fifty Witnesses Are Summoned," *The Basin Republican,* Apr. 30, 1909; O'Neal, *Cattlemen v. Sheepherders,* 95, 120. See also Davis, *A Vast Amount of Trouble,* 10.

3. In its Apr. 30, 1909, and May 7, 1909, issues, the *Basin Republican* printed the entire charge to the grand jury, apparently verbatim, and the entire discussion here comes directly from what was published in this newspaper.

4. Morton, grand jury testimony, n. p.; Alston, grand jury testimony, n. p.; trial transcript, 47. This map is not found in any of the court documents, but in January 1989, the Northwest Chapter of Professional Land Surveyors of Wyoming replicated the map using the original field notes of Clyde Atherly. This map is printed in Davis, *A Vast Amount of Trouble,* 163.

5. Bounce was at Dietz, near Sheridan, at the ranch of a sheepman, Bill Wagner. See trial transcript, 195. C. D. Helmer, grand jury testimony, 17, 19, 23; Cafferal, grand jury testimony, 7, 9, 10, 13; Lamb, grand jury testimony, 3, 4, 10–14; Fred Greet, grand jury testimony, 2, 8, 14–20.

6. See Walt Ritchie, grand jury testimony, 3–6; W. G. Colethorpe, grand jury testimony and trial testimony, 304–306; George Rogers, grand jury testimony, 2–3; Lizzie Lamb, grand jury testimony, 1; Davis, *A Vast Amount of Trouble,* 79–81.

7. See Davis, *A Vast Amount of Trouble,* 81–82.

8. Summary of grand jury testimony, Lola Homsher Collection; Billy Goodrich, trial testimony, 337.

9. Anna Goodrich, grand jury testimony, 6, 7, 9.

10. Davis, *A Vast Amount of Trouble,* 83–84.

11. Cole, grand jury testimony, 2, 3, 8, 11–13.

12. Brink, grand jury testimony, 4–6; Davis, *A Vast Amount of Trouble,* 86–87.

13. Davis, *A Vast Amount of Trouble,* 71, 88, 92; trial transcript, 373; Percy W. Metz, speech to the Natrona County Historical Society, Nov. 2, 1961, Archives Division, Wyoming Department of State Parks and Cultural Resources, Cheyenne, Wyoming.

14. "More Arrests in Tensleep Case," *Thermopolis Record,* May 8, 1909; "Witness Before Grand Jury Takes Own Life," *Big Horn County Rustler,* May 7, 1909; "William Garrison Commits Suicide," *Basin Republican,* May 7, 1909.

15. Davis, *A Vast Amount of Trouble,* 95–103; G. W. Walker, grand jury testimony, 4, 6. Dr. Walker later concluded that the wound was probably caused by a ricocheting bullet. Trial transcript, 88–96.

16. "Grand Jury Names Seven," *Cheyenne Daily Leader,* May 8, 1909.

17. "Seven Men Are Held for Murder," *Big Horn County Rustler,* May 7, 1909; "Four Indictments for Each Man."

18. Alston to Brooks, May 7, 1909, Sheep Raid File.

19. Percy W. Metz, speeches to the Park County Historical Society, June 9, 1961, and the Big Horn County Historical Society in Lovell, Mar. 1, 1962.

20. Trial transcript, 207–243, 252–256, 258–59, 260–64.

21. See Baber, *The Longest Rope*. For contrast, see David, *Malcolm Campbell, Sheriff*, 313–20, which presents an antiseptic version of the taking of two trappers, Jones and Walker.

22. "Two Thought to Have Confessed," *Big Horn County Rustler*, May 14, 1909; "Say Two Confess Murders," *Billings Gazette*, May 12, 1909; "Two Make Confession," *Thermopolis Record*, May 15, 1909; and "Confessions by Two Murderers," *Cheyenne State Leader*, May 11, 1909.

23. Trial transcript, 188.

24. Davis, *A Vast Amount of Trouble*, 25; Joseph Reculsa, grand-nephew of Chabot, interview by author, Jan. 7, 2003; Big Horn County 1903 tax assessment roll, 48; Chabot to the ambassador to France, Apr. 16, 1909, Sheep Raid Files.

25. Embassy of the French Republic to Chabot to the ambassador to France, Apr. 24, 1909, Sheep Raid Files; Brooks to Parmelee, May 7, 1909, Sheep Raid Files.

26. Brooks to Wilson, May 7, 1909, Sheep Raid Files.

CHAPTER FOURTEEN

1. The figures cited ranged from $20,000 to $200,000. O'Neal, *Cattlemen v. Sheepherders*, 143; "Militia Called to Stop Intimidation in Tensleep Cases," *Denver Post*, Oct. 31, 1909; "Herbert Brink Arrested," *Big Horn County Rustler*, Apr. 23, 1909. Eaton was not in good financial shape; he was trying to put together a cattle herd after a business in Basin, the Luxus Bar, did not work out. Rhodes, "The Rest That Came," 13; Davis, *A Vast Amount of Trouble*, 23.

2. "Charge to the Grand Jury," *Basin Republican*, 30 Apr. 30, 1909; "Address to Grand Jury," *Basin Republican*, May 7, 1909.

3. Alston to Brooks, July 1, 1909 and July 8, 1909, Sheep Raid File; Davis, *A Vast Amount of Trouble*, 265. The Republican Party was closely identified with big cattle interests in 1892, and the voters of Wyoming punished the party after the Johnson County Invasion. See Larson, *History of Wyoming*, 284.

4. "Broken Political Promises," *Basin Republican*, May 21, 1909.

5. "Judge Metz Puts It Up to Commissioners," *Big Horn County Rustler*, May 28, 1909.

6. Ibid.; "The 'Explanation' Was Made," *Basin Republican*, June 4, 1909.

7. "The Story of Percival the Young," *Basin Republican*, June 4, 1909.

8. Henderson to Brooks, May 20, 1909, Sheep Raid File.

9. "The 'Explanation' Was Made." The cattlemen employed more lawyers than the prosecution, some ten or twelve, and in the one demonstration of a raider's attorney fees, those fees were higher than those taken by any of the lawyers for the state. In *Stotts v. Saban*, Big Horn County civil case 1007, Joseph L. Stotts brought an

action for fees, indicating that his total fee was $4,500. Stotts was not even the principal trial attorney for his side, as were William Metz and E. E. Enterline.

10. Alston to Brooks, May 7, 1909, and May 11, 1909, Sheep Raid File; Percy W. Metz, speeches to the Big Horn County Historical Society, Mar. 2, 1962, and to the Natrona County Historical Society, Nov. 2, 1961; Brooks to Alston, May 11, 1909, Sheep Raid File.

11. *Basin Republican,* May 21, 1909.

12. Biennial Report of the Adjutant General, 1909–1910, Archives Division, Wyoming Department of State Parks and Cultural Resources.

13. "Why Has Militia Been Employed?" *Basin Republican,* June 11, 1909; Davis, *A Vast Amount of Trouble,* 123.

14. "Why Has Militia Been Employed?"

15. The man providing all the jailhouse reports was the author of *Sweet Smell of Sagebrush,* published by Friends of the Old Pen, who was probably William Stanley; see *Sweet Smell of Sagebrush,* 90, 92, 94.

16. W. L. Simpson to Brooks, Oct. 16, 1909, Sheep Raid File.

17. Brooks to W. L. Simpson, Oct. 18, 1909, Sheep Raid File; Enterline to Mullen, Oct. 29, 1909, Percy W. Metz Collection. See also Davis, *A Vast Amount of Trouble,* 139–40.

18. "Soldiers Guarding Tensleep Murder Case Witnesses," *Denver Post,* Oct. 30, 1909, and Oct. 31, 1909; W. S. Collins to Brooks, telegram, Nov. 2, 1909, Sheep Raid File; "Recall the Militia," *Basin Republican,* Nov. 4, 1909; Gatchell to Brooks, undated, Sheep Raid File; Brooks to W. S. Collins, telegram, Nov. 8, 1909, Sheep Raid File.

19. W. L. Simpson to Brooks, Oct. 16, 1909, Sheep Raid File.

20. "Trial of Alleged Slayers of Ten Sleep Men Is On," *Denver Post,* Nov. 3, 1909; "Recall the Militia."

21. Davis, *A Vast Amount of Trouble,* 142.

22. Plea in abatement, *State v. George Saban,* Big Horn County criminal case 401.

23. See "Attacks Grand Jury," *Basin Republican,* Oct. 22, 1909; "Saban Charges Win," *Basin Republican,* Oct. 29, 1909; and "Defense Attacks Legality of Jury List," *Big Horn County Rustler,* Oct. 22, 1909; "Information Filed Against Five Men," *Big Horn County Rustler,* Oct. 29, 1909.

24. "Saban Charges Win"; "District Court Proceedings," *Worland Grit,* Oct. 28, 1909. The *Republican* and the *Worland Grit* used identical phrases about ozone and the "most righteous" decision.

25. "The Rapid Growth of Big Horn County," *Worland Grit,* Nov. 4, 1909.

CHAPTER FIFTEEN

1. Davis, *A Vast Amount of Trouble,* 147–48. Regarding the guns, see Nelson, *The Big Horn Basin,* 43. Appearance Page, trial transcript, *State v. Brink.*

2. "Brinks Jury's Ready," *Basin Republican,* Nov. 5, 1909; "Trial of Herbert Brink Is Now On," *Big Horn County Rustler*, Nov. 5, 1909; Davis, *A Vast Amount of Trouble,* 156, n. 16. It is stretching the point to include W. W. Rhea of Shell, but people in the Shell area, although not within the deadline, were of a like mind to those along the Nowood. "Ten Sleep Trial Open; Get Jury in Record Time," *Denver Post,* Nov. 5, 1909; G. S. Walker, comp., *Sheep Owners of Wyoming.*

3. See the discussion in Davis, *Vast Amount of Trouble,* 140–41, regarding a letter by C. M. Jones to Governor Brooks, wherein Jones told the governor that the people from Shell to the head of the Nowood were "insane" regarding sheep and sheepmen.

4. Davis, *A Vast Amount of Trouble,* 151; Record of Challenges, *State v. Brink.*

5. Record of Challenges. Regarding Denver Jake Winslow, see Davis, *Worland Before Worland,* 2–3.

6. Davis, *A Vast Amount of Trouble,* 153; Percy W. Metz, speeches to the Natrona County Historical Society, Nov. 2, 1961, and the Big Horn County Historical Society, Mar. 1, 1962; 1900 census, Hyattville Precinct.

7. "Surprised to Secure Jury at Once," *Cheyenne Daily Leader,* Nov. 5, 1909; "Trial of Herbert Brink Is Now On"; "Keyes Makes a Confession," *Thermopolis Record,* Nov. 6, 1909.

8. Until 2001, I had no notion that a photograph of the jury existed. In early 2001, though, Karma Smith of Salt Lake City wrote and informed me that her grandfather, C. E. Nielson, had been on a jury involving a clash in the sheep and cattle wars, and she had a picture showing her grandfather and other jurors. There is no question that this photograph is of the Spring Creek Raid jury. Nielson, in fact, was listed as member of the jury; in addition, the foreman, W. H. Packard, is identifiable, as is the sheriff, Felix Alston. Further, Smith knew of another man on the jury with her father, Charles Duncan, and there was a Charles Duncan on the Spring Creek Raid jury. See Saxton, *The Packard Legacy,* 137; 1910 census for Park County and Big Horn County, Wyoming. Of the men in the photograph, only three have been identified, Packard, C. E. Nielson, in the front row (seated second from right), and Sheriff Alston (standing).

9. Regarding Duncan, see Big Horn County 1910 census. Nielson was identified by his granddaughter, Karma Smith, who stated that he had married her grandmother in Draper, Utah, in 1897. Cowley has been a Mormon colony from the beginning, and even today, most of its population consists of members of the Church of Jesus Christ of Latter Day Saints. In his long lectures about the Spring Creek Raid, Percy Metz never mentions the religious faith of the jury, not even that the eventual foreman, W. H. Packard, was the first bishop in Burlington.

10. "Brink's Jury Ready," *Basin Republican,* Nov. 5, 1909; "Trial of Herbert Brink Is Now On"; "Brink Is Guilty," *Big Horn County Rustler,* Nov. 12, 1909; "Is Guilty of Murder," *Basin Republican,* Nov. 12, 1909.

11. Trial transcript, 2–34, 37–38.

12. Ibid., 47–50.

13. Ibid., 55, 63, 66, 69, 78–82, 99.

14. Ibid., 86–88.

15. Ibid., 88–98, 103.

16. Ibid., 108–109, 111, 113–24.

17. Ibid., 127.

18. "Brink Shot Allemand Confesses Cattleman on Stand at Basin," *Rocky Mountain News,* Nov. 7, 1909.

19. C. D. Helmer, grand jury testimony, 1, 10, 14–17, 19, 20, 23; Davis, *A Vast Amount of Trouble,* 102–103.

20. Trial transcript, 175–77.

21. Ibid., 179, 181, 184.

22. Ibid., 186.

23. Ibid., 188–89, 191, 195–200. See the subpoena dated November 2, 1909, issued on behalf of Herbert Brink in the case of *State v. Brink,* Big Horn County criminal case 443.

24. Trial transcript, 201–203.

25. See Davis, *A Vast Amount of Trouble,* 176, 188–89.

26. Trial transcript, 205–208, 210–211, 221, 223–24, 227; Percy Metz, speeches to the Natrona County Historical Society, Park County Historical Society, and Big Horn County Historical Society, Archives Division, Wyoming Department of State Parks and Cultural Resources.

27. Trial transcript, 233, 236, 239.

28. Ibid., 245. Faris did not tell the jury of one interesting aspect of his life, that he had been born in Montana in 1872, meaning that his parents had come to Montana when that country was raw, and that he had lived his whole life in the West. 1903 tax assessment roll, 49.

29. Trial transcript, 255–58.

30. Ibid., 258–61. Regarding the testimony that Allemand was "stooped," Allemand had probably been hit by a ricocheting bullet in his collarbone and had great difficulty standing straight and raising his hands.

31. Ibid., 266–67, 271–72.

32. "Is Guilty of Murder"; "Eye-Witness Tells of Murder of Unarmed Men," *Denver Post,* Nov. 7, 1909.

CHAPTER SIXTEEN

1. See *Clay v. State,* 15 Wyo. 42, 86 Pac. 17 (1906).

2. Trial transcript, 274–81.

3. Ibid., 281–90, 294–301. The witnesses were John Rogers, Walt Richie, John Buckmaster, and Mary Buckmaster.

4. Trial transcript, 302–315.

5. See Davis, *A Vast Amount of Trouble*, 30, 206; trial transcript, 321–29.

6. Billy's nickname was "pis-ant." Howard McClellan, interview by author, Mar. 15, 1991. Goodrich was slight, about five foot three or five foot four. See Davis, *A Vast Amount of Trouble*, 29–30.

7. Trial transcript, 331–35.

8. Ibid., 336–38.

9. Ibid., 339–40.

10. In the opening statement in the case of *State v. Dixon*, the prosecution did announce that Dixon had made admissions to Goodrich. "Trial of Thomas Dixon Has Begun," *Big Horn County Rustler*, Nov. 19, 1909; "Jury for Second Murder Trial in Basin Is Secured," *Denver Post*, Nov. 12, 1909.

11. Trial transcript, 347–49, 367, 378; Davis, *A Vast Amount of Trouble*, 212.

12. See John I. Tierney, "Both Sides Rest in Brink Murder Trial at Basin," *Denver Post*, Nov. 9, 1909; trial transcript, 355.

13. Ibid., 356–61.

14. Ibid., 361–67, 372–74, 378–79, 381.

15. "Astonishingly Weak Defense Set Forth on Behalf of Brink," *Cheyenne Daily Leader*, Nov. 9, 1909; Davis, *A Vast Amount of Trouble*, 218.

16. Instruction nos. 1, 24, 26–28, *State v. Brink*.

17. W. S. Metz to Jennie Metz, Nov. 14, 1909, Percy W. Metz Collection. See also "Leading Features of the Argument," *Big Horn County Rustler*, Nov. 12, 1909, which sets out this argument in great detail and is the source of the following discussion about the argument.

18. "Attorney Grills Accused Slayer of Sheep Herder," *Denver Post*, Nov. 10, 1909; "Is Guilty of Murder." See the surveyor's map in Davis, *A Vast Amount of Trouble*, 163, which shows the location of places where shots were fired. The .30–30 shells, the caliber of Faris's rifle, were found at more southerly spots. See also Davis, *A Vast Amount of Trouble*, 58, n. 43.

19. W. S. Metz served as the district judge between 1893 and 1897, when he resigned in the face of impeachment proceedings before the Wyoming legislature. "Judge Metz Resigns," *Wind River Mountaineer*, Feb. 8, 1897.

20. The *Basin Republican*, in its November 12, 1909, edition ("Is Guilty of Murder"), provided thorough, almost verbatim coverage of the arguments of the defense attorneys.

21. Just as the *Basin Republican* provided thorough coverage of the defense arguments, the *Big Horn County Rustler*, on November 12, 1909, provided thorough coverage of all the prosecution arguments ("Leading Features of the Argument").

22. "Brink's Life Forfeit for Murder of Joe Allemand," *Cheyenne State Leader,* Nov. 12, 1909.

23. "Brink Is Guilty"; Davis, *A Vast Amount of Trouble,* 247; "Brink's Life Forfeit for Murder of Joe Allemand."

24. See Wyo. Stat. Ann. § 7–11–107 (2002).

25. "Brink Is Guilty"; John I. Tierney, "Brink Guilty of Murder, Says Jury," *Denver Post,* Nov. 11, 1909.

26. "Brink Is Guilty."

27. Tierney, "Brink Guilty of Murder, Says Jury"; "Brink is Guilty"; "Brink's Life Forfeit for Murder of Joe Allemand"; "This Morning the Jury Returned with a Verdict of Murder in First Degree."

28. See Davis, *A Vast Amount of Trouble,* chap. 17, n. 16; Lewis is incorrectly identified as being a carpenter from Byron. "Trial of Thomas Dixon Has Begun," *Big Horn County Rustler,* Nov. 19, 1909. Like Byron and Cowley, Kane was another predominately Mormon area.

29. Friends of the Old Pen, *Sweet Smell of Sagebrush,* 98; John I. Tierney, "Murderers of Sheep Men All Plead Guilty," *Denver Post,* Nov. 13, 1909; Davis, *A Vast Amount of Trouble,* 231–32.

30. Tierney, "Murderers of Sheep Men All Plead Guilty"; Percy W. Metz, speech to the Natrona County Historical Society, Nov. 2, 1961; "Four Plead Guilty," *Big Horn County Rustler,* Nov. 19, 1909. For a detailed discussion of all the negotiations, see Davis, *A Vast Amount of Trouble,* 230–31.

31. "Enact Final Scenes," *Basin Republican,* Nov. 19, 1909; "Four Plead Guilty"; Sentence, *State v. Saban*; Sentence, *State v. Milton A. Alexander*, Big Horn County criminal case 433; Petitions for Pardon (Brink) File (the date of the commutation was December 18, 1909); Sentence, *State v. Thomas Dixon*, Big Horn County criminal case 435; Sentence, *State v. Ed Eaton,* Big Horn County criminal case 449.

32. "Brink's Life Forfeit for Murder of Joe Allemand."

33. See Davis, *A Vast Amount of Trouble,* 244, 261.

34. Coons, Editorial, *Rocky Mountain News,* Nov. 5, 1909; "Two Confess a Part in Murder of Sheep Men," *Denver Post,* Nov. 6, 1909.

EPILOGUE

1. "State Witnesses Depart," *Big Horn County Rustler,* Nov. 19, 1909; "Enact Final Scenes"; O'Neal, *Cattlemen v. Sheepherders,* 146–47.

2. See citations and discussion in Davis, *A Vast Amount of Trouble,* 237. See also "State Witnesses Depart."

3. "Herbert Brink's Feelings," *Sheridan Enterprise,* Nov. 23, 1909; "The District Court," *Worland Grit,* Nov. 25, 1909; "'Bitter Fate,' Says Herbert Brink," *Basin*

Republican, Nov. 26, 1909; Rhodes, "The Rest That Came," 46; Percy W. Metz, speech to the Natrona County Historical Society, Nov. 2, 1962.

4. "The District Court," *Worland Grit,* Nov. 26, 1909.

5. Davis, *A Vast Amount of Trouble,* 239–40; "Will Take Down the Coin," *Basin Republican,* Dec. 10, 1909, citing Cody Enterprise.

6. "Summary of Incomplete Unofficial Vote Big Horn County," *Basin Republican,* Nov. 11, 1910; Rhodes, "The Rest That Came," 46; Friends of the Old Pen, *Sweet Smell of Sagebrush,* 125; Saban, *He Wore a Stetson,* 63.

7. See *Alexander v. State,* 20 Wyo. 241, 250, 123 Pac. 68 (1912); *State v. Saban,* Big Horn County criminal case 444; Petition for Writ of Error Coram Nobis, ¶¶ 9–12, records of the Wyoming Supreme Court.

8. Davis, *A Vast Amount of Trouble,* 244; Ed Eaton, Penitentiary Records; "Discharge Notice," Nov. 25, 1912, Files of Gov Joseph M. Carey; Thomas Dixon, Penitentiary Records; Gage, *Ten Sleep and No Rest,* 219; Rhodes, "The Rest That Came," 46; O'Neal, *Cattlemen v. Sheepherders,* 148; Robinson, "Ten Sleep Raid," 3. Eaton's tombstone is still found in the Ten Sleep Cemetery, which abuts the northwest corner of the town.

9. Davis, *A Vast Amount of Trouble,* 245–47.

10. "Judge Orders Investigation," *Big Horn County Rustler,* Jan. 2, 1914.

11. Gage, *Ten Sleep and No Rest,* 221; Jack Seaman, grandson of George Saban, interview by author, Feb. 15, 1992; Davis, *A Vast Amount of Trouble,* 264; Jean Groshart, interview by author, Oct. 20, 2003.

12. Petitions for Pardon files for Alexander and Brink, Files of Gov. Joseph M. Carey.

13. Milton A. Alexander, Penitentiary Records, "Convict Discharged or Removed"; "Aged Pioneer Buried Sunday," *Worland Grit,* Jan. 29, 1931; Davis, *A Vast Amount of Trouble,* 265.

14. Loveland, *Sagebrush and Roses,* 400; Saxton, *The Packard Legacy,* 174–83.

15. See the affidavits of E. E. Enterline and Felix Alston attached to Motion to Quash and Dismiss Proceedings, *State v. Saban,* Big Horn County criminal case 401; Robinson, "Ten Sleep Raid"; Gage, *Ten Sleep and No Rest,* 220; Davis, *A Vast Amount of Trouble,* 263.

16. Davis, *A Vast Amount of Trouble,* 263; Sherry Cunningham, Joe Allemand's granddaughter, to John W. Davis, letter, July 1998; Gage, *Ten Sleep and No Rest,* 222; "Famous Tensleep Massacre During Sheep Cattle Feud Recalled By Lone Survivor," *Cody Enterprise,* Jan. 22, 1953.

17. See Deeds, Book 41, p. 234, and Book 45, p. 279, both relating to lots one and two of block 140, City of Casper; Mortgages, Book 30, p. 285; Deeds, Book 55, p. 273, all in Natrona County Clerk Records, Casper, Wyoming. I came across this reference

to Maggie while searching the entire set of Wyoming Supreme Court decisions, using the term "Margaret Gorman"; I found a case in which Margaret Gorman, along with a number of other people, was involved in a paving controversy relating to residential lots in Casper. In the course of researching this book, I have undertaken searches using the name "Margaret Gorman," and even within the social security system, which, of course, extends to the entire United States, the name turned up only a few times. Regarding the population, see Larson, *History of Wyoming,* 413.

18. Davis, *Sadie and Charlie,* 52. See also Davis, *A Vast Amount of Trouble,* 262, regarding Metz's earnings from the Elk Basin field, and 263, regarding the fate of Joe LeFors; details about Alston appear in Percy W. Metz, speech to the Natrona County Historical Society, Nov. 2, 1961.

The grand jury papers, which I finally found in Lola Homsher's collection (Lola was Percy Metz's niece), included some notes showing chapter headings for a book, apparently in Metz's handwriting. Lola was the first head of archives in Wyoming, and Percy Metz might have bequeathed these papers to her in the hope that she would use them to write about the Spring Creek Raid.

19. "Black Page in Basin's History," *The Basin Republican-Rustler,* Mar. 19, 1936.

20. "Black Page in Basin's History"; Rhodes, "All the World's a Stage," Apr. 4, 1940.

21. 355 US 184, 2 L.Ed.2d 199, 78 S. Ct. 221; Annotation, "Conviction of Lesser Offense as Bar to Prosecution for Greater on New Trial," 61 A.L.R.2d 1119.

22. *Green v. United States,* 61 A.L.R.2d 1128, 1130.

23. See ALR Later Case Service for 61 A.L.R.2d 1141. *Green* has been distinguished in other contexts, but I am not aware of any case in which prosecuting authorities have insisted upon trial for greater offenses when there has been an acquittal or implied acquittal of those offenses.

♦
Bibliography

ARCHIVES AND PUBLIC RECORDS

Big Horn County Clerk of the District Court, Records. Basin, Wyoming.

Big Horn County Commissioner's Journal. Records of the Big Horn County Clerk, Basin, Wyoming.

Carey, Governor Joseph M., Files. Archives Division, Wyoming Department of State Parks and Cultural Resources, Cheyenne.

Chatterton, Governor Fenimore, Records. Archives Division, Wyoming Department of State Parks and Cultural Resources, Cheyenne.

Fremont County Board of Commissioners, Records. Lander, Wyoming.

Johnson County Board of Commissioners, Records. Records of the Johnson County Clerk, Buffalo, Wyoming.

Johnson County Clerk of the District Court, Records. Buffalo, Wyoming.

Journal Proceedings of Commissioners. Records of the Johnson County Clerk, Buffalo, Wyoming.

Lola Homsher Collection. American Heritage Center, Laramie, Wyoming.

Office of the Big Horn County Treasurer. Big Horn County Courthouse, Basin, Wyoming.

Penitentiary Records. Wyoming State Penitentiary, Archives Division, Wyoming Department of State Parks and Cultural Resources, Cheyenne.

Percy W. Metz Collection. American Heritage Center, Laramie, Wyoming.

Percy W. Metz, Speeches. Archives Division, Wyoming Department of State Parks and Cultural Resources, Cheyenne.

Petitions for Pardon File. Governor Bryant B. Brooks Files, Archives Division, Wyoming Department of State Parks and Cultural Resources, Cheyenne.

Sheep Raid File. Governor Bryant B. Brooks Files, Archives Division, Wyoming Department of State Parks and Cultural Resources, Cheyenne.

Sweetwater County Clerk, Records. Green River, Wyoming.

Victor Arland Collection. Buffalo Bill Historical Center, McCracken Research Library, Cody, Wyoming.

Wyoming Attorney General Records. Archives Division, Wyoming Department of State Parks and Cultural Resources, Cheyenne.

Wyoming Department of Commerce. Archives and Records Division, Wyoming Department of State Parks and Cultural Resources, Cheyenne.

UNPUBLISHED MANUSCRIPTS

Carter, C. Dana. "C. Dana Carter, Pioneer Doctor." unpublished autobiography, Archives Division, Wyoming Department of State Parks and Cultural Resources, Cheyenne.

Gustafson, Carl Stanley. "History of Vigilante and Mob Activity in Wyoming." Master's thesis, University of Wyoming, May 24, 1961.

Rhodes, Marvin B. "The Rest That Came: A History of the Ten Sleep Raid." Unpublished manuscript, Archives Division, Wyoming Department of State Parks and Cultural Resources, Cheyenne.

Robinson, Arlene G. "Ten Sleep Raid." Miscellaneous Files, WPA #1307, Archives Division, Wyoming Department of Parks and Cultural Resources, Cheyenne.

Simpson, Peter Kooi. "History of the First Wyoming Legislature." Master's thesis, University of Wyoming, Laramie, August 1962.

BOOKS AND ARTICLES

Ainsworth, Mrs. Bert. *To the Wilds of Wyoming: Pioneers of the Big Horn Basin in Wyoming.* College Place, Wash.: Self-published, 1983.

Arrington, Leonard J., and Davis Bitton. *The Mormon Experience.* Urbana and Chicago: University of Illinois Press, 1992.

Baber, D. F. *The Longest Rope.* Caldwell, Idaho: The Caxton Printers, 1953.

Black, Henry Campbell. *Black's Law Dictionary: Definitions of the Terms and Phrases of American and English Jurisprudence, Ancient and Modern.* 4th ed., by the publisher's editorial staff. St. Paul, Minn.: West Publishing, 1951.

Bowes, Verona. "Vigilante Vengeance: Western Justice Rides a Death Trail." *Daring Detective,* December 1938.

Brown, Larry K. *You Are Respectfully Invited to Attend My Execution.* Glendo, Wyo.: Prairie Press, 1997.

Carlson, Chip. *Tom Horn, Killing Men is My Specialty: The Definitive History of the Notorious Wyoming Stock Detective.* Cheyenne, Wyo.: Beartooth Corral, 1991.

Clover, Sam T. *On Special Assignment.* Boston: Lathrop Publishing, 1903.

Cutler, James Elbert. *Lynch Law: An Investigation into the History of Lynching in the United States.* New York City: Negro Universities Press, 1905.

David, Robert W. *Malcolm Campbell, Sheriff.* Casper: Wyomingana, 1932.

Davis, John W. Comment, "The Lesser Included Offense Instruction, Problems With Its Use." 3 *Land and Water Law Review* 587 (1967).

———. *Sadie and Charlie.* Worland, Wyo.: Washakie Publishing, 1989.

———. *A Vast Amount of Trouble: A History of the Spring Creek Raid.* Niwot: University Press of Colorado, 1993.

———. *Worland Before Worland.* Worland, Wyo.: Northern Wyoming Daily News, 1987.

DeVoto, Bernard. *The Year of Decision, 1846.* Boston: Little, Brown and Company, 1943.

Dimsdale, Thomas J. *The Vigilantes of Montana, or Popular Justice in the Rocky Mountains.* Butte, Mont.: McKee Printing, 1950.

Doob, Leonard W. *Social Psychology: An Analysis of Human Behavior.* New York: Henry Holt and Company, 1950.

Edgar, Bob, and Jack Turnell. *Brand of a Legend.* Cody, Wyo.: Stockade Publishing, 1978.

———. *Lady of a Legend.* Cody, Wyo.: Stockade Publishing, 1979.

Friends of the Old Pen. *Sweet Smell of Sagebrush: A Prisoner's Diary, 1903–1912.* Rawlins, Wyo.: Friends of the Old Pen, 1990.

Frison, Paul. *First White Woman in the Big Horn Basin.* Worland, Wyo.: Worland Press, 1969.

———. *Under the Ten Sleep Rim.* Worland, Wyo.: Worland Press, 1972.

———. *When Grass Was Gold.* Worland, Wyo.: Worland Press, 1970.

Gage, Jack. *Ten Sleep and No Rest.* Casper, Wyo.: Prairie Publishing Company, 1958.

Golden, Michael. "Journey for the Pole: The Life and Times of Fred H. Blume." 28 *Land and Water Law Review* 196 (1993), 511.

Hanson, Margaret Brock, ed. *The Papers of J. Elmer Brock: Powder River Country.* Cheyenne, Wyo.: Frontier Printing, 1981.

Hofstader, Richard, and Michael Wallace. *American Violence.* New York: Alfred Knopf, 1970.

Holden, W. C. "Law and Lawlessness on the Texas Frontier: 1875–1890." *Southwestern Historical Quarterly* (October 1940).

Hufsmith, George W. *The Wyoming Lynching of Cattle Kate, 1889.* Glendo, Wyo.: Prairie Press, 1993.

Larson, T. A. *History of Wyoming*. Lincoln: University of Nebraska Press, 1959.

LeFors, Joe. *Wyoming Peace Officer: An Autobiography*. Laramie: Laramie Printing Company, 1953.

Lindsay, Charles. *The Big Horn Basin*. Lincoln: University of Nebraska Press, 1932.

Loveland, Carla Neves. *Sagebrush and Roses*. Lindon, Utah: Alexander's Digital Printing, 2003.

McGrath, Roger D. *Gunfighters, Highwaymen and Vigilantes: Violence on the Frontier*. Berkeley: University of California Press, 1984.

McPhee, John. *Rising from the Plains*. New York: Farrar, Straus, and Giroux, 1986.

Milek, Dorothy J. *Hot Springs: A Wyoming County History*. Basin, Wyo.: Saddlebag Books, 1986.

Moulton, Candy. *Roadside History of Wyoming*. Missoula, Mont.: Mountain Press Publishing, 1995.

Murray, Ester Johansson. "Short Grass and Heather: Peter McCulloch in the Big Horn Basin." *Annals of Wyoming* 51, no. 1 (Spring 1979): 98–129.

Nelson, Dick J. *The Big Horn Basin*. San Diego: Dick J. Nelson, 1957.

O'Neal, Bill. *Cattlemen v. Sheepherders*. Austin, Tex.: Eakins Press, 1989.

Pence, Mary Lou, and Lola Homsher. *Ghost Towns of Wyoming*. New York: Hastings House, 1956.

Pendergraft, Ray. *Washakie: A Wyoming County History*. Basin, Wyo.: Saddlebag Books, 1985.

———. "The Road of Yesteryear," *Annals of Wyoming*. 24, no. 2 (July 1952): 88.

Robertson, Charles Fremont. *A History of the Worland Valley*. Worland, Wyo.: Self-published, 1941.

Rollins, George Watson. *The Struggle of the Cattlemen, Sheepmen and Settler for Control of Lands in Wyoming, 1867–1910*. New York: Arno Press, 1979.

Saban, Vera. *He Wore a Stetson: The Story of Judge Percy W. Metz*. Basin, Wyo.: Big Horn Book Company, 1980.

———. "20th Century Vigilante Justice." *Old West* (Winter 1977): 12.

Saxton, Lowene Packard, comp. and ed. *The Packard Legacy, Family History and Genealogy (In Memory of my Grandparents William Henry and Cynthia Ernestine Perry Packard)*. Sacramento, Calif.: Saxton Press, 1992.

Skovgard, Lylas. *Basin City*. Basin, Wyo.: Timbertrails, 1988.

Smith, Helena Huntington. *The War on Powder River: The History of an Insurrection*. New York: McGraw-Hill, 1966.

Stephens, Press, and Gretel Erlich, eds. *The Shell Valley: An Oral History of Frontier Settlement*. Cody, Wyo.: Rustler Printing and Publishing, 1986.

Walker, George S., comp. *Sheep Owners of Wyoming: 1910 Directory*. Cheyenne, Wyo.: S. A. Bristol, 1910.

Walker, Tacetta. *Big Horn Basin: Stories of Early Days in Wyoming.* Casper, Wyo.: Prairie Publishing, 1936.

Wasden, David John. *From Beaver to Oil.* Cody, Wyo.: Pioneer Printing and Stationery, 1973.

Wentworth, Edward Norris. *America's Sheep Trails.* Ames: Iowa State College Press, 1948.

Wister, Owen. *The Virginian.* New York: Pocket Books, 1956. First published 1902 by Macmillan.

Woods, Lawrence M. *Wyoming's Big Horn Basin to 1901: A Late Frontier.* Spokane, Wash.: Arthur H. Clarke, 1997.

Zangrando, Robert L. *The NAACP Crusade Against Lynching, 1909–1950.* Philadelphia: Temple University Press, 1980.

NEWSPAPERS

Basin Republican, April 23–May 21, 1909; June 4–June 11, 1909; October 22–December 10, 1909; December 24, 1909; November 11, 1910; December 14, 1913; January 2, 1914; January 23, 1914.

Basin Republican-Rustler, March 19, 1936; March 7–April 4, 1940.

Big Horn County News and Courier, November 1, 1902.

Big Horn County Rustler, April 9–May 14, 1909; May 28, 1909; October 22–November 12, 1909; January 23, 1914.

Billings Gazette, May 12, 1909.

Buffalo Bulletin, April 16, May 7, May 21, June 18, July 30, August 20, 1891; November 25, November 30, 1893.

Buffalo Echo, August 2, 1883.

Casper Derrick, July 23, 1903.

Cheyenne Daily Leader/Cheyenne State Leader, June 13, November 10, 1902; May 4, July 20, October 25–November 1, 1903; April 20, April 23–24, April 27–29, 1904; April 7, April 13, April 10, April 21, May 6, May 11, November 5, November 9, November 10, November 12, November 16, 1909.

Cody Enterprise, January 22, 1953.

Denver Post, April 21, May 11, October 13, October 26, October 30, October 31, November 3–November 7, November 10–November 13, November 16, November 17, November 19, November 30, 1909.

Fremont Clipper, November 19, 1887; June 28, July 19, 1888.

Garland Guard, August 25, 1909.

Lander Clipper, June 28, 1888.

Laramie Boomerang, July 19, July 21–July 22, July 24–25, 1903.

Rocky Mountain News, November 5, November 7, 1909.

Sheridan Enterprise, June 21 (supplement), November 8, November 15, 1902; November 23, 1909.

Sheridan Post, July 23, 1903; April 29, 1904.

Thermopolis Record, October 17–October 31, 1902; November 7, 1902; May 8, July 25, 1903; May 8, 1904; May 15, 1909; October 23, 1909; November 6, 1909; November 13, 1909.

Wind River Mountaineer, February 8, September 13, 1897.

Worland Grit, April 8, April 22, May 6–May 20, October 28–November 11, November 25, December 2, 1909; January 29, 1931.

Wyoming Derrick, June 19, 1902; November 6, 1902; July 23, 1903.

Wyoming Dispatch, June 13, July 4, 1902.

Wyoming Eagle, February 7, 1930.

Wyoming Tribune, July 19, July 21–July 23, July 26, July 28–30, 1903; April 19–April 20, 1904.

◆
Index

Absarokas (mountains), 7
Adams, Tom, 16
Alamo (election precinct), 31
Alexander, Milton A., 138, 202;
  after raid, 203; Brink's identification, 144, 185; caliber of gun,
  139; conviction and sentencing,
  193–95; involvement in raid, 143,
  146–48, 178, 179, 188; writ of
  coram nobis, 200
Allemand, Adeline (Ada), 186, 188,
  189, 206
Allemand, Jacque, 136, 146
Allemand, Joe, 124, 125, 143, 151,
  155; Brink's statement, 170;
  Chabot, 149; driving sheep to
  Spring Creek, 127–31;
  newspaper reports, 133–36; shot,
  148; testimony of Ada Allemand,
  186; trial testimony, 172–74,
  179–81, 183, 184, 188

Alston, Felix, 82, 149, 152, 168, 177;
  after raid, 208; elected sheriff
  (1908), 124, 125; election of 1910,
  198, 200; friendship with Saban,
  113; grand jury, 143–47;
  investigation of raid, 129–32,
  137–40; militia, 154, 155; jury
  photograph, 241n8; plea in
  abatement, 159, 160; testimony of
  Billy Goodrich, 184, 185; trial
  testimony, 170, 172, 173, 177;
  warden; 202
Anable, Harry, 16
Anderson, A. A., 18
Anderson, Neil J., 94
Andersonville, Wyo., 34, 35
Angus, W. C. (sheriff of Johnson
  County), 27
Antlers Hotel, 90, 94
Arland (election precinct), 31
Arland, Victor, 10, 14, 15, 17, 19, 20, 22

Arland, Wyo., 15, 18, 19, 29
Arnold, Benedict, 197
Arnott, John P., 43, 45, 63, 73, 114
Arrington, Leonard J., 36
Atherly, Clyde, 143, 172
Attorney general (Wyoming), 76,
    107, 110
Averell, Jim, 105

Bader, Fred, 4, 5, 42
Baker, Maude, 15
Basin City (Basin), Wyo., 38, 60,
    121, 124, 149, 154, 192, 195–98,
    208; after lynching, 95–98; before
    Brink trial, 156–58; county seat,
    5, 37; Felix Alston's return, 139;
    Jim Gorman's walk, 52, 55;
    lynching, 80–82, 85–87, 89, 93;
    newspapers, 134; Percy Metz's
    return, 132, 137; railroad, 123;
    site of Brink trial, 162, 163; site of
    first Jim Gorman trial, 45; site of
    1903 grand jury, 110; site of 1909
    grand jury, 141, 143, 146
Basin Republican, 134, 151–56, 158–60,
    162, 189
Basin Republican Rustler, 208
Baxter, George, 8
Bay State Ranch, 33, 138, 234n2
Bear River City, Wyo., 103, 104
Beck, W. E., 50
Becker, J. M., 164
Bedford, Jack, 31
Big Horn Basin, 40, 42, 47–50, 86,
    95, 99, 100, 114, 116, 121, 123,
    132, 151, 197, 198, 207, 208;

Alexander not to return, 203; Big
    Horn County, 26, 29–38; Brink
    jury, 192–95; early history, 7–22;
    1890 population, 24; Governor
    Brooks visits, 140; Judge Carpen-
    ter's connection, 63; new judge-
    ship, 200; railroad entered, 45;
    Saban on a work crew, 202; sheep
    and cattle interests clash, 117–19;
    site of Gorman home, 3; Spring
    Creek Raid, 134, 137
Big Horn Canal, 121
Big Horn Cattle Company (Bar X
    Bar), 8, 16
Big Horn County, Wyo., 7, 58, 71;
    Billy Goodrich, 184; Brink jury,
    192; Brink trial, 162; creation, 24,
    29, 35; debt, 159; Enterline letter,
    76; factions regarding lynching,
    112; French interest, 149, 150;
    Gov. Chatterton's pronounce-
    ment regarding lynching, 109,
    110; grand jury (1909), 141;
    Hoover murder, 73; increase in
    jury list, 161; lynching, 80, 81;
    makeup of 1900 population, 48;
    militia, 155; new counties, 124;
    Republican-Rustler 1936 comments,
    208; site of Gorman murder, 5,
    41; Spring Creek Raid, 134–36;
    Tom Gorman arrived, 39; vote
    for county seat, 37; Will Metz
    fees, 152, 153; Worland Grit
    comments, 195
Big Horn County commissioners,
    43, 137, 140, 153

Big Horn County Courthouse, 87, 89
Big Horn County Rustler, 51, 134,
    147, 152, 153, 162, 163, 195
Big Horn County Woolgrowers
    Association, 135, 202
Big Horn Mountains, 3, 112, 120,
    126; Bedford-Burch killings, 30,
    31; eastern wall of Big Horn
    Basin, 7; horseback trip over, 34;
    Jim Gorman's escape route, 83,
    84; part of deadline, 118; part of
    Johnson County, 11
Big Horn River, 19, 34, 120; allega-
    tion re: Rose Gorman, 42; Edna
    Wilson disappearance, 21; Jim
    Gorman escape, 82, 83; move of
    Worland in 1906, 123; settlement
    associated with irrigation projects,
    121; retreat of mob, 92; site of
    Hoover murder, 73; Tillard ferry,
    87; western border of Johnson
    County, 11–13; western border of
    Sheridan County, 22
Big Trails, 19, 126, 138, 149, 183,
    198, 203
Billings, Mont., 14, 45, 197
Birdseye Pass (Wyo.), 10
Bitton, Davis, 36
Blackman, Edward, 34
Black Mountain, 85
Blair, Jacob B. (district judge), 18
Blake, M. L., 43, 45, 57, 65, 66
Blume, Fred, 46, 222n13
Boggs, (Missouri Governor)
    Lilburn W., 100
Bonanza (election precinct), 31

Bonanza, Wyo., 26, 27, 31, 49, 152
Booth, William, 18
Bozeman, Mont., 203
Brady, Thomas, 20
Brigam, Bert, 92
Brigham, F. T. (justice of the peace), 5
Brink, Herbert, 159, 161, 206; after
    raid, 203; conviction and sentencing,
    190–96; Faris's statement, 148;
    grand jury, 143–45; indictment,
    147; prison, 202, 203; pushed
    sheepwagon over knoll, 119;
    suspect, 138–40; trial, 164, 165,
    166, 170, 172, 174, 177–79, 181–88
Brokenback Creek (Dry Fork), 3, 5,
    41, 49, 50, 67, 207
Brooks, Bryant B.: Alston letter,
    147; county clerk Enders's letter,
    133; militia, 154–58, 198; owner-
    ship of newspapers, 152; reward,
    136; secretary of state letters, 149,
    150; veto of Washakie County bill,
    124; visit to Big Horn Basin, 140
Brown, Eliza and Frank P., 183,
    184, 189
Brown, J., 33
Buckingham, J. F., 16
Buffalo Bulletin, 27, 28
Buffalo, Wyo., 3, 10, 11, 13, 16–18,
    26, 30–33, 35, 136, 208
Bull, Jim and Topsy, 213n3
Bunce, Austin M., 21, 22
Burch, Dab, 22, 30
Burke, Milo, 8, 193
Burlington, Wyo., 36, 141, 166
Byron, Wyo., 141, 192

Cache Valley, Utah, 36
Cafferal, Pete, 127, 128, 131, 139, 143, 173, 175, 177
Callahan, John, 183, 185, 189, 206
Campbell, Malcolm, 106
Camplin, M. B., 73
Canton, Frank, 16, 20, 217n5
Canyon Creek, 19
Carbon County, Wyo. 10, 105
Carey, Joseph M. (governor), 200, 202, 203, 235n16
Carpenter, Charles E. (district judge), 63–66, 68, 70, 71, 81
Carter, C. Dana, 5, 67, 92, 93, 94, 229n31, 230n39
Carter, William A. (judge), 8
Carthage, Ill., 100
Casper, Wyo., 4, 106, 206, 207
Casper Derrick, 109
Casper Mutual Building and Loan Association, 207
Chabot, Virgil, 149
Champion, Nick, 30
Chapman (election precinct), 31
Chapman, Alfred, 34
Chapman, Melvin, 33, 34
Chapman, W. J., 50, 96
Charles and Ghodderton, 29
Chatterton, Fenimore, 109–11
Cheeseman, Harry, 21
Cheyenne, Wyo., 30, 98, 103–105, 110, 155
Cheyenne Daily Leader: Brink trial, 162, 187; editorial regarding Faris and Keyes, 197; first Gorman trial, 50, 51–56; first

story regarding the Gorman murder, 41; Gov. Chatterton comments, 109, 110; lynch mob, 89; prosecution of lynchers, 114, 115; second trial, 65, 67, 70; Spring Creek Raid, 134; Will Metz remarks, 194
Chicago, Burlington & Quincy Railroad, 45, 121, 123
Church of Jesus Christ of Latter Day Saints, 59, 168. *See also* Mormons
Clark, Wyo., 166
Clear Creek, 11
Clifton, "Diamond Slim," 106, 108
Cloud Peak (Big Horn Mountains), 11
Cody, William F., 115
Cody, Wyo., 10, 13, 16, 23, 36, 38, 45, 63, 96, 164, 166, 168, 192, 206; arrival of railroad, 45; county seat election, 37; militia, 155
Cole, Farney, 138, 144, 148, 178, 183
Colethorpe, W. G., 183
Collins, Hugh, 51, 52, 54, 55, 57, 69
Collins, Winfield Scott: attorney for Spring Creek Raid defendants, 162; Basin mayor during Brink trial, 152, 158; founder of Basin City, 37; prosecuting attorney (Jim Gorman), 43–45, 51, 57
Converse County, Wyo., 106
Conway, John, 34
Coons, Arlan W., 195, 196
Copps, E. W., 10
Corbett, John, 14
Corbett, Wyo., 16, 21

Cottonwood Creek (on the Stink-
  ing Water), 14
Cottonwood Pass (Wyo.), 10
Cowley, Wyo., 141, 166, 168, 192
Crook County, Wyo., 120, 121
Crosby, 50
Crow, Joe, 18–20
Cutler, James Elbert, 99, 111

Dadant, Camille, 19, 20
Davis, J. J., 192, 193
Deadline, 85
Deadwood, S. Dak., 104
Deane, John William ("Josh"), 12,
  17
Declaration of Independence, 101
Delfedler, J. A., 135, 136
Denver, Colo., 198
Denver Post, 162, 180, 181, 191
DeVoto, Bernard, 8
Dewey, Admiral, 97
Dimsdale, Thomas J., 101
Ditmer, Willis, 111
Dixon, Tommy: after raid, 200, 201;
  Brink trial, 178, 183, 185, 188;
  caliber of gun, 139; conviction
  and sentencing, 193–95; grand
  jury mention, 143–45; indict-
  ment and arrest, 147; return to
  bunkhouse, 148; seen at Spring
  Creek, 138
Donahue, John 166, 168
Double jeopardy, 60, 61, 209
Drewry, Belle, 29, 32, 33, 37, 220n23
Duncan, Charles, 168
Dungeness, Wash., 149

Dutch Charlie (lynched in 1879), 105
Dyer, John, 23

Eaton, Ed: after raid, 200; almost
  shot Ken McClellan, 39; Brink
  trial, 175, 177–79, 188; conviction
  and sentencing, 193–95; grand
  jury, 143, 144, 146–48; initial
  appearance, 151; investigation,
  138–40
Election precinct, 11
Elk Canal, 121
Ellsberg, Wash., 206
Embar (election precinct), 31
Embar, Wyo., 86
Emblem, Wyo. (Germania), 5
Emge, Joe, 151, 155, 188; became
  sheepman, 124, 126–28; established deadline, 118; gold teeth,
  172; Greet's testimony, 173, 174;
  Helmer testimony, 175; killed in
  raid, 130, 131, 133; newspaper
  stories, 134; threats, 143, 183
Ender, Peter, 133
Enterline, E. E. (Edward Elmer),
  72, 162; after lynching, 98; Brink
  trial, 170, 179, 180, 184–86, 189,
  190; Crook County prosecution
  of raiders, 121; defense of Joseph
  Walters, 73, 75–80; first Gorman
  trial, 49, 53–55; grand jury, 143;
  Jim Gorman defense attorney,
  45, 46; militia, 156; prosecutor,
  State v. Brink, 137, 139; second
  Gorman trial, 62, 64–66
Ewing, William J., 34, 35

Faris, Charles: after raid, 203; Brink trial, 186–89; confession, 148; Goodrich grand jury testimony, 144; indictment and arrest, 147; leaves Basin, 197; suspect, 138, 139; trial testimony, 175, 178–82

Fenton (election precinct), 31

Fenton, J. J. (sheriff of Big Horn County): charges against lynchers, 114; first Gorman trial, 65, 66; to and from Thermopolis, 85, 86, 95, 97, 98; warned of lynching, 81, 82

Feuder, Walter, 112

First National Bank of Meeteetse, 159

Fiscus, Walter, 129

Fisher, E. C., 91

Fister, J. B., 21

Flitner, Arthur, 120

Fort McKinney, 30

Fort Washakie, 15, 17

Franc, Otto, 8, 17, 31

Fraternal Hall, 170,

Freemason, 90, 91

Fremont County, Wyo., 13, 16, 17, 20, 24, 26, 29, 31, 63, 206

Fremont County Board of Commissioners, 16, 17

Frison, Jake, 175

Frison, Paul, 39

Fullerton, James (justice of the peace), 32

Gallagher, Bill A., 29, 32, 33; defendant in *State v. Galigar*, 219n12

Gantz, Louis A., 119, 124

Garland (deputy sheriff), 97

Garland, Wyo., 45, 94

Garland Canal, 121

Garrison, Bill, 144–46, 183–85

Gatchell, P. A., 157, 158

Gebo, Wyo., 123

Gibson, William, 182

Gillam, C. M., 92

Gleaver, John, 50

Glenwoodville, Alberta, Canada, 203

Goodrich, Ade, 131, 146

Goodrich, Anna, 143, 144, 183, 184, 189, 197, 203

Goodrich, Bob, 177

Goodrich, William D. ("Billy"), 148, 172; Goodriches return, 203; grand jury testimony, 143–45; H. S. Ridgely's closing argument, 189; sawmill burned, 197; trial testimony, 183–87

Gooseberry (election precinct), 16, 31

Gooseberry Creek, 8, 12, 19

Gorman (elder, father of Jim and Tom Gorman), 98

Gorman, James (Jim), 7, 40, 80, 107, 117; attorney general records, 221n5; burial, 98; escape, 81–86; Felix Alston, 124; first trial, 50–57; *Green v. United States*, 209–11; kills brother, 4, 5; lynching, 89–95; newspaper stories about Tom Gorman killing, 41–47; newspaper stories about lynching,

109; Saban's arrest, 113; second trial, 58–66, 69–72

Gorman, Margaret (Maggie) (McClellan), 39, 197; appearance in Basin, 60; comment by Topsy Bull, 245n17; first trial, 43–46, 50–58; killing of Tom Gorman, 3–5; in Casper, 206, 207; newspaper stories regarding Tom Gorman's killing, 41, 42; raid on jail, 93–95; second trial, 63, 67, 69

Gorman, Rose, 5, 42

Gorman, Thomas C. (Tom), 3–5, 38–42, 44, 50–55, 57, 94, 221n5

Gormand, Henry, 20

Grand jury (1903), 111

Grand jury (1909), 140, 141, 147

Grass Creek, 8

Green River, Wyo., 10, 12, 13, 15

Green, Everett, 208

Green v. United States, 208, 209

Greet, Frank, 128, 129

Greet, Fred, 128, 129, 143, 173, 174

Greybull, Wyo., 22, 82, 123, 141, 166, 192, 198

Greybull River, 8, 15, 21, 24, 36, 118

Gross, Christopher (deputy), 17

Guffy, John, 92

Guthrie, S. A., 121, 154

Hale, Dudley (sheriff of Big Horn County), 5, 50, 51, 95–97, 111

Hamilton, Ill., 19

Hamilton, Ira, 15

Hanover Canal, 121

Hardee, Orville, 112

Harvard, Clyde, 138, 144, 145

Helmer, Charles David ("Bounce"): after raid, 206; grand jury testimony, 143; importance of testimony, 182; kidnapped, 131, 132; recognition of Eaton, 139, 140; Ridgely closing argument; sent away, 149; sheep herder, 127, 128; testimony of father, 186; trial testimony, 175, 177, 178

Helmer, Frank, 146, 185, 186

Henderson, Harry B., 153, 154

Hill, Jack (deputy), 20, 218n19

Hill, T. P., 34

Hollywood, Jack, 31, 32

Hoover, Agnes, 70, 72–74

Hoover, John, 72

Hoover, Maude, 87

Horn, Tom, 70, 110, 225n23, 232n7

Hot Springs County, Wyo., 124

Houlihan, "Blind Bill," 32, 33

Hyatt, S. W., 16

Hyattville, Wyo., 19, 32, 85, 112, 118, 130, 138, 145, 166, 173

Hyde, Thomas W., 162

Inglas, J. C., 20

Jackson, Andy ("Broken Nose"), 19, 23

Jackson, Bob, 37

James, Frank (deputy), 5, 95

Jimmerfield, Dan, 50

Johnson County, Wyo., 135, 136; 1880s, 16, 17, 22; 1890s, 26, 29–31, 34; inception, 11, 12; killings in 1891, 1892, 106

Johnson County Board of Commis-
    sioners, 17
Johnson County Invasion (Johnson
    County War), 20, 30, 106, 148,
    154
Joliet, Ill., 16
Jones, J. T., 163
Jones, W. J., 193
Judge Lynch, 30, 81, 211

Kane, Wyo., 192
Keffer, James, 70
Kendrick, John (governor), 203
Keyes, William: after raid, 203;
    Brink trial, 175, 178–80, 182, 183;
    closing arguments, 187–89;
    grand jury, 144–48; leaves Big
    Horn Basin, 197; suspect, 138,
    139
King, Samuel, 200
Kirby Creek, 118, 119
Kirwin (election precinct), 31
Knight, Jack, 16
Knight, Jesse (judge), 75

Lamb, Porter, 128, 129, 143, 174,
    175, 184–87
Lander, Wyo., 13, 19, 22, 137
Laramie Boomerang, 90, 96, 97, 108
Laramie Mountains, 103
Laramie, Wyo., 64, 103
Latham, I. B., 177, 178
Laurel, Mont., 202
Lazier, Jules, 127, 128, 131, 133–35,
    151, 155, 173, 188
Leavitt, W. W., 50

LeFors, Joe, 121, 143, 148, 198, 199
    (photograph), 208, 234n15
Lewis, William (W. H.), 67, 190, 192
Lincoln Land Company, 123
Lindsay, Charles, 20
Linton, Alex, 160
Little Canyon Creek, 16, 18, 19
Lonabaugh, E. E., 66, 113
Lone Tree Creek, 118
Lost Cabin, Wyo., 118
Loveland, Carla Neves, 95
Loveland, John W., 95
Lovell (election precinct), 31
Lovell, Henry Clay, 8, 12
Lovell, Wyo., 121, 141, 166, 168
Lower Shell (election precinct), 31
Luman, John, 8
LU Ranch, 8, 21, 29, 218n24, 234n2
Lynn, J. L., 120

Madden, Peter, 26, 28
Madden, Tom, 26–28
Magill, Joe, 113
Mahogany Buttes, 17, 184
Maloney, William, 105
Manderson, Charles D. (justice of
    the peace), 33
Manderson, Wyo., 146
Manhattan, Mont., 203
Mansfield, Billy, 104
Marquette (election precinct), 31
Martin, A. J., 50
Martin, Charles, 103
Martin, Helen, 26
Massey, Alice, 73
McCabe, B. R., 73–75, 78

McClaughlin, Archie, 104
McClellan, Annie, 39, 55
McClellan, George B. ("Bear George"), 4, 34, 118, 175, 193, 198
McClellan, Jennie, 38, 39
McClellan, John, 39
McClellan, Kenneth (son), 39
McClellan, Kenneth, 38, 39, 55, 206
McClellan, Oscar, 185
McCloud, Jim (Driftwood Jim), 85, 86, 96–98
McComb, Al, 21
McCulloch, Pete, 8, 16
McDermott, James, 26–29
McDermott, Mary, 26, 27
McDermott, Phil (son of James and Mary), 26–28
McDonald, Angus, 8, 12, 16
McGregor, Jack, 18
McKenzie, Colin F., 112
McPhee, John, 3
McWallace (killer of George Smith), 15, 16
Mead, George, 86, 87, 89, 93, 190
Medicine Bow, Wyo., 11
Meeteetse (election precinct), 16, 31
Meeteetse, Wyo., 13, 24, 96, 141, 166, 200
Meeteetse Creek, 14, 15
Mercer, Ralph, 112
Meredith, John, 174
Metcalfe, George, 105
Metz, Percy, 125, 162; after raid, 207; appointed district judge, 200; confessions of Faris and Keyes, 147; criticisms, 152–54;

elected county attorney, 124; flowers from Denver, 198; grand jury, 139–41; Helmer interview, 177; planned book, 246n18; Ridgely's reaction to juror, 166; special prosecutors hired, 137; to Spring Creek, 129–32; trial testimony, 173
Metz, William S., 162; attorney fees; 152, 153, 198; closing argument, 188, 189; comments regarding significance of convictions, 194; Enterline comments, 76–78; Guthrie raids, 121; questioned Alston, 170; pledges to help Percy, 124; represented Saban, 113; resigned as district judge, 243n19; special counsel in Brink case, 137, 139; Walters' prosecutor, 73
Militia, 154–58, 198
Miller, Henry E. (Ed), 3, 4
Minnick, Ben, 85, 86, 98, 119
Minnick, William, 85
Montana Vigilantes, 101
Mormons, 36, 59, 67, 100, 141, 193, 225n16, 241n9. See also Church of Jesus Christ of Latter Day Saints
Morrison, Lincoln A., 119
Morse, Daniel Lee, 112, 115, 136
Morse, Henry, 37
Morton, Al, 129, 130, 143, 172
Mosier, Henry, 105
Mountain View Hotel, 90, 91
Mullen, W. E., 157, 200
Murray, Earl D., 33

Nard, Albert ("Slick"), 35
National Woolgrowers, 135
Natrona County, Wyo., 106, 206, 207
Natrona County Tribune, 42
Newcastle, Wyo., 106
Nichols, Jeff, 96
Nickell, Willie, 70
Nielson, C. E., 168, 241n8
Noble, Warden, 8
Northern Pacific Railroad, 14, 202
Nowood, Wyo., 118, 173
Nowood country, 16
Nowood River, 8, 16, 17, 26, 48, 118, 124, 128, 137, 138, 164

Old Meeteetse, 15
Old West (magazine), 94, 95
Olney, Tom, 91
O'Neill, Jack, 104
Osborne, John, 105
Osborne, Tom, 15
Otter Creek, 126, 131, 137, 138, 144, 148, 178, 183, 188
Otto (election precinct), 31
Otto, Wyo., 36, 37, 67, 73, 112
Owens, Ella, 32
Owl Creek, 21, 34
Owl Creek, Wyo., 95
Owl Creek Mountains, 7, 13, 17
Owl Creek Precinct, 16

Packard, William H., 36, 168, 190, 203, 241n8
Paint Rock (election precinct), 31
Paint Rock, 82

Paintrock Creek, 8, 17, 118
Park County, Wyo., 124
Parmelee, C. H. (district judge): Brink trial, 166, 172, 174, 187, 189, 191, 193, 194; Gov. Brooks's letter, 149; grand jury, 140–42, 151, 210; plea in abatement, 160, 161
Parrott, George (Big Nose George), 104, 105
Patch, D. A., 16
Pease County, Wyo., 11
Peay, Walter (justice of the peace), 31
Pennsylvania, 3
Penrose, Wyo., 166
Peremptory challenges, 49, 50, 67, 165, 192
Peverly, John, 31
Picket's Creek, 24
Pickett, George, 186
Pickett, William Douglas, 24, 29
Pitchfork Ranch, 8, 24, 37
Plea in abatement, 159
Plummer, Henry, 101
Potter, Charles N. (judge), 75, 91, 208
Powder River Basin, 11
Powder River Pass, 12
Powell, Wyo., 121
Powers, Jimmy, 104
Price, C. C. (captain), 95
Price, Christopher Earl, 211; buried, 98; coroner's jury, 93; deputy county clerk, 86, 87; Mead memories, 190; notification of parents, 95; public comments, 107, 109; Saban arrested, 113; shot dead, 89

Price, John, 218n19
Pulliam, David T., 121

Rawlins, Wyo., 10, 70, 105, 116, 198,
   202
Ray, Nick, 30
Rebidaux, Jack, 184
Red Bank (election precinct), 31, 198
Red Bank Ranch, 34
Red Lodge, Mont., 23
Red River Kid (shot Tauhoundus),
   18
Reed, James, 104
Reimann, Joseph (justice of the
   peace), 28
Rhodes, Marvin D., 111, 228n19
Rice, D. J., 29
Richards, DeForest, 66, 68, 69
Richards, William A., 34, 37
Ridgely, Hilliard S.: Brink defender,
   166, 172, 174, 179, 180, 181, 183,
   185, 189; jail raid grand jury, 114;
   Jim Gorman prosecutor (second
   trial), 63, 64; Spring Creek Raid
   defense attorney, 151–53
Ritchie Brother Ranch, 17
Robertson, Charles Fremont, 121,
   123, 162
Robinson, A. J., 20
Rock Springs Massacre, 105
Rock Springs, Wyo., 46
Rocky Mountain News, 175, 195
Rodgers, Joseph, 31
Rogers, Pistol Billy, 22, 30
Ross v. State, 75, 77, 80
Russell (clerk of court), 191

Rustlers, 30
Rutrough, John, 166, 190

S. A. Guthrie Company, 120, 121
Saban, George, 204, 205 (wanted
   flier); Brink trial, 178, 179, 185,
   188, 193–95; early sheep raid,
   120; escape, 202, 203; jail raid
   charges, 112–15; militia, 156; plea
   in abatement, 159; Spring Creek
   Raid, 138, 144, 145, 147, 148; writ
   of coram nobis, 200
Sackett, Carl L., 66
Sagebrush and Roses, 95
Schuelke, Dr. Julius, 74
Schwoob, Jake, 116
Shaw, Charles, 178
Shaw, Charles E., 127
Sheldon, F. M., 164
Shell, Wyo., 82–86, 112, 120, 138, 198
Shell Creek, 17, 83, 118–20
Shell Creek (election precinct), 31
Shell Creek Canyon, 83, 84
Sherard, Henry (constable), 33
Sheridan, Wyo., 45, 46, 114, 143
Sheridan County, 22, 24
Sheridan Enterprise, 41, 60
Sheridan Post, 98, 108, 109, 115
Simpson, Will L., 151; before Brink
   trial, 157–59; dons Allemand coat,
   188; Fremont County attorney, 33;
   justice of the peace, 29; posterity,
   219n12; redirect of Helmer, 178;
   refuses reward, 198; special prose-
   cutor, State v. Brink, 137, 162; Spring
   Creek Raid grand jury, 143

Slick Creek, 35

Smith, Adeline, 126

Smith, C. C. (juror), 50, 84, 85

Smith, George, 15

Smith, Helena Huntington, 106

Smith, Joseph, 100, 168

Smith, W. H., 110, 193

Sommers, Ora, 67

South Pass, 13

Spring Creek, 125, 132–34, 137, 143,
153; cowboys seen in, 138, 183;
Gross kills Stevens, 17; Harvard's
presence, 145; homestead claims,
19; Joe Emge builds fence, 126;
Spring Creek Raid, 128–30, 148,
178, 188

Spring Creek (election precinct), 31,
198

Spring Creek Raid, 135, 138, 142,
184, 207

State v. Alexander, 200

State v. Brink, 164, 170, 188, 192, 194

State v. Thomas Dixon, 192

State v. James Gorman, 209, 214n8

Stevens, George, 17

Stewart, Mary, 21, 22

Stinking Water (Shoshone River),
14, 15, 17, 121

Stinking Water Precinct, 16

Stone, A. L. (deputy), 86

Stotts, Joseph L. (district judge), 77;
alleged comment about Jim
Gorman, 58; defense counsel,
State v. Brink, 163, 189; fees,
239n9; future partner of
Enterline, 46; open venire, 50;

presides over first Gorman trial,
45; presides over 1904 raiders'
cases, 115; sworn off as judge, 63;
tribute to Gov. Richards, 68

Sundance, Wyo., 121, 156

Sunlight, Wyo., 192

Sweeney, Hal, 85

Sweeny, Harry, 113

Sweetwater County, Wyo., 10, 12, 13

Sybille Creek, 105

T. A. Ranch, 30

Tatlock, James G., 112–15

Tatman (stockman on Grey Bull),
27

Tauhoundous (Mexican shot by the
Red River Kid), 18

Taylor, Tynacum T., 112

Ten Sleep (election precinct), 31, 38

Ten Sleep, Wyo., 3, 4; Alexanders,
203; Bay State ranch, 33; deadline,
118; Ed Eaton residence, 138;
Jack Hollywood, 32; precinct
established, 16, 17; residence of
jail raiders, 112; Tom Gorman
arrives, 40; witnesses summoned
to grand jury, 141

Ten Sleep Cemetery, 200, 203

Ten Sleep Creek, 8, 12, 16, 127

Thermopolis, Wyo., 32, 63, 73, 85,
86, 95–98, 124

Thermopolis Record, 63, 86, 93, 96,
97, 109, 119

Tillard, John M., 87

Toluca, Mont., 38, 45

Torrey (election precinct), 31, 33

Torrey, J. L., 112, 113

Torrey, Robert A., 29
Trapper Creek, 120

Union Pacific Railroad, 10, 46, 101, 103, 104
United States Supreme Court, 208, 209
Upper Nowood, 127, 132, 137–40, 146, 184, 203

Van Orsdel, J. A. (attorney general of Wyoming), 76–79
Vigilantes, 103, 104, 211
Vogel, Joseph, 168

W. H. Hunt Ranch, 17
Waggoner, Tom, 106
Walker, George W., 130, 146, 173
Walls, W. L., 163
Waln Brothers Ranch, 17
Walters, Joseph P.: appeal, 77, 80; buried, 98; convicted of first degree murder, 72–75; in jail for Agnes Hoover killing, 70; lynched, 89–93, 117, 229n29, 229n30; moved from jail, 82, 85, 124; newspaper comments, 109; raiders charged with murder, 113; report of Attorney General, 107; questionable conviction, 210, 211
Warner, Mark, 164, 166
Warren (election precinct), 31
Wasden, David John, 10, 19, 97
Washakie County, Wyo., 35, 124
Watkins, S. A., 50
Watson, C. H., 50

Watson, Ella, 105
Welling, Wyo., 95, 230n47
Wentworth, Edward Norris, 119
West, R. B., 162
West, William, 37
Weston County, Wyo., 106
Whaley, Bertha, 113
Whaley, W. T., 138
Wheatland, Wyo., 105
Wheaton, William, 32, 33
White, Jim, 11, 84
Whitney, F. A., 50
Wickham, James, 31
Wickwire, B. F. (constable), 19
Widmeyer, Fred, 183
Wigfall, Frank, 195, 200
Williams, Rose, 19, 22, 32
Wilson, Edna, 21
Wilson, Huntington, 149, 150
Wind River Canyon, 26, 124
Winslow, "Denver Jake," 166
Winter of 1886–1887, 19
Wister, Owen, 11
Wood River, 119
Wood River (election precinct), 31
Woodard, Charles Francis, 106, 108
Woodruff, J. D., 7
Woods, Bert, 34
Workman, Cornelius, 50, 59
Worland, Wyo., 10, 21, 34–36, 94, 121, 123, 124, 164, 166, 198
Worland, C. H. ("Dad"), 93, 94
Worland Grit, 134, 160, 161, 195
Wyoming Dispatch, 42
Wyoming Eagle, 103
Wyoming State Bar Association, 46

Wyoming State Penitentiary, 198, 200, 208
Wyoming Stock Growers Association, 20
Wyoming Supreme Court, Big Horn County formation, 29, 35, 37; Charles N. Potter, 91; Enterline case, 46; Jim Gorman appeal, 61, 65, 67, 71, 81; jury qualifications, 48; open venire, 50; Sheridan County formation, 22;

State v. Alexander, 200; Walters appeal, 75, 79, 80, 107
Wyoming Tribune, 84, 89, 109, 115
Wyoming Woolgrowers Association, 120, 135

Young, Frank, 168

Zaring, Clarence A. (C. A.), 5, 51, 56, 64, 162

CPSIA information can be obtained
at www.ICGtesting.com
Printed in the USA
BVOW10s2147080217
475713BV00001B/6/P